what a girl wants

a novel

by kristin billerbeck

WestBow
P R E S S
A Division of Thomas Nelson Publishers
Since 1798

visit us at www.westbowpress.com

Published by WestBow Press, a division of Thomas Nelson, Inc., P.O. Box 141000, Nashville, TN 37214.

WestBow Press books may be purchased in bulk for educational, business, fund-raising, or sales promotional use. For information, please e-mail SpecialMarkets@ThomasNelson.com.

ISBN 0-8499-4458-9 (softcover)
ISBN 1-5955-4185-3 (mass market)

Printed in the United States of America
06 07 08 09 10 QWB 5 4 3 2 1

Acknowledgments

Thank you to everyone who believed in this book. First and foremost, thank you to Colleen Coble, who brought me encouragement when I needed it most. Your friendship is incomparable and truly a gift. Thank you to Ami McConnell for taking a chance that the Christian market was ready for Chick Lit. And thank you to Lisa Tawn Bergren for her incredible work in making this a better manuscript. You are all godly women, and I praise our heavenly Father for allowing our paths to cross.

Thanks to Colleen Coble, Denise Hunter, Carol Cox, and Nancy Toback for reading this manuscript when it wasn't ready to be read. And thanks to the youthful readers, Kara Coble and Gina Siegle, who helped me know when a reference was far too old for Ashley's generation.

To my husband, Bryed, who had to put up with my "chick" attitude far too often, and to our precious four children—Trey, Jonah, Seth, and Elle—you make life worth living.

Thanks to Steve Laube, my gifted agent, and to Chi Libris for your daily conversation (for putting up with my outlandish opinions and political rants, etc., when I was bored).

And finally, thank you to my best friend (since I was five), Beth Harke. How would I ever find the chick within without you? I'm eternally grateful God brought such an awesome person into my life, and helped us both to find Him together. (After the gummy bear incident, of course.)

*T*his is Rick Ramirez, reporting for Entertainment This Evening." *The announcer rolls his "R's" to emphasize his Latin heritage; he's a cross between Ricardo Montalban and the used car salesman up the street.*

"*We're live in Silicon Valley at the celebrated wedding of Ashley Wilkes Stockingdale to the world's most eligible bachelor, John Folger, heir to the coffee fortune. Not since JFK, Jr. have the world's single women mourned a wedding as today, but Ashley is the woman who stole his heart—the woman who left the sworn bachelor no other option but marriage. And we hear the ladies cry, 'Who is this woman?' For more on Ashley, we go to Jen Jenkins in 'copter 7.*"

"*Rick, we're live over the Stanford University chapel, awaiting the much-anticipated arrival of the enigmatic Ashley Stockingdale: a woman who brought Manolo Blahnik, shoemaker to the stars, all the way to California to design her diamond-encrusted bridal slippers. Who is this Ashley?*" Jen leans into the camera's lens, "*I'm glad you asked.*

"*Ashley Wilkes Stockingdale came from humble beginnings and grew up in a quaint California bungalow. The child of a homemaker and a carpenter, Ashley always knew she was destined for something great. Although there was time for frivolity, like high school cheerleading, Ashley was a serious student, passing the California bar her very first time out. And she hasn't forgotten her roots; when asked if Franklin Graham might perform the ceremony, Ashley declined, choosing her beloved pastor instead. Rumor has it she'll arrive in a cream-colored, body hugging Vera Wang gown. The world waits . . . back to you, Rick."*

Yes, the world waits. And so do I. *There's single for a season, and single for a reason.* My singles' pastor used to say that and laugh like staccato SpongeBob. I remember thinking it was hilarious until the day I turned thirty. Then my thoughts turned much darker, like hey, maybe *I* am single for a reason. That's a depressing day, when you realize Prince Charming isn't riding in on a white horse, and J. Vernon McGee is starting to sound awfully handsome on the radio.

I gaze around the singles group, and it's rife with its reasons. Tim Hanson has those hair plugs that look like he's sprouting rows of corn on his head. Jake Henley has been pining over an ex-girlfriend that no one's ever seen, for going on three years now. He still talks to her on the phone, and I just want to say, "Wake up, dimwit! She's moved on!" To waste your life on an emotional relationship that is going nowhere is such an easy out, don't you think? It makes him unavailable, and avoiding commitment is now that much simpler.

There's Kay Harding, resident organizer and anal-retentive of the group. She can run everyone's life perfectly and is content to do so. The sad thing is we all go along, without enough will of our own to plan our social lives. Kay does a fine job, and we always have something to do on Saturday night, so who's complaining? Kay's home looks like Martha Stewart lives with her, but she's alone. Just like me. So here I'm left to wonder, if all their reasons are so blatantly obvious, what's mine? And why can't I see it when I see everyone else's so clearly?

When I graduated from law school from Santa Clara University and became a patent attorney, I thought the world was my oyster. My head had a hard time fitting through the doorway, it was so grossly oversized. It's been shriveling ever since with the daily rejection that is my reality.

My mother told me that no man wanted to marry a lawyer. "You're too educated," she'd say. Like I was supposed to dumb myself down for Mr. Right. I laughed at such a ridiculous concept. After all, I'd dated plenty in college, but I waited on real romance because I knew there was someone out there who would make my feet tingle and my brain fog. Alas, I'd settle for a phone call at this point. My mom's intellectual theory is starting to gel like her aspic. But I live in Silicon Valley—it's not like intellect is a bad thing here— so where's my knight in shining silicone?

Family support is everywhere. Besides my mother, there's my brother who calls me "bus bait"—as in, I have more chance of getting hit by a bus than married after thirty. They've proven that study is totally bogus, but does that mean anything to my brother? Absolutely not. I just pity the poor woman who eventually gets stuck with him.

He's a bus driver, by the way. And probably the one to run me down just to prove his point.

Don't get me wrong. I live a full life as a Christian single, and I'm not waiting for life to start when I get married. I just can't stop wondering, what is *my* reason? Do I have some glaring flaw that I cannot be witness to? This kind of thing just drives me crazy, like when men my age marry twelve-year-olds fresh from college. Okay, so they are in their early twenties. But I remember rooting for *The Bachelor* when he chose a woman who was twenty-seven. Finally, a man who saw a little age like a fine wine, rather than vinegar past its prime.

Yet here I sit, with all the same single people I've been sitting near for years. Once in a while, we'll get some cute young thing in her twenties and some single guy swoops out of nowhere and whisks her away. Leaving us "reason" people wondering what strange scent we give off. Maybe it's desperation.

I don't feel desperate. I sing in the worship band, I work at the homeless shelter, and I'm busy nearly every night of the week. Granted, my busyness translates into which reality television show is on that night, but I still have my routine.

Kay Harding has taken the podium, and her familiar voice breaks into my thoughts. "Saturday night we're going to the local Starbucks for a talent night. If anyone wants to sign up, please see me after Sunday school." Kay takes the pen from behind her ear and attaches it to the clipboard. "I'll send the sign-up sheet around, but see me if you're performing."

The thought of invading a local coffee house and

humiliating myself sends my stomach surging. At the same time, I know I'll be there. What else do I have to do? I'm in such a rut. It's like when an engineer tries to explain a new segment of technology to me. I know I'll eventually get it, but the early frustration leaves me wondering why I do what I do.

Jim Henderson is clapping. I call Jim "Wild at Heart Man" because he can't seem to say a thing without quoting John Eldredge. Trouble is, I think Jim missed the message of that book because he's not more masculine, just more annoying. Of course, I'm not one to judge because I've been sitting here, same as him, waiting for someone to bear witness to my feminine wiles.

Seth Greenwood stands up. Seth is the one anomaly in the group. He's handsome, albeit bald, but that doesn't bother me. He has crystal blue eyes and a heart as big as the San Francisco Bay. He's a programmer—read: Geek. But who isn't in the Silicon Valley? He's thirty-four—granted his baldness makes him look a little older—but he's always there for anyone who needs him. Including me. Right now, he's got an out-of-work salesman friend living with him. And that guy brought two cats along. Seth's "reason" is probably just fear of commitment, the universal fear of single men everywhere, but something tells me he won't stay in that trench forever. So I guess maybe he's a "season" man. Time will tell.

Seth takes center stage over the rickety music stand. "On Wednesday night, after Bible Study, we're watching *Notorious*. It's an old movie with Cary Grant" (the women coo here) "and Ingrid Bergman" (now a few guys whistle). "Anyone interested"—Seth looks over at Kay and her organized clipboard and winces just a bit. "Well, anyone interested can just show up on Wednesday night. We'll know why you're there. Bring a snack, or be at the mercy of my fridge." Seth sits back down, and I feel my smile break loose. Seth encapsulates an invisible charm, like Fred Astaire. You can't really see his attractiveness in a Hugh Jackman way, but there's something about him that throws you off, in a good sort of way.

The singles' pastor stands up. "If that takes care of all the announcements, I have one of my own." Pastor Max Romanski is dreamy to look at, sort of a cross between the quarterback in high school and the president of the student body all grown up. Not the cool guy who peaked in high school, but the one whose gift transcends adolescence.

Max is tall and radiates this vibrant love for the Lord. Just by the way he looks at his wife—all googly-eyed, like a lovesick teenager—makes you appreciate him. And maybe covet just a little bit.

Max's wife, Kelly, is a beautiful, blond, doe-eyed princess. Sweeter than caramel, there is no mistaking why Kelly married. She was the girl in high school we all wished we could be, with the right clothes and the stylish haircut. I can't imagine Kelly ever *not* knowing how to look.

Max beams a grin, ideal for one of those BriteSmile ads. "Kelly and I would like to announce we are expecting a baby, and we're due in July."

Everyone claps. A polite round of applause that implies joy for the new gift of life, yet an irritable jealousy that no one wants to feel, but who can help it? Every time someone gets pregnant it's just another reminder: There's Absolutely No Chance of That Happening in My Life

Anytime in the Near Future. Unless God is planning another Immaculate Conception, and I'm thinking He's done with that kind of miracle.

So I clap a bit more than the others and smile. It's one of those plastered, fake smiles, but it's all I can manage. I am happy for them, really I am, and I know that envy is a sin, so I force such feelings away. But when I help throw another shower, and when I hold their perfect bundle of joy, it will hurt—and I hate that I feel that way.

I notice that I do better at reacting than Kay Harding. I can't imagine what it's like for her with everything in her life so ordered. You almost believe she could snap up a baby by putting a line item in her Palm Pilot. But it hasn't happened yet and she's past forty. The age that invokes panic in us all.

We move on to prayer. Same old stuff. If we were any shallower in our prayers, we'd be floating. It's all about jobs, and job changes, and maybe moving from one apartment to another. But who among us would dare to bare their soul? It's as though announcing our loneliness is like making it a reality. Heaven forbid we discuss something publicly that actually means something to us. Like, it's been six months and I haven't had a date, or that, as sad as the coffee house talent show is, it's the highlight of our week. But we don't say any of those things. We either say everything's fine, or we whine about our jobs and apartments.

Truthfully, I can't really complain about work. I picked a boring profession, and it is a real snoozer most of the time. Since my expectations weren't high in the first place, I'm content. Being a patent lawyer and working with engineers, you'd think I'd have beaus galore to choose from for potential husbands. However, at work, engineers are on a different plane. They're not thinking about dates or women, they are thinking about an integrated circuit they must procure, and since they can only open one mental compartment at a time, my chance of getting a boyfriend at work is about as slim as Ally McBeal's neck.

After prayer, we go into Bible study. Right now we're studying submission to authority. Maybe Pastor Max is hoping to defer some job prayer requests, but so far it isn't working. Submission, to a single, is a bit like explaining commitment to a male. It makes sense, but you don't really have much of an opportunity to test-drive the sermon without a partner.

We go home to our separate apartments, and we think about submission, but unless the neighbor's cat walks by and we bow before it, the good intentions drift away. I have no trouble being submissive to my boss. She tells me what to do; I do it. It's not a hard concept for me, really. Since there's no one else in real authority over me, I guess I'm okay there.

Max winds up his lesson with a hearty, "Go rejoice and be glad in this day!"

His invocation announces Sunday afternoon has arrived. Now, as a collective entity we will head to a local restaurant, most likely Chili's or Applebee's, and prove to the waitress why we are all single. Kay will order like she's at a San Francisco five-star restaurant, *Hold this, this on the side, blah, blah, blah* . . .

Someone will inevitably snap at the waitress, usually right before we all pray for the meal. The bill used to come up short, so now Kay ensures that all bills are tallied separately, yet another reason for the waitress to hate us. Someone used to assume that tax and tip is taken off the tally, rather than added, and a few of us had to add an extra dollar. It's never worth the argument, but it makes me cringe at the witness good Christians can be: willing to sacrifice their faith for that extra buck.

So I'm in a rut. And short of jumping from an airplane, which I'm not inclined to do, or planning a vacation, which I can't afford to take, lest someone else takes my position, I have no idea how to get out of my current situation. I've considered on-line dating, but then I think, do I want my computer to reject me, too? Remembering Meg Ryan's excitement when she had e-mail in *You've Got Mail*, I can't help but think what an empty in box might do to me. Like, "I can't even see you and you're still a loser!"

Maybe I need a makeover, but I already got one of those cute blunt cuts. One thing to remember when you get your hair chopped like a movie star is that they still have that face, and you still have yours. So while it may look cute for Halle Barry to get shorn like a hairless Chihuahua, it is simply not a good look for me. I was going for a Reese Witherspoon look this time, but Reese lives a charmed life. Her hair flips right; mine is in a perpetual state of confusion.

"Are you going to lunch with us, Ash?" Seth asks.

I don't want to admit I have nothing better to do, so I answer, "Of course I am. Wouldn't miss it." I'm downright perky with cheerleader enthusiasm.

"Sam is driving. Do you want to come with us?"

Now, I'd like to think of this as chivalry, but parking is limited at the restaurant and in all probability, it's a logistical issue that drives Seth to ask me about a ride.

"Sure." I shrug, but my heart does a little cartwheel. It's those blue eyes of his. They are like a gemologist's dream of aquamarine and sapphire. The perfect jewel created by God alone, and when they're pointed at you? Well, at the risk of being cliché, my knees go weak. Seth and I have a long history. He calls me when he gets dumped. I call him when no one calls me. We've been friends for years. And friends is all we'll ever be.

So I grab my Prada bag, a gift to myself when I passed the bar, and I follow Sam and Seth to the car. I say follow, because unfortunately, chivalry is dead in Silicon Valley. I know from experience that Seth won't open my door, and he'll make me sit in the back while he rides shotgun. It's hard to overly romanticize an engineer. They are what they are: practical above all else. And at six foot two, sitting in the backseat is wholly impractical for Seth.

I look into those blue eyes, and I envision a future where Seth thinks of me as a girl. He may have his Master's Degree in Engineering Management, but he's in the first grade when it comes to women. I can picture him pulling my hair before I can picture him kissing me. Of course, this infers I have hair left to pull and sadly, I don't. I used to have cascading tresses like the romance books say, but a picture of Reese Witherspoon in *InStyle* and I was a sheep to the slaughter.

We pile into the Saab, Sam's beat-up version of the European sedan, and we head to our familiar hangout. The waitresses are probably fighting now as to who will get us in their section.

2

Lunch is just as I expect. The waitress practically falls to the ground in worship when we depart. Who says we're not witnessing to the outside world when we go out? When you can leave a waitress lying prostrate on the ground, you have yourself some serious faith-spreading.

Seth is back to discussing video games with Sam in the front seat of the Saab. They're talking about some secret key in some corner chamber, and I smile dumbly, like I have any notion as to what they're talking about. Or any care.

When I was in eighth grade and boys discussed video games, I understood. Now that I'm thirty-one I think to myself, *If you boys would grow up, you might be having sex by now instead of playing Super Mario XXXIV.* But as an aging virgin, who am I to judge?

"You want me to drop you off at church or home?" Sam looks at me in the rearview mirror. His Asian eyes are pleading with me silently to save him the extra jaunt to church.

"I kinda need my car," I say, trying to keep the

"You're an Imbecile" out of my voice. Although it should be obvious that I'd like to be taken to where I left my vehicle, I've learned that engineers do not understand simple math: A+B = C. After all, B is an unknown, right? And if B takes an engineer out of his desired path, then the equation just doesn't add up.

I rail on engineers, but if you lived here in Silicon Valley where the men are engineers, and the women are hopelessly single, you'd understand my point. When a new science-fiction movie opens here, it's an event worthy of a costume. A nice dinner out is considered Dave & Buster's, the local grown-up arcade. Just once I want to meet up with a man who knows it's good manners to open a lady's door and let her enter first. Not a race.

Seth turns around, his blue eyes shining with laughter. He instinctively knows where Sam should be driving, but he keeps it all inside. As though he enjoys the private joke of how clueless his friends are. "We're watching *The Matrix* tonight, Ash. You want to come over?"

"No thanks. I'm doing dinner at my mom's house tonight." *My birthday dinner.* I don't add that I'll be home in time for *Masterpiece Theatre,* or that I think *The Matrix* is stupid. That's blasphemy around here. "Don't you guys ever get tired of our lives in Silicon Valley?"

We're at a traffic signal, and they both turn around and stare at me as if I have whipped cream on my nose.

"What do you mean?" Sam asks.

"I mean, we always do the same things. We hang out at the coffee shop, we see the same movies, we—you know, I can't even think of what else we do. We should plan a trip to the beach and have a wild volleyball game or something."

The light has changed, but they're both still staring. "*The Matrix* is an allegory, a worldview, if you will."

"We've still seen it a few times," I try half-heartedly. I've started it. Now we'll get into the deeper discussions— like why Spock, without feeling, would sacrifice himself for mankind in *Star Trek Genesis.*

"Do you want to watch *Lord of the Rings?*" Seth asks.

I can't help my audible sigh. "No. I'm going to my mom's. Never mind. I was just thinking out loud." That must be the burning smell in the car.

Seth's face screws up into a tight knot. He cannot understand my problem today, and I can't fathom my own lack of interest in the life around me. Engineers have their own language, their own culture. My fear is that I speak it fluently, and if I ever leave, will I still be able to speak English? Or will I revert to discussions about the battle for Middle-earth? These are my people.

"Maybe you need a vacation, Ashley," Seth says.

"Maybe I do." I shrug. "But I can't take one now. We're right in the middle of six new patents at work. There might be some kind of bonus when I'm done . . . maybe then my boss won't be so crazed." But in my heart, I don't hold out much hope. Vacation is a dirty word in the Valley. It's for weaklings and the unem- ployed. The money in Silicon Valley is great, but the most valuable commodity is time, and my boss owns it. Hence, she owns me.

Affording a vacation means taking the risk you'll come back to the same money and stock options when you leave—and that isn't likely. Choosing a Hawaiian beach over employment somehow feels irresponsible. And finding your next job in a down economy, fresh from the dot-com implosion, is not fun.

If I were a robot, I'd be better suited for life here. In many ways, I used to be robotic, but something in me snapped. Maybe it's my birthday, another year older and wiser and all that. All I know is that I'm suddenly aware of all the colors around me, the beautiful rolling hills and majestic oaks that surround me. It's just like in *The Wizard of Oz*, where everything comes to life, and I'm aware of my own blatant black-and-white coloring. The green in my bank account has sprung to life, taunting me with its chlorophyll while I wither and die.

We arrive at my car, and both men are still looking at me like I've eaten a fish farm.

"Thanks for the ride. Enjoy the movie." I clamber out of the backseat and open my Audi's trunk. Granted, I do it to see if they'll wait and make sure I'm safely into the car. They don't, of course, and I just can't help but see the humor in the situation. I'm laughing in the church parking lot, looking like the weirdo I have become.

My best, and now married, girlfriend, Brea, also happens to be in the parking lot, and she's shaking her head at me. There are just a few vehicles left in the lot, and her minivan is near my Audi.

Brea is smiling; her dark wavy hair and trendy glasses make her model caliber. Terminally enthusiastic, Brea is the type of person you don't want to be sitting next to in a meeting because everything out of her mouth is encouraging. She makes us practical people feel like the death knell. But I love her. And so does everyone else. She's impossible not to love.

"You're laughing by yourself. Should I be worried?" Brea crosses her arms and lifts her perfectly-waxed brows.

"I'm weird. Since when did you not know this?" Tactfully, I switch gears. "Where's Prince Charming?"

"John has a meeting with the elder board about the Easter program. Did you do lunch with the gang?" Brea used to be part of "the gang" until John whisked her off into marital bliss. I know there must be realism to marriage that I don't see, but with Brea and Pastor's Wife Kelly, it's invisible. The two of them would be happy if they were each married to Attila the Hun. They'd tell him how powerful and sexy he was.

"Did they do anything special for your birthday?" Brea asks, pulling off her sunglasses and staring at me with earnest hope.

"No. No birthday celebrations. The gang went to Chili's again. The waitress despises us, the Middle-earth battle will rage forever, and *The Matrix* is playing again tonight at Seth's. Typical day."

"Oh, you! Why didn't you go to Seth's house? It sounds like fun, and you know you like him. I've seen the way you look at him." Brea slides her sunglasses into her thick hair like a casual headband. Her green eyes stare into mine. "Admit it."

"Will you pass a note for me in homeroom?" I jump up and down, thoroughly enjoying my moment of humor.

"Oh, Ash, it's okay if you like someone, you know. Since when did you become so cynical?"

After a long, quiet thought, the accusation brings the sting of tears to my eyes. "Cynical—that's an ugly word. But it's true. I don't know what's happening to me . . ." I pace back and forth in front of her, trying to work it out in my own head as well as explain it to her. Maybe she can help me see straight again, calm my topsy-turvy brain.

"I'm struggling, Brea, and I don't know why. I have everything I thought I wanted . . . but my life seems so empty. I wish I knew what to do next. I guess all my goals have been met, and they haven't been replaced with any-thing new."

She takes my hand in her overly-concerned way. I love Brea. "You don't think a husband will change that, do you, Ash?"

I shake my head. "I know it won't. But it's not just the Husband Hunt that haunts me. On the outside, I look like Miss Success, don't I?" I place the shape of an *L* on my forehead with my fingers. "I thought I'd change the world. And here I am eating at a chain restaurant every Sunday with people who don't truly care if I come. Or if I'm another year older."

"I think you're just in a mood, Ashley. I've never known you to feel sorry for yourself. And the Reasons love you. Everyone loves you."

"Why shouldn't I feel sorry for myself? I just spent my birthday Dutch treat at Chili's." I'm thinking Brea got a diamond tennis bracelet for her last birthday. That somebody made her a cake from scratch. Does she not see the dichotomy here?

Brea doesn't mean anything by it, of course. She doesn't possess an evil bone in that size-four frame of hers. Brea's whole face suddenly lights up. "I need to tell you some-thing that will cheer you up," she whispers.

Just by the way she says it, I know. "You're pregnant!"

Her smile fades. "How'd you know?"

I laugh. "Something about your glow, I suppose. That and the new minivan you bought after your honeymoon. It's not like you haven't been waiting for this very moment since I met you."

Brea smoothes her stomach. "Can you believe it's finally happening though?"

"No!" I squeal appropriately, pulling her into an embrace. "I'm so happy for you, Brea." I fight the nausea as I stare past her perfect hair and into the empty parking lot. Pastor's Wife Kelly and my best friend. Two preggers announcements in one day is a bit much for me to take. *Lord, did you forget it's my birthday? You said you wouldn't give me more than I can handle, but com'on!*

I take a deep breath and compose an appropriate smile so I can let my best friend out of my death grip. Brea was created to be a mother. She has all those nesting instincts, like buying a minivan before children. Her constant mothering of me is testament to her abilities: taking me to church, rescuing me from a drunken high school party, and showing me that even though my parents didn't seem to care, God did. I don't know what I would have turned out to be without Brea and her young love of God. Perhaps a slightly high bus driver like my brother.

Brea's children will look like Baby Gap models. She will never dress her kids like nerds, and unlike my own mother, she innately understands the disaster of wearing floods in junior high school or the wrong brand of jeans at all. Brea's kids will be leaders, and Christ in them will be cool. That's a pretty awesome legacy. It makes me wistful and misty-eyed just to think of it.

"When do we get to go shopping for her?" I ask.

"It might be a boy, you know." Brea lifts her eyebrows.

"She wouldn't dare be a boy. Auntie Ashley wants to buy her very cute things in pink." I shove a fist to my hip.

"If he's a boy, John won't appreciate pink. Men are funny that way."

I clap my hands, "We can buy her little Lilly Pulitzer sweaters! And Oilily mother/daughter dresses. I can hardly wait! Pop this kid out!" I rub her tummy.

Brea crosses her arms. "Don't get me all excited. If I have a boy I want to be happy, not disappointed."

I relent. "Okay, so we have to shop at Baby Gap if it's a boy. Still cute! We can get those little chambray caps and maybe some sunglasses. Hey, what about little itsy-bitsy Old Navy jeans?" We both squeal.

Brea's shoulders relax. "I can hardly wait, Ashley." She rubs her tummy again.

"Me either." And I can't. I have heard of Brea's dreams for twenty-five years. Her ultimate goal was always to be a mother, to put into practice all that homemaking she acted out when we played house. (I was always the husband. What does that tell you?)

Brea lives to be Mrs. John Wright. They've left the singles group and are now happily imbedded in the couples group, which will no doubt turn into the young families group. I wish I could go with her, if only because I'm sick of standing in the same place. Being single is sometimes like this great drawn circle. I have all the freedom I can imagine yet this inability to step outside that line, which amounts to no freedom at all. I want to see what it's like where I fear to tread.

Brea hugs me again.

"What was that for?"

"I'm so proud of you, Ashley. I always knew you'd be someone really important. I'm praying my children won't be ditsy like me, but smart like their Auntie Ashley."

I shake my head. "You've always said that, Brea. But you've always been the intelligent one. The one who knew drunken football players didn't want to be just my friend. The one who knew my brother wasn't hiding botany plants for biology in my back-pack . . ."

"Maybe I should home school?" Brea laughs and tosses her dark brown curls. Out of the corner of my eye, I see her husband, John, catch a glimpse of the movement from the top of the church steps. He watches Brea as if he has a hummingbird in his possession, and he just can't believe he caught her.

Brea knows everything she needs to know about making those around her happy. It's something you can't learn in school, but the world around you changes with such a gift.

I say good-bye and jump into my little two-seater Audi. *Two seats*. Without my briefcase, I'd only have need of one.

3

Dinner at my mom's house is always quite the occasion. My brother shows up, only because it's quite convenient, living there and all. The bus driving business doesn't pay much in the Valley, unless you count easy access to new marijuana dealers. And I don't count that. My brother, Dave, apparently did when he got the job.

Thankfully, random drug testing is part of his career, and we all breathe a sigh of relief over that little law. Dave's been allowed to live with my parents rent-free as long as he has viable employment. Never underestimate the motivation of sheer laziness.

Dave is like a "how-to" on lenient parenting. I honestly think my parents should take him back to the high school where he was "Mr. Jock" and show the current students what peaking at sixteen does for a person's long-term career. You know, to give the band nerds some hope.

"Happy birthday, you old maid." Dave slaps me on the back, laughing his little brother snicker. Except he's twenty-eight. "How's it feel to have another year of bus baithood ahead of you?"

"Grow up." I put my hand over my mouth and pretend to yawn. "Oh, I forgot, you did grow up. It's just not that obvious because you're, like, living with your mama!"

"Ashley Wilkes Stockingdale, you be nice to your brother." My mother comes out of the kitchen carrying what looks like a side of beef, ringed with potatoes. She's wearing her homemade apron and reminding me that marital bliss is definitely not all I dream it will be. Mom kisses my cheek. "Happy birthday, dear."

Dad is watching football in the family room, too immersed to bother saying hello or even acknowledge his firstborn's birthday. My brother sits down in front of the pot roast and stretches his arms behind him. "I'm starving," he says.

"You just wait, Dave. Your father will come in on commercial and pray for us."

Prayer. That is just what this family needs. So we wait. My brother can hardly resist the temptation of razzing me, and he preys like a crouched lion until the opportunity presents itself. My mother walks into the kitchen to get the rest of my birthday feast—which will no doubt include Strawberry Angel Food Cake, my favorite since kindergarten.

"Hey, maybe this is the year you'll find some sucker— I mean, *guy*—to marry you."

I don't say what I want to say. I give my Christianity credit for that. "Do you really think I need some man to rescue me?" I ball my fists under my chin, "I guess my brand new Audi TT convertible and my apartment in Palo Alto are really hard to deal with—my life is a trial, an utter trial! I guess you're right, Dave, I do hope a man will rescue me soon." I add a wistful sigh for effect. "But when is someone coming to rescue you?"

As ever, my mother comes out at the worst possible time. "Ashley, it's not becoming to hurt your brother that way." My mother has never caught Dave saying a word against anyone. "Ashley wouldn't talk that way about another."

Ashley is Ashley Wilkes of *Gone with the Wind* and my namesake. Why my mother thought to name me after the mealy-mouthed male character, rather than Rhett or Scarlett, is a Big Question. But it does explain her undying devotion to Dave, who possesses Ashley's useless ways in spades. I suppose too much spark is dangerous in a person, and my mother, Mary Stockingdale, never could handle conflict. I should count my blessings I won't be asked to marry one of my cousins. Wilkeses always do, you know.

"Hey Mom, you know the rents are coming down lately." I look at my brother, and the corner of my lip lifts ever so slightly. Dave's eyes thin as if to make his dark threat known. "Dave might go ahead and look for his own place soon."

"Now Ashley, you know your brother is in the service industry. He's just never going to make the kind of money a patent attorney does because he helps people." She pats my shoulder as she places Jell-O salad on the table. The service industry. Like cutting off a Mercedes for the sheer joy of it is service oriented.

Dave gives a sardonic smile. "Some of us were out living life while others wasted all those beautiful summer days in a classroom."

"Classroom?" I ask dryly. "You make law school

sound like elementary school. But then that's all you've known, right?"

"Hey. I went to the school of reality. I can explain *my* job."

"David," my mother says. "Your sister worked hard for her job. You should be proud of her." I barely conceal my shock that she's standing up for me. Her reproach makes Dave take pause, at least. "Hank!" my mother yells to my father. "Come pray so we can eat!"

"It's in overtime! Start without me," he shouts back. Praying is not exactly my dad's specialty. I'm appreciative they put forth an effort when I'm over, but the last time my father graced a church with his presence was when he married my mother. His prayers are usually those rhyming numbers that sound like an Irish limerick.

My mother smiles awkwardly, wondering if she should try to pray, then obviously decides against it. "Well, let's eat then." She sits down. "So Ashley, tell us about your work. Have you written any new documents yet?"

"Patents, Mom. Yes, I'm doing about three a month, but six right now."

"That's nice. Hank! Come in here before your food gets cold!" She turns back to me, and I notice, not for the first time, that my mother is really beautiful. She has nearly no wrinkles, and her skin is supple like a fresh apricot. Her gray eyes hold a certain sparkle that belies their bland color. Why she put up with my father all these years mystifies me. Although he did let her name me Ashley Wilkes Stockingdale, so maybe she had more choices than I give her credit for.

My father comes lumbering out of the family room

zipping up his pants. Why watching TV with his pants zipped is too great a feat, I'll never know. I'd buy him some bigger trousers, but they already hang on him like an elephant's backside girth.

He looks at my mother, while smoothing his hand over his balding head. "You couldn't wait five minutes?"

"It's your daughter's birthday."

Dad looks at me and nods. "Happy birthday."

"Thank you." And there you have it. The longest conversation we will have all year.

"So are you seeing anyone, honey?" My mom's eyes grow wider with hope.

Dave nearly spits his potatoes out through his nose, but he stays quiet for once. What's the deal? Usually he'd say something like, "Ashley dating someone? Not unless you've seen bacon in midair. Did pork take flight today, Dad?"

Dad laughs at his unspoken joke anyway and then Dave laughs out loud. Sophomoric humor reigns in the Stockingdale family, and once it's begun it will quickly degenerate until my mother intercedes. Suddenly I'm longing for the intellectual stimulation of a good allegory discussion on a science-fiction movie. I should have gone to Seth's.

My father's laughter mingled with Dave's raucous cackle creeps into my invisible barrier. My nose stings as I ward off the tears. Not because of the idiotic humor; I'm used to that. Because no one truly cares that I'm thirty-one today. Not one person. My best friend has left me for a husband, and I'm standing in the world all alone with the three people I resemble the very least in this world. There has to be a place for me. There just has to be.

All three of them, with forks halted, stare at me with gaping mouths. "No, Mom, I'm not seeing anyone." The silverware begins to clink again.

"What about that nice guy you were with at Brea's wedding?"

"He was the best man, Mom. He's married."

"Well, for heaven's sake," my mother says with exasperation. "Who isn't married these days? Are you trying at all? You're a pretty girl, Ashley. The boys must look your way sometimes."

Trying at all? Now I cough back a laugh. "Well, I'm thinking of dressing like Lara Croft and Tomb Raiding in my spare time. Do you think that might catch Mr. Right's attention?"

Dave laughs with me, and it's odd, this sudden feeling of kinship with a man I wouldn't normally choose to be with. Ever. But then we are laughing at me, after all. Still . . . I glance his way, but he's deep into the roast.

"Is Lara like Scarlett O'Hara?" My mom's gray eyes blink repeatedly. She is not stupid . . . so why does she pretend that I can still be the belle of the ball? In her day, women got married out of high school. It was simple. Everyone did it. It's not the same game anymore, now that masters and doctorates are as common as ants, and church weddings are scarcer than valuable stock options.

I decide it's best to drop the Lara line of thinking. "What about you, Dave? Is there anyone special in your life these days?"

My parents' heads whip around like metal rushing to its polar opposite. "Is there someone, honey?" my mom asks.

I have to cover my mouth to avoid the thrill I garner from such a childish and cheap trick. I'm thirty-one, but get me with my brother and I am immediately eight years old again, taking inordinate amounts of pleasure in watching him squirm. If I ever hope to grow as a Christian, I think I need to avoid my brother.

Dave acts the part of lecherous playboy, but in reality he's scared of women. He seems attracted to the type who can't question his authority. Most of his dates have been from third-world Asian countries, and they rely on Dave for English translation. I'm sure driving a bus in a place where American cars are considered substandard doesn't afford him the best opportunities for meeting women, but when I think this way I actually feel sorry for him. So I avoid it at all costs.

Dave shakes his head and grunts; a perfectly acceptable form of communication in the Stockingdale home. I'm an avid creationist, but that's not to say I don't see the argument for evolution in my brother.

My mother's attention quickly turns back to me. After all, it is my birthday. Why should Dave have all the fun? "Ashley, I saw in the paper that boy you dated in college got married. His wife is just a darling, little blond thing. I saved the paper for you."

"Thanks, Mom." Because that's what I really wanted to see to make this birthday complete.

Mom rises from the table, as if she cannot wait to show me the wedding day that should have been mine. I give her a tight-lipped smile as she hands me the newspaper, pointing to my ex-boyfriend and his "darling" bride. She is darling, and that ticks me off because she's probably about ten years younger than Eddie. At least I receive the satisfaction of seeing that Eddie has lost most of his hair.

"They're a cute couple," I say, sliding the paper back toward my mother.

"Did you see her dress?" She slides the paper back toward me. "It looks very rich."

I was thinking more like Barbie meets *American Idol*, but I keep my opinion to myself. Why must I be a Christian in my own childhood home? It's the hardest test of them all. I try Dave's *modus operandi* and grunt a reply, but it doesn't produce the desired result.

"Ashley? Did you see her dress?" my mother asks again.

"Yes, Mom. It's beautiful. She's a peach." Another clamped-mouth smile injected here. "I'm sure Eddie is ensured pure bliss with such a gorgeous dress as that beside him."

"Now Ashley, what did Eddie ever do to you?"

Um, dump me because I wouldn't sleep with his slimy self after a drunken binge at a fraternity party. "Nothing, Mom."

"Sometimes I think that religion of yours makes you so judgmental. We didn't raise you to not enjoy other people's good news." My mom pats my hand. "It's not becoming. I would think God wants us to love one another and be happy for another's happiness."

Mom, your God resembles Winnie the Pooh more than the biblical model. "Love rejoices with the Truth," I say. The truth is that Eddie slept his way through Santa Clara University while he used me for all his "intellectual" dates. I was the *girlfriend du jour* when the occasion called for some semblance of professionalism.

I look up across the table to see Dave studying me then glance down guiltily to his food. He shovels in the rest of his meat and potatoes, pushes back from the table, and, still chewing, swings his arms into his leather jacket— the only decent piece of clothing he owns.

"Are you going out, Dave?" Mom asks, her voice going up an octave.

"Yeah, I got plans," he says, ducking his head to actually help swallow the enormous amount in his mouth. His eyes flicker to me. "Happy birthday, Ash."

"But, Dave, you haven't had cake!" Mom cries.

"Later. I'll catch a piece later." He's out the door, leaving me flabbergasted that (1) he was somewhat decent for a minute and (2) he gets to leave on my birthday and I'm stuck here.

My father grunts and then belches. Apparently having made more room, he finishes his meat and slogs back to his never-ending football fest without a word to me or a thanks to my mother for preparing his meal. I see my mother's spark die. It's been thirty-four years, and every night she's hopeful something in my father will change. Yet it never does. How I wish I could tell her what Brea told me about expectations and not having them if you want happiness, but I can't. I cry every time I try, and emotion is not tolerated in the Stockingdale home.

I help my mother clear the dishes, and then together we sit down to eat some cake. I eat quickly. I just want this over. "I should get home, Mom. Tomorrow is Monday."

"I'm glad you could join us for dinner, Ashley. You don't look a day over twenty-six." She pats my back.

That's little consolation to me today, considering I

feel fifty-six. "Thanks, Mom." I watch her take my father his coffee and my world shifts. Brea is off and married. My family doesn't really know me, and I'm a full-fledged, card-carrying member of the Silicon Valley Reasons. "This is not how I intend to spend my thirty-first year on this earth."

"What, dear?"

"I'm going to get a makeover," I announce. She smiles her "Isn't that sweet?" grin. I kiss her cheek and get ready for the Real World after a brief visit to this alternate universe. Oh yeah, Mama, bring on the engineers, fresh-roasted coffee, and snaking traffic. Monday in Silicon Valley: Go!

4

It's seven a.m. and I schlep all the files from my car to my office. Jim Bailey, the mail guy, rescues me at the doorway.

"Ashley, how was the weekend?" Jim clucks the side of his mouth and winks. "Did you do the wild thang?"

It's far too early for this. In what guy manual is it written that women want to be talked to like this? Because I really need to get my hands on that book and put it in the section called Ways to Make Sure You Never Have a Woman in Your Life.

"The wild thang? What's that, Jim?" I flutter my eyelashes innocently. I am not known around these hallowed halls as the church girl for nothing. To his credit, he visibly blushes, and his freckled face turns into one bright shade of autumnal red.

"Don't mind me, I was just being friendly. You got anything going out yet?"

I shake my head. "Not yet." Watching him slink away, I now feel guilty. I didn't mean to take the John Wayne out of his day. Call me old fashioned, but I just don't care to be asked if I did *it* this weekend. Is that too much to expect? But now, of course, I feel guilty for making him feel so bad about himself. And I hear my mother's voice chastising me for being judgmental.

Purvi Sharma, my boss, waltzes in with an equal bushel of legal-sized envelopes to the ones I brought home with me and drops them on my desk. "What's wrong with Jim? Are you picking on him again?" She laughs. Purvi is a dream to work for. She's from India, glad to be here in America, and makes the most of every day and every situation.

She doesn't let the uptight VPs rile her when they need something. After watching people starve in the streets of Calcutta, she sees creating technology patents as rearranging deck chairs on the Titanic. Stress is not something that gets to her. But of course, half the time it doesn't get to her because she rolls it down to me. Still, I wish I possessed her inner calm. Not her workaholic, insane hours. But her peace.

When a VP comes storming in my office, I just freak about the deadlines and other companies swooping in to steal the deal because I haven't fought hard enough for patent approval. My whole world goes into a tailspin as if technology as we know it—nay, that fate of all humankind—will cease to exist.

I really need to get out more.

Purvi has one son by a husband who is still in India, and everything revolves around the boy. There's a lot to admire about Purvi, but her stance on sexual harassment—and the mail guy's comments—is decidedly rooted in historical eras, and not one of her better qualities. She thinks of SH as an American thing, and she finds the whole concept hilarious. *You sue when a man notices you're beautiful and makes stupid comments? Only in America. Only in America. In my country, they'd give your family many cows, you'd say goodbye to your family, and we'd be done with the entire mess. Case closed.*

But, of course, in some parts of her country, women are supposed to cover everything with skin on it and walk behind their husbands, so I don't make mention of the hypocrisy. Or the fact that she's not living in her country, nor that her husband isn't living with her. Purvi shoves more files toward me, and I watch and wonder over her as she exits.

Dianna Kendal is outside Purvi's office. A bit of a stereotype, this one. Purvi's opposite in many ways. She dresses quite provocatively at work, and she's a single mother to a four-year-old girl. No mother should dress like she does. By Dianna's mere, yet carefully-measured actions, she lets every man know she's available. I watch the dance she does with both fascination and disgust because she's the type of woman that no man would take seriously. She practically shouts that she's the kind you sleep with but don't marry.

I know so many single mothers at the church. They are solid Christians who made a mistake and devote themselves entirely to their children. Dianna is not that type of mother. She's the kind who would make the same mistake again and again if given the opportunity. And she looks for it at every corner.

Whenever Dianna speaks to a man in the office, she must suddenly bend over for something to give them a glimpse of her cleavage, which is pressurized in a torture chamber of a bra. If there's an easier way to tell a man you're the kind who sleeps around readily, I don't know what it is. But I'm watching Dianna, and she's leaning against her desk with her head swaying, licking her lips slowly.

Jim Bailey is losing the battle not to stare, then fumbling around to gather her mail. It's like watching a bad beer commercial in my very own office setting. Oh, the joy.

My office phone rings, and it's Brea, according to caller ID. I know Brea is probably at home in hysterics because she's worried about me and the news of her pregnancy. She's left me ten messages and three e-mails already. I must get it through to her that I am Ecstatic about The News.

I pick up the phone without a hello. "Enough already. I'm so stinkin' happy for you, I want to run through the forest in a tiger-striped thong and shout my enthusiasm through the trees!"

"Ashley?" John's voice sounds confused and I wince. I have just given my best friend's husband a visual. *Blech.*

John has never understood my relationship with his wife. But we have emerged from a parallel childhood. Brea and I practically speak our own language, and it's hard for John. I know it drives my own parents crazy.

"John, sorry. I thought you were Brea." I'm hoping I've given him enough time to shake the visual of me in a thong. *Heaven knows I want to shake it.*

"Listen, Brea's in the hospital. She had a miscarriage this morning, and she's crying her eyes out."

I gasp. Mouth the word no, but say nothing. There is no air.

"I wish there was something I could do, but I just keep saying the wrong things. She wants you, Ashley."

My stomach roils. If I could do anything to take this burden from Brea, I would. No one wanted a baby more than she did. No one deserves a baby more than she does, and I'd give up my own right to bear children if it would help her. I clutch my ailing tummy which aches with empathy.

I find my voice. "Is she all right? Physically, I mean?" I ask.

"She's worn out. She made them do two ultrasounds before she would believe the baby wasn't there anymore. They want to do a D&C tomorrow and told her we could try again in a few months, but she's brokenhearted, Ashley. It feels like she'll never be happy again." John's voice cracks, and I feel myself tear up. To know Brea is so loved by a man lifts my spirits like nothing else could. There will be more babies, but this one will always be Brea's first. I know her.

"I'll be right there, John. Tell her I'm on my way."

I'm tentative, but I make my excuses to Purvi and grab a few envelopes I'll work on late into the night. For once, my heart doesn't care about work or how many hours this day will cost me. My best friend has just lost the only thing she ever wanted, and I want to rail at the injustice of it all. While crack-heads can spew out children, my precious Brea loses hers.

I try to calm down in the car and wipe away any remnants of emotion. The last thing Brea needs to see is my tears. Lord knows she has enough for both of us right now. I stop by Starbucks and order her a Frappuccino with a double shot. When all else fails, there's no pick-me-up like a good double-dose of caffeine. The only drug we've ever done. The only drug we'll ever need. Except, of course, for an epidural when the day comes. Oh! An epidural . . . I tear up all over again.

I find Brea at the hospital, stuffed into a tiny room with two other people. Both speak some form of Chinese—and loudly. Brea's lovely face is red, and her eyes and nose are swollen from weeping. She breaks down again when she sees me and her whole body begins to shake. John is sitting beside her and immediately sees his chance to retreat.

"I'll be back later," John says as he makes a mad dash for the door.

"It's okay, Brea," I say through tears as we cling to one another. "There will be other babies. This one just wasn't ready yet, that's all. That man"—I point to the doorway—"who just ran out of here like a lead greyhound loves you with his whole heart."

We giggle through our tears.

She sniffles again. "Is that Frappuccino for me?"

I pull it away and pretend to sip. "No. Did you want one?"

"I'm betting it's got extra shots in it, and you're too much of a worm to drink that much caffeine."

I hand it over. "See, that's one plus. You can drink caffeine again."

"Only for today. Then I'm going on the cleanest diet you ever saw me do. This is going to be the healthiest womb known to modern science." She pulls another Kleenex from the box on her bed. "Other pregnant women will have to fear me as their babies yearn for the comforts of my luxury suite."

"Sheesh, you'd better stay away from my brother, then. Dave finds out there's no rent and he's there." We both break into cackling laughter, and the Asian roommates give us a look as if we've swallowed something whole. "I'm so sorry, Brea." We hug again tightly.

"Do you think John is okay?" Brea asks as she leans back against her pillows.

I nod. "He loves you so much, Brea. He only wants you to be okay."

"I didn't know what to say to him, Ash. He looks at me with those puppy dog eyes, and I feel like I've let him down. I just feel so guilty I can't look at him."

Her brutal honesty stabs me in the chest. Here John knows he's got the best deal in town, and Brea is worried she's letting him down. "John knows that God has His plan," I say. "I can't for the life of me imagine what it is right now, but there's a reason for this." Why does faith sound so empty at times like this? I know the words are true, but there's sometimes a sting to them when you're hurting. Try as we might, words can't make pain go away.

"John could have married someone who could give him babies right away, someone who could use a big word in a sentence. Why did he marry me?" She sniffles again and pulls another tissue from the box.

"Need I remind you that John wasn't the only guy who wanted to marry you, Brea? He did not marry you for how many kids you could pop out in the shortest amount of time. And I'm sick of you saying you're stupid. You're one of the smartest people I know and definitely the highest caliber. I know I'd trade some IQ points for a date."

Brea smirks at me but then the smile fades. She stares

out the window, chin quivering. "Did you see John's face just now? He wants a baby."

How can Brea not see his pain for her? His love for her? I'd die to have a man look at me like that. "He's crushed. But he's only concerned for you right now. Doesn't that tell you anything about how people feel about you? You're not a surrogate. He's not out ten thousand bucks. You're the woman he loves." I sigh and try to attempt some humor. "Now I know you're hurting big-time. You haven't even touched your Frapp."

She ignores my brilliant quip. "What if I can't have any kids ever?"

"I'm not going to discuss that because that's ridiculous. The doctors haven't said anything like that, right? Miscarriages happen, what, one in four pregnancies, or something? It's just a fluke."

Brea shakes her head. "Maybe God is waiting for you to get married so we can be pregnant together."

"Hmmm. I'm thinking you and me hormonal together is not a good thing. Let's just let you have your day, and you can tell me how it's done. How's that?"

I sit with Brea for maybe an hour, and then I see it in her eyes. She wants John now. He's pacing down the hallway like a tiger at mealtime. It's funny that John and I should have such a hard time starting a conversation when we have Brea in common. I guess we both want all of her; sharing Brea is like taking a sliver of cheesecake and leaving the rest for someone who might not fully appreciate it.

But she belongs to him. "She's all yours," I say to John when he comes bounding over like an oversized Saint Bernard puppy.

"Thanks, Ashley." John pats my shoulder and then grips me in an awkward hug. "We'll have more babies. You told her that, right?"

I look through the doorway at Brea and then John. "I told her. God's told her, too. Right?" I stare at her until a small smile appears on her face. She knows. God has not left her side.

Once out of the room, I wander the hallways to the maternity ward. Is there anyone who can visit the hospital without going to the hope ward? The place where new life is fresh and smells baby-powder sweet.

There are three little babies in the viewing window. One is small and pink, and apparently angry at his new accommodations. The other is blessed with a shock of black hair and dark eyebrows, and I can't help but think that it's a good thing he's a boy because waxing all that would just be painful. Then there's one little girl. She's got a touch of strawberry blond hair and creamy skin with a healthy pink tone, and my heart clenches all over again for Brea.

Just when you think you've got life all figured out, God throws a curve ball. *You're out!*

5

After an extended day of work after my morning off, the other gang (not The Reasons, but a group of paralegals and administrative assistants with a few female engineers for good measure) is going out to get drinks. I generally go along, even though I only hit the hard stuff: Diet Coke on the rocks. If I'm feeling really bold, I go all out and add a twist of lemon. But tonight, I'm just too distraught over Brea, and I've read the same patents over and over again, but they just appear as word salad. I'd go sit with her and cheer her up but that's John's job now, and I feel genuinely useless. So I'll just go home and pout. Besides, *The Bachelor* is on tonight and what better way to forget *my* life than to watch a bunch of inflated females vie for faux princess-ship?

My apartment is dark when I enter, except for that scarlet beacon of hope: the answering machine blink. The temptation of the red flash—it speaks to me, beckons me nearer, asks me *ARE YOU BUSY ON SATURDAY NIGHT?* In its own primitive Morse code it hypnotizes me, and I come to it with my arms outstretched zombie-like.

I breathe deeply. For three years running, I've made a New Year's resolution that I will not tie my worth to this cruel appliance, but I've never been able to curb my over-eager enthusiasm. This bubble of hope grows and grows until I am certain Colin Firth has left his gorgeous Italian wife for me, or Rupert Everett has suddenly gone straight and can think of no one but me: Ashley Wilkes Stockingdale. Yes, I know it's not the most Christian dream, but it's there all the same.

Generally, I press the answer button, only to be offered a great phone plan or told I have just won a fabulous, all-expense-paid trip to Vegas. So I should learn, right? I'm a Smart Girl. Yet I continue to dream and, even now, my heart races with the possibilities. I try to ratchet my hopes down a bit. It will not be a date. It will probably not even be someone I know, but rather one of those friendly-sounding guys on tape pushing weather-proof windows.

Dropping my purse, I press the button and brace for the worst.

"Ashley, hi. It's Seth. Listen, I was wondering if you might be free for a movie or dinner this week. I wanted to talk to you about something."

I press the button three more times just to make sure I've heard him right. A movie. Now does that mean he wants me to come over for the old movie night with the gang? Okay, but he said dinner. Maybe he wants me to bring dinner with me before the movie?

"I should just give him the benefit of the doubt. Maybe he's asking me for a date." I hold my shoulders up high and dial his work number. Seth works until all hours of the night, like me, so I figure that's my best shot.

"Seth Greenwood."

"Hi Seth, it's Ashley."

He pauses for a moment, and in that split second I wonder if I misunderstood his message, that the last person he wants to hear from is me, that—

"Ashley, good to hear from you. You got my message then, good. I was wondering if we could do something later on this week. I want to ask you about something."

He wanted me to call! "You can ask me anything," I say like an idiot middle-schooler. *Mental note: Do not try to be cool.*

"How's Wednesday night? Maybe we could meet at Fresh Choice."

"Great," I answer with little enthusiasm. Fresh Choice is a salad bar. No waitresses, no tips, definitely no reservations. Now I'm wondering if I'm not worthy of a sit-down restaurant, does he expect us to go Dutch, too? And there's no mention of the movie. *Two whole days of questions. How will I get through it?*

"I'll see you there at seven. Is that okay?" Seth asks.

He'll see me there. He can't pick me up?

"Perfect. I'll see you then." Now of course, I'm dying to call Brea. But I wonder if she's up to hearing about my paltry love life. I reason she probably needs a good laugh, and I call her at home, hoping she's not asleep yet.

Expecting John, I'm surprised when Brea's voice answers groggily. "Hello?"

"Brea, hi. It's me."

"Oh, Ashley. Finally someone who's speaking in English! Tell me something I can understand. Please. Please. That hospital room made me want to run screaming by the end of the day. I've been listening to non-stop chatter in a foreign language for the entire day. Did you know they bicker like Italians?"

"Great. So you felt right at home."

"Very funny."

"Hey, I'm not sure if this qualifies as something you can understand, but Seth called and asked me out for Wednesday night."

"Where?"

"Dinner at Fresh Choice."

"Oh."

"Well, it's better than nothing," I say brightly.

"True, but not much better." We both laugh. "What are you going to wear? I wish I could go shopping with you, but I don't think I'm going to feel up to it after tomorrow and the procedure. Will you bring the outfit by before you wear it?"

A date is, first and foremost, a reason to shop. Ann Taylor calls my name, and I know I must find that perfect outfit, the cross between *I look good*, and *Hey, I'm not trying to look good*.

"Ann Taylor has this darling pantsuit I saw in the window last week. It's kind of a maroonish color with beading."

"Maroon is not your color, Ash. You need something bright like red or white on top. Besides, beading at Fresh Choice? I think you'll feel a little self-conscious when some toddler splashes Hi-C on you."

She's right, of course. I hate that. "Okay, there's a cute nautical outfit at Talbot's. I saw it in the catalog. It's red." And so we dance. The negotiation of the perfect ensemble. Since Brea won't be there in body, she must be there in spirit, and we discuss everything right down to the earrings and lipstick shade. The talk cheers us both up.

After I hang up, I make myself a gourmet meal of Cup-o-Noodles and Diet Coke and settle in for a night with the fake Prince Charming *Bachelor*. Unfortunately, I can only stomach about five minutes of the show and its pathetic jiggling collection of women, since it's early in the season.

No wonder men think we're pitiful. I cannot imagine I'm from the same species as these women, much less the same gender. If my mom thinks I'm too smart for the average male, no wonder. According to this show, Anna Nicole Smith is too intelligent for the average male.

Clicking off the television, I grab a women's magazine only to find out the rest of the world is entirely immersed in their sex lives. At some point over the years women's magazines become a litany on STDs and how to have good sex despite them—no longer fashion-oriented. Unless you count the latest lingerie styles. If women are from Venus, I'm living on Pluto.

Being celibate in today's "forward-thinking" society makes me feel like the freak I am, and yet every time I read these mags, I thank my Lord He's kept me pure. I go on faith that someday, some man somewhere will recognize my virginity for the gift it is, and not ask what's wrong with me. Brea found her man, and somewhere mine is searching for me. Maybe it's Seth. At least I'm not completely tainted. There's a dash of hope in me yet.

I settle back in my chair and force away the thought that Seth sounded very businesslike on the phone. *Ah, we*

have arrived at the phone analysis portion of our day. What
he said, what he meant. What I said, what I meant, what I
could have said differently . . .

His business tone is what I'm left with. He didn't
sound overly gushy, but he was at work. He can't exactly
fawn over a date when he's sitting in a cubicle. And he is
Seth. So it's not like he has the emotional capacity to coo
anyway. In the end, I decide there's nothing to worry
about. Seth asked me out.

Looking at my watch, it's 8:30 already. Too late to go
to the mall, so I grab up a few mail-order catalogs for ideas
and plan my grand entrance at Fresh Choice. I will be
radiant. What's that word they only use in romance novels? Oh yeah, *exquisite.* I will be exquisite. Or resplendent.
Either one is fine by me. I will render Seth speechless at
the mere sight of me. He will not hear the screaming tod-
dlers, nor notice his chain-restaurant surroundings. No,
he will have eyes only for me.

By Wednesday, I still haven't found an outfit. You can
never find anything when you're looking for it. When will
I learn this? So I've spent two lunch hours at the mall to
no avail. My date is in four hours and what I'm now wearing—a white ribbed sweater and fitted red skirt from Ann
Taylor—is looking awfully good to me at this point.
Sadly, I'm not resplendent, I'm more what you'd call tolerable. But hey, Elizabeth Bennet was tolerable, and she
nabbed Mr. Darcy. Maybe it's better that I don't knock
Seth over with my appearance. Maybe it's better to seem

average and let him see my inner spark—which will ignite like a fireworks finale.

I've tried on a few pairs of pants, but the low hip thing is made for, well, I don't know who it's made for. Certainly not a woman with hips. I saw a picture of J. Lo in low-cut white jeans and they looked awful. Now if a style doesn't look good on J. Lo, chances are very slim it looks good on anyone else, so why is this all you can purchase in the stores? I mean, if the average woman is a size ten, and J. Lo is, say, a small six, why are these pelvis-baring jeans available in a size sixteen? It's a cruel joke on the women of America. And we purchase the punch line like lemmings.

Rather than go home and get ready for my date, I just finish a few projects at work. Taking tonight off is going to cost me. But before I know it, it's time for Fresh Choice and I'm rushing out the door. I pat a little powder on my face and apply a sheer red lipstick. My look says I tried, but not too hard. It says, I'm your friend, but I'm open to more. Let's talk.

When I get to the restaurant, Seth is there waiting in the foyer. Those eyes just make my heart stop with their icy blue color. His smile catches all the way to his eyes. Seth and I have known each other for years. We've worked the singles committees together, and while there's always been this underlying current, neither one of us has ever acted on it. Clearly that's all about to change. Never has he looked at me this way. I'm sure of it. Pretty sure. Almost sure.

"H-hi," I sputter. So graceful! I pull my chin up, fighting to recover.

"Hi. I'm glad you could make it." He grabs me a tray and lets me go first in the salad bar line. Okay, that's kind of chivalrous.

We go through the entire line in silence, and once we get to the register, I start to panic. Should I take out my wallet? It's not like nine dollars is going to set him back, but is it tacky to expect it? I nibble on my lip for a brief moment, then decide he's invited me; he can pay for it. I smile as he takes out his wallet, complete with coupon, and gets us a deal.

"Thanks for dinner."

"My pleasure." We find a table, and he ignores the tray in front of him, concentrating on my nose. Never has he looked at me so intently! And those eyes! I'm seeing him in a tux at our wedding, his eyes in our son's head, a head covered with hair that is my color, definitely in more abundance than that atop Seth's—

"I suppose you're wondering what I wanted to talk to you about."

Now, I'm close to panting. I didn't know there was an agenda. Should I have caught some clue that there was an agenda? If Brea was feeling better, she would have caught it. I should have analyzed the conversation more. *Mental note: Listen to the answering machine at least six times.*

"No, I wasn't really wondering. I thought you just invited me out for dinner. We've been friends a long time now, right?" My hope is that this dissuades him from telling me something I don't want to hear.

He spills his Coke—he's endearingly clutsy at times— and rises to go fetch some napkins. I shove an olive in my mouth and imagine our conversation to come.

"I need patent help on a project I'm working on. There was no one else I could call. No one else I could trust." Seth looks away for a moment. The emotion is too great.

"You know I'm here for you, Seth." I curl my hand over his. "Do you have the drawings yet?"

"Right here." Seth pulls out schematics, and our eyes meet again, as if for the first time. He shoves aside the blueprints and kisses me hungrily over the table.

I return his kiss feverishly.

My eyes drop to the paperwork on the floor. "Your product is incredible. An unmet market. You'll be wealthy beyond your wildest dreams," I say, breathless from macking.

"It will make us wealthy, Ashley. Which is why I bought you this to say thank you." He holds up a two-carat princess-cut diamond ring—set in platinum, of course. "Will you marry me?"

"Oh yes, Seth. Yes."

"Ashley, are you all right?" He sits down across from me again and mops up the mess. "I thought it would be good to talk over dinner," he says, his eyes all business once more.

My heart's pounding, and I try to steady my breathing. It wouldn't do to die of a heart attack now. Not now. "Go ahead, Seth."

"You've been singing in the worship band sometimes."

"Yes," I say slowly, flushing a little in pride. "I'm no Jaci Velasquez or anything, and my work schedule doesn't allow for the practice time lately, but—"

He cuts me off. "The other gal who sings with you, Arin?"

My smile fades. "Yes?"

"Do you think," he pauses. "Well, do you think she would ever go out with me?"

Breathe. Breathe. Don't show disappointment. But I can't talk. I can't force the words I don't feel, and I realize why I could never be a trial lawyer or a poker player. I shrug an answer, but my heart is broken. I didn't realize until this very moment what Seth meant to me. His quiet intellect . . . and searing blue eyes . . . and gentle smile captured a part of me. It happened so subtly over the years I never had time to notice. We have so much history, I took it for granted.

"Has Arin ever mentioned me?" Seth prods, puncturing that sharp object into my heart farther.

"She's only twenty-four," I say, feeling the distinct desire to point out his baldness and age, but I clamp my mouth shut, hoping *her* age will be enough to stab his over-inflated, egotistical, insensitive balloon . . .

He nods eagerly, blindly. "She's beautiful, don't you think?"

Oh, to wring his neck. To just reach my hands around his scrawny little throat and shout, *YOU ARE SINGLE FOR A REASON. I THOUGHT YOU WERE A SEASON MAN, BUT YOU ARE A REASON MAN IN THE WORST WAY!* My salad suddenly looks wilted and I'm debating how to get through the next half-hour, but my anger is simmering, brewing to a slow boil.

But suddenly I have this surreal calm. I am in control. I continue with all the composure in the world, like Glenn Close, Academy-Award-winning actress, with maybe a little *Fatal Attraction* thrown in. Without the bunny. "Arin is very beautiful," I say calmly. Maybe a little scarily calm. "Arin also has a boyfriend at Stanford. In medical school," I add. But I get nowhere. If Seth had any sense of Season in him, it's long since buried under the multitude of Reasons. He could teach Clueless 101.

"Is it serious?" Seth asks. "Between Arin and her boyfriend?"

"Are you serious?" I don't mean to sound nasty, but can this man be so completely dull-witted? Can he possibly think a gorgeous twenty-four-year-old woman, with a boyfriend who resembles Hugh Jackman in doctor form, would be interested in his balding science-fiction self? Every part of me wants to start shouting his list of reasons off for the benefit of the restaurant's crowd.

"So you're saying you don't think she'd go out with me." Seth stabs a cherry tomato with vigor. He obviously still has hope within him despite my non-answer, and I want to snuff it out with my heel.

"I can't really say what she'd do. Why don't you ask her?"

"I don't want to make a fool of myself."

Too late. The crying kids in the restaurant become louder. Unbearably loud. And I can't stomach the thought of one more bite sitting across from Seth. "You know, I'm not feeling very well, and I have a lot of work that I brought home with me tonight. Good luck with Arin. Sorry I can't be more helpful, but I don't know her that well. She's a little young for me to be close friends with. And maybe for you to date."

He doesn't catch on that I'm gathering up my things, preparing to flee. "I thought maybe because she liked allegory and science fiction we might make a good match. She also likes to ski, I heard."

I like to read romance novels, but you don't see me calling up Fabio.

I rise, preparing to let loose a comment worthy of this night. But my heart softens at his furrowed brows, and my fingers massage my purse strap. *Lord God, give me Your grace here when I feel like slicing him to ribbons!* "Seth, um, you're a . . . great guy. Who's to say what Arin might do? But you don't seem like the kind of person to go after another man's girl."

"Thanks, Ashley. I appreciate your honesty." *He doesn't believe a word of it, but he appreciates it all the same.*

"No problem," I breathe, singing "Chain of Fools" in my head. "See you Sunday?"

"Sunday," he affirms.

I wouldn't mind if I never see a Reason again. I leave the restaurant thankful I didn't spend one red cent on this "date." This wasn't even worth a new lipstick. I'm embarrassed to call Brea and tell her what a yutz I am, but I won't make it through the night without her emotional support. Besides, she'll have some good bald jokes, and tonight I will relish every one of them. *Two-carat princesscut*—Seth would buy a cubic zirconia and tell me about the deal he got on QVC just to add insult to injury.

Mental note: Do not expect blood from a turnip.

6

Saturday night arrives—if I had a date it would take forever to get here but, alas, I don't, and it's snuck up on me like a deadline. It's talent night at the local Starbucks, and I debate a thousand times if I should go. Seth will be there, which discourages me, but I figure I can't run from him forever. He doesn't know what I feel any more than Arin knows about his secret crush.

I check the TV guide first, and there's nothing worth staying home for. Which is really saying something. It wouldn't have taken much; even a *Growing Pains* reunion would have worked. Kirk Cameron in puberty was all I was asking for, but I got nothin'.

I head to the coffee shop, determined that I will not perform under any circumstances. I'm thankful I never signed Kay Harding's infamous clipboard under duress. The blank clipboard is my ticket to freedom.

First Community Church's Open Mic Night at Starbucks is our attempt at showing the world we Christians are fun without the alcohol, without the drugs, without the sex. We *are* in Silicon Valley, so fun is relatively tame anyway.

If it weren't for the sales and marketing people, the Christians would blend right in. It's perfectly acceptable for a weekend's entertainment to include video games or RISK. You don't have to be Christian. Being an engineer is quite enough.

I'm a Trivial Pursuit gal myself, but engineers, while they know the universal language of math, are quite naive on useless facts. The singles group has played a few times, and I'm always left realizing I barely know that WWII took place but can repeat verbatim a cover story from *People* magazine back in 1988. There has to be a market for that kind of talent somewhere, wouldn't you think? Maybe there's a don't-repeat-this-fashion-era-mistake think tank or something in Washington.

Entering the coffee house, I order a tall double latte and find my way to one of the tables next to the other singles without better plans. We smile at each other, a bit embarrassed we're here, but then Kay starts the show and things loosen up a bit. Kay's great as emcee because she loves what she does, and she doesn't care what anyone thinks. To have that ability must be so liberating. I covet it. To be able to get up in front of this group and belly dance would be so empowering.

"Welcome to the second bi-annual Open Mic Night for First Community's singles group!"

Shouts and hollers rise, and it's sounding like the Trigonometry Olympics from high school. I'm hanging out with the Mathletes now! The baristas behind the counter roll their eyes, and I'm wishing I could just ignore stuff like that, just not even notice it happening. Our group doesn't get that we're comical. Why do *I* have to see it? Apparently, I'm the only one who does. *God, could You*

*just give me some special blinders for that? Make me socially
inept too, so I can enjoy myself?*

I want to go through life thinking Christian Colin
Firth will be along anytime I'm ready. That he'd gladly
put up with my bigger-than-J. Lo bum and sorry social
schedule, stealing me away to an idyllic life on some trop-
ical island, where he would be endlessly awed by my
unyielding knowledge of Johnny Depp trivia.

Sigh.

"First up for tonight's show is Seth Greenwood."

I clap politely, wondering if Seth has any idea he
dissed me. Seth has two beakers in his hands, and he proceeds to show us how salt added to water makes an egg
float. I raise my eyebrows. Now that ought to impress
Arin. It's too bad she's not here. I'm having Glenn Close
bunny thoughts again. Let's move on, shall we?

"Next up," Kay consults her trusty sidekick, the clipboard. "Please welcome Sam Wong, who will be performing the Spock Dying Scene from *Star Trek.*"

Sam has dressed his portly self in a *Star Trek* uniform
and, quite frankly, he looks more like a navy Teletubbie
than a Vulcan, but I suspend reality for the enjoyment of
the scene.

Sam sputters and wrinkles his drawn-on Vulcan eyebrows for emotion, talking to an unseen Captain Kirk.
"Don't mourn. My sacrifice is logical. The needs of many
outweigh the needs of the few, or the one." The drama
increases as Sam pretends to die, gives Spock-the-Vulcan
fingers, and tells him to live long and prosper. Then he
pushes the button on a tape machine where a rousing edi-
tion of "Amazing Grace" is played on the bagpipes.

The crowd goes wild, and I wonder how anyone is going to follow this—the grand finale of all engineer performances.

"Jake, you're up, buddy," Kay says.

Jake stands up and bows before actually doing anything. I swear I do not turn for the barista's reaction this time. Progress. I'm making progress.

"May I have a beautiful assistant, please?" Jake is looking directly at me, and I immediately check my purse for something I must have left at home. It's useless though; Jake comes toward me. "Ashley, will you do me the honor?"

He takes my hand and lifts me up. Unfortunately, playing with my purse has wrapped the strap around my ankles, and I feel the top half of me going forward but, unable to untangle my feet, the bottom half is firmly planted back at the chair. I grasp Jake's hand, desperately trying to stay off the hard tile floor, but it's useless. I tumble into an ungodly pretzel position and pull Jake down on top of me. Immediately followed by my double, thankfully-cold latte. The whole room roars with laughter, and for once, we have the approval of the baristas who are clapping wildly.

As ladylike as possible, I wait for Jake to remove himself from my torso, and then uncross my legs and lift myself off the floor gingerly. I smile as if I'd enjoyed the whole scene, but I am mortified and can't bear to look up. Jake, being a typical Silicon Valley male, quickly makes matters worse.

"Correction. I need an attractive assistant who can stand up by herself." He laughs and grabs another woman from the giggling audience, wiping the excess coffee from his jeans. I sheepishly climb back into my seat and take the ribbing that is so richly deserved. Patting the coffee on my khakis, I know the exercise is futile. Color-safe bleach is my only option.

The worst part is that now I'm committed for the entire evening. I cannot possibly leave early without risking another big laugh.

Jake reads, from memory, a sonnet by Keats to his new, better-coordinated assistant. She blushes, and I wonder if maybe bowing out in clumsy fashion wasn't the better alternative to having Jake under the delusion that he is a romantic. With all the waitresses he's stiffed and extra dollars that have been added to bills for Jake's sake, he fails miserably in the role of Romeo. Unless there's a woman who finds home-cooked canned-chicken burritos a sexy alternative to gourmet dining.

Just when I think my evening can't get much worse, in walks Arin sans Boyfriend. She's wearing a darling pair of colorful capris on her size-two frame and a fitted T-shirt with flip-flops—in January—and it's a look that works for her. She sits beside me and twists her gorgeous long blond hair. The action catches the attention of the entire room, and Seth is practically hyperventilating.

Her smile is bright and excited. "What did I miss?"

"Seth Greenwood did a science experiment, Sam Wong died as Spock, and now Jake is reading poetry." My voice is monotone.

"Which one is Seth again?"

Ah, vindication. "He's the bald guy over there."

"Oh." She looks and turns away uninterested. "Nothing too exciting yet, huh?"

Kay Hard.ng laughs, overhearing our conversation. "Well, Ashley did some gymnastics for us. Don't be so modest, Ashley, it was the best thing all night. She tripped all over her own feet."

I grin and give one of those half-laughs. Arin gets it, and she knows it's not funny. Even though she's twenty-four and darling and men bow at her feet as if she's royalty, I like her anyway. Sue me.

"Ashley fell and spilled coffee, and you all thought that was funny?" Arin asks with almost a Southern drawl to the question.

"Of course it was funny," Kay explains like a math equation. "You're too young to remember, but Nancy Reagan was always doing that in her day. The news would play it at night and we'd laugh."

"I think that's terrible. Ashley could have been hurt, burned even. Not to mention her feelings from being laughed at. Isn't this a Christian group?" The cutesy smile leaves Arin's face, replaced by an angry frown. She has this Rene Zellweger quality. Both guys and girls love her, and despite my history with Seth, I like her, too.

Kay clicks her tongue and goes back to emceeing.

"Ashley," Arin says loudly. "Let's sing a song up there!"

I shake my head wildly. "I couldn't. I have no talent. Where's your boyfriend?" I ask, hoping to put off the idea of me performing anything other than a patent explanation.

Arin pouts. "The boyfriend is studying. On a Saturday night. Can you beat that? I told him it's a good thing he's cute." She places two tiny fists on her non-existent waist. The last time my waist was as small as hers, I was graduating from sixth grade. I look again. Maybe not even then.

"Come on, Ashley. It will be fun. What do we have to lose? We sing every Sunday."

"That's different."

"The karaoke machine is up there. Come on." Arin gets up and pulls me out of my seat. Keep in mind, I'm still soaked with coffee, and now I'm standing next to a darling, size-two blond. We won't even mention Seth's presence. *Mental note: Don't be so picky about television entertainment on a Saturday night.*

Kay's clipboard suddenly clears as everyone is mystified by the sight of the young, enigmatic Arin joining our group and heading to the stage. We are The Reasons, after all. She hasn't a one.

She opens the karaoke book and finds us a song. The music starts, and before I know it, we're crooning a kissing song by Cher.

"Ooooh Oooh Oooh," I sing, as Arin goes for the wild part. At the end we break into a pile of giggles, and I realize with total shock that I really enjoyed myself. "Let's do it again!"

"You pick this time." Arin and I are still giggling, and our humor is infectious because this crowd of stagnant engineers is going crazy. More so than for Spock's dying. At this rate, we could outpace *The Matrix.* My ego is soaring by the minute.

"'The Macarena!'" I yell.

The music starts, and our hand motions are immediate. Who would have guessed this group would have known "The Macarena"? We shimmy and wiggle until the song ends, and once again I can barely breathe from laughing.

"Ashley, I didn't know you could dance." Seth is standing beside me.

"'The Macarena' isn't really dancing," I explain. "Even a patent attorney can do it."

"Hi," Seth says to Arin. "I'm Seth Greenwood."

Arin nods. Even the way she nods is cute. "Nice to meet you. Wasn't Ashley great? I knew she rocked inside that lawyer front. There's a wild woman just waiting to get out."

I swallow past an enormous lump in my throat waiting for his answer. He's not looking at Arin, but at me, and I suddenly can't believe I danced and sang in a local Starbucks. Do I have no shame? I start to laugh again at the thought.

"I've seen glimpses of her wild side before," Seth winks. "You should have seen her at the water slides last summer."

I feel my face burn. "I need an iced tea." I bolt for the counter.

As I look back, I can see that Seth and Arin actually do make a nice couple. She's listening to him like his words are pure gold, and I feel my own heart pound at the sight. *God, if this is the part where I give up what I want so someone else can be happy, umm, can You rethink that whole idea?*

Arin joins me at the counter without Seth. "He seems like a nice guy, Ashley. Have you ever dated him?"

"Seth? No, I haven't. I'm not really a big dater, actually."

Arin tosses her hand. "Me neither. What's the point?"

I shrug. "Don't you want to ever get married?"

"Ha!" Arin tosses her blond, healthy, youthful hair. "Not in this lifetime. Well, not before I'm thirty-five, anyway. Not unless I could find someone who wanted to travel the world. Someone who relished life and wasn't content to just have a day-to-day job like all the robots here."

"Wait until you're thirty to say that. Those feelings will change." I sound like the Scrooge I have become.

"No, really. I'm going to Costa Rica next month on a short-term mission. Then I want to do Africa and a safari. Kevin is too into his work for my tastes, and I've really enjoyed my time with him, but if we were both honest, we'd admit we've just been keeping each other company." Arin's little features crinkle under the dim Starbuck's light. "Besides, he's too serious for me to take seriously." She laughs, a lighthearted tinkling sort of laugh.

"You're in Silicon Valley, Arin. Everyone's serious." A serious, handsome doctor. Maybe she'll toss him my way.

"I know. And isn't that the problem? When I was in Italy last summer, people actually took the afternoon off to have a little wine and antipasto. Here, people barely remember to eat. I don't think I'm cut out to be here."

"I think I am. But lately I've been wondering," I admit. "I don't mind working twenty-four/seven. At least, I didn't used to mind." I look over at Seth who's laughing with Sam about his *Star Trek* performance. I have a longing I just don't care to feel, and Arin's indifference to him—her focus on the future, the beyond—only reminds me I'm not comfortable in my own skin. It hasn't been so long since I'd said the same thing about marriage. And now, according to my brother, and the men of First Community Church, I am bus bait. That Arin still has options about getting married ticks me off.

"Someday my prince will come . . ." she sings.

Ah, to be that naive again. Must change subject before I hurt her. "So, Costa Rica? What are you going to do there?"

"I've always wanted to see the rain forest and this mission provides the opportunity. With the economy being what it is, there are no jobs—not that an English Lit major is hot property in this town—so it's not like I'm missing out on anything." She blows her long bangs from her face. "If I'm going to be unemployed, I might as well do some good."

Ah. If only my brother Dave had had her gumption . . .

"What's to do in Costa Rica?" I ask.

"I met up with this group of dentists who just need hands. I'm going to be helping them work on the locals who live near the coast. I'll get to go into the rain forest and see the monkeys and the birds . . . we'll cover quite a bit of territory."

"Wow," I say, truly in awe. Here I thought I was adventurous going to the movies without prepurchasing tickets on the Internet.

"You're lucky this kind of life makes you happy, Ashley."

I look at Seth who's still laughing with Sam. "Am I?"

7

I have spent this Sunday morning in meditative prayer. With fasting, the whole bit. I have discerned God's will for my day, and I am ready to handle anything—peace like a river and all that. I am so darn pacified, I'm positively comatose.

Like driftwood floating on the surf, I feel my melancholy history pass away. Maybe I'll now be the life of the party like Arin. I have released bad memories from my body into the abyss of my ocean. I leave them on the altar of God's throne and move forward. Today is the first day of my new faith. I will live without upset. I will not be anxious for anything, but in prayer and petition, I will present my requests to God. And the peace of God, which transcends all understanding, will guard my heart and mind in Christ Jesus. Life is good, and I feel alive.

The phone rings.

"Hello," I say breathily to show off my new-found pacifist attitude. What good is having it if I can't share it?

"Ashley, it's Mom."

Breathe. This is my first test. "Hi, Mom!" I have vigor.

Throw it at me! Tell me I'm old, tell me I'm bus bait, tell me I'm too smart, I can handle it all. I am swathed in prayer, baby!

"Ashley, sorry to hold you up before you go to church, but I didn't want to miss you. You seem to be at church all the time anymore."

"That's okay, Mom." I should be starring in a La-Z-Boy commercial. I am downright giddy, I'm so at peace.

"I'm calling about your brother."

"He's lost his job." I let out a long breath.

"No, nothing like that. Why would you say something like that, Ashley? Your brother is a fine bus driver." She clicks her tongue. "Sometimes I just don't know what to make of you. You've had everything at your fingertips. Your brother was never as gifted as you, Ashley Wilkes Stockingdale."

Ack! The full name treatment. "Sorry, Mom. I didn't mean anything by it. Dave is a great bus driver," I say through clenched teeth. My peaceful front is leaving me. *No! Reset.*

"I'm calling because Dave is getting married, honey."

My knees buckle, my stomach nearly wretches. Did I hear her correctly? My pot-smoking, homeless, no-ambition brother is getting married before I do. My younger brother. *Okay, God, I know I just spent the morning talking to You, but I am so not talking to You right now!*

"Since last week? Did he get someone pregnant?" Where is this peace I prayed for? My calm, Christ-like reaction? I sound like I'm on Ricki Lake, not Billy Graham.

"Ashley! What a horrible thing to say. Nobody's pregnant. We like her very much. She's a nice girl."

"Does she speak English?" *There it is again, that uncontrollable mouth!*

"A little bit, why do you ask?"

"Put Dave on the phone, Mom. I want to congratulate him."

I wait a bit while the shuffling goes on. Clearly, Dave is still in bed. And why wouldn't he be? It's only nine a.m.

My brother and I have had this invisible, yet all-consuming, competition since we were children. It's time to move past it. I'm going to congratulate him, and I'm going to be happy about it. Even if it kills me.

"Hey, ever-a-bridesmaid." He laughs so hard he snorts. "What do you think of my news?"

I know he's just jealous. I know he's just jealous. Rise above this; it's the only way to move out of a desperate pattern. Lord God, help me out here!

"Dave, this really is great news. Where did you meet her?" My voice is calm. But then my mouth is moving again: "The immigration department?" *Ack, I meant to say that silently.*

Dave is nonplussed by my attack. "Just because I'm getting married and you can't get a date is no reason to be angry with me, Sis," he says with all the gentleness of a psychologist. "Someone will come along someday. I hear Florida is a good place to find wealthy widowers. Maybe you should put in for a transfer. Of course, I hear they go pretty quickly. Both to marriage and death! Better hurry." He laughs again

I ignore him. "What's your fiancée's name?"

His tone changes. "Mei Ling. She's from Hong Kong. Her father passed away when they got here, and she's been living in Michigan for the past ten years."

My heart swells for this woman. I don't know her, but she's marrying my brother. If that isn't enough to garner sympathy, I don't know what is. If Mei Ling was a citizen, I might be more inclined to think she knew what she was getting into, but her immigrant status makes me seriously worried for her long-term happiness. And my brother's. Yet, I still force thoughts away of myself dancing at their fiftieth wedding anniversary wearing a Haversham gown, bitter that my own day never came.

"Mei Ling. That's a pretty name."

Now he speaks in a voice I've never heard before. It's gentle and concerned and, quite frankly, freaking me out a bit. "She doesn't know anyone in the family, Ash. She's going to need a maid of honor, a bridal shower, and whatever else goes on. The whole routine. It's a long story, but she's here now, and of course her family can't come. China won't let them go—the commies think they won't return."

"Did you say she's from Michigan?" I ask, but I'm selfishly picturing the bridesmaid's dress and terror strikes my heart. At its base level, it's about loss of control. No bridesmaid has control, and what Silicon Valleyite can stand that? "Does she know that maids of honor pick their own gowns? I can take her shopping with me."

"Nah, she doesn't know any of those rules," he says blindly, and my heart starts beating again. If I have to be maid of honor for a sister-in-law I don't know, I might as well look gorgeous. "You'll have to fill her in. She was raised in pretty sparse circumstances."

My guilt overwhelms me. "Dave, that's not really true. The bride picks everything out."

"Oh, well, whatever. Mei Ling just wants our family to be happy. Hers won't be here obviously, and that makes her sad. You'll do what you can for her, right?"

The softness in my brother's voice makes me realize that Mei Ling is not just some sucker on the wrong path of life. He cares about her, and for the first time, I think my brother might not be a total screw-up. A heart really beats inside that lumpy chest of his. Do I dare face that? It's so much easier to write Dave off for the loser he is and leave him for God to fix.

"I'm really happy for you, Dave. I really am." And now I'm tearing up, which ticks me off. Partly because I don't want to mess up my makeup, and partly because I realize I really do love my brother. I just want him to be a grown-up, and maybe this is God's way. Allowing him to do what I wanted most, first. *Oh, the humiliation!*

"You know, I don't really think you're bus bait," Dave says.

Okay, now I'm totally freaked out. Dave, reaching out to me? After practically being civil for whole minutes of time at Mom's last week? "Let's not go overboard," I say quickly. Unless a woman over thirty does Dave's laundry, he sees no use for their walking the planet. "Put Mom back on the phone, will ya?"

There's more shuffling, and my mother comes back on the line. "It's so nice to hear you and your brother talking. Aren't you thrilled to be the maid of honor?"

"Of course I am." What does one say to the honor of being held in an esteemed position for someone you've never met? It's strange. But my brother's getting married. Surely Roswell folklore has nothing on my life.

"She's such a sweet girl. I think you'll really hit it off. She reminds me of that little gal you work for, just a bit."

"Purvi?"

"Purvi, that's right. Of course she's Indian and Mei Ling is Chinese, but they're both small and . . . what's the word?"

"Asian?"

My mom laughs. "No, dear, not Asian. They're both . . . Oriental."

I bang my head on the table. Indian may be technically Asian, but overly-educated, self-sufficient Purvi Sharma and Mei Ling probably have about as much in common as Pamela Anderson and myself.

"Mom, Oriental is kind of considered rude nowadays." As if living in the Asian rim of California amid a myriad of specialty grocery stores would not tell her that.

"Mei Ling doesn't mind. You've been in that politically correct business world too long. It's starting to color your speech. Honestly, Ashley, it's a wonder you grew up in this house at all."

"Mom, I'm going to be late for church. When's the wedding so I know when to plan the shower?"

"They're having a small wedding next month in the Chinese Church. On Valentine's Day."

They have a church? And on Valentine's Day? Now there's a depressing thought. I will be wearing a bridesmaid's gown on the International Day of Love. If that don't beat all.

"Got it, Mom. I'll talk with you later about plans. Gotta run." I hang the phone up, desperate to get to church and pray again. Because I'm already running on fumes here. I want to be happy for my brother, but there's this petty child inside me screaming at how unfair life is. I'm the oldest; I should be first!

Once at church, I try to listen to the focusing part of the sermon—that message God wants me especially to hear today—but my mind is completely preoccupied. I'm not singing today, which is a good thing, but Seth is seated beside me, which is a very bad thing. He keeps leaning over and whispering to me about Arin and their possible budding relationship. This strange thought floats through my mind, like if I had an old clothespin in my purse like on that old game show, I could clamp his lips shut. *Let's make a deal.*

"Did you talk to Arin about me?" he whispers.

"Kind of," I whisper back. *Yes, I told her that you were the bald one.* I just shake my head. Nuff said, right? Wrong. This is Seth we're talking about. And one thing can be said about engineers: They may be clueless in the romance department, but they're also fiercely competitive. Arin has suddenly become the finish line, and if Seth has to use every last one of his follicles, he's going to keep running the race.

"Did she say anything about me?"

I can almost see his tail wagging. "Seth, she has a boyfriend." I whisper too loudly, and my neighbor gives me a dirty look. "Doesn't it bother you just a little bit that you're after someone's girlfriend?"

His eyes widen. Ah, those gorgeous, sparkling, gem-toned eyes. Such a pity they mask the incredible blindness Seth possesses. Life is definitely not fair.

"She's only twenty-four, Ash. How serious could it be?"

He's got me there. "Not serious enough to keep her here, I guess. She's leaving for Costa Rica soon on a mission trip. To work with dentists." I secretly wonder if foreign mission trips have increased with the *Survivor* shows. It all sounds so horribly romantic now, doesn't it?

Arin's a cappella solo interrupts our conversation, and Seth immediately turns silent. He's gazing dreamily toward the altar, and I feel my stomach turn. He listens with his hands clasped as if he's hearing the angels sing. I can see his chest heaving as he watches her. I feel for the guy, but there's a little seething mixed in when I think back to my recent princess-cut diamond fantasies.

The Bible outright *tells* men that beauty is fleeting, yet they seem to chase after it like a leaf in a rogue wind, stumbling and grasping, while another more intricate and colorful leaf dangles on the tree.

Arin's solo ends, and he quickly restarts our conversation. "She's going where?"

"Costa Rica. On a mission trip," I repeat. Following Seth's gaze to Arin, I must admit her beauty is mesmerizing. It's not her looks. She just has that invisible quality that makes it impossible not to notice her in a room. I wish, just for one day, I could possess that spark. Eyeing Seth now, I know it has its privileges. Seth's interest, for one.

My statement has just hit Seth full force. He snaps his head like a Roman soldier's whip. "She's leaving Silicon Valley?"

I feel the distinct need to soften the blow. "Seth, you barely know her. What if you don't like her personality? I know she's pretty but—"

Seth looks at me wistfully. "You know, Ashley, I've

lived my whole life doing the safe thing. What if there's some great opportunity out there and I miss it? When you sang the other night at Starbucks, I saw this whole other side of you again. And I wondered what would happen if I took that kind of risk."

Great. He's holding me responsible for pursuing Arin.

His gaze catches mine, and I feel as though he's looking straight through me. To Arin. "I don't want to miss God's will for me because I was too wimpy to act, Ash."

God has Arin in mind for Seth? Weirder things have happened, I guess. It's just terrific. While Arin frolics in the Central American rain forest, with Seth anticipating her return, I will be wearing an off-the-rack bridesmaid's gown for an unknown Asian bride who speaks very little English. And Seth will probably call me or e-mail me, asking for my advice on dates he'll actually spend money on when Arin returns.

My life reeks like an onion.

8

After church, the singles gang meets up at Chevys, a Mexican restaurant. *Vive Mexico!* I have seated myself at the middle of the long table, and I watch as Seth jockeys for a position next to Arin. Of course, I'm talking to the woman next to me, and she has no idea my attention is directed elsewhere. Do you think there's a name for this mental condition I so evidently have?

Arin sees me and waves like the princess she is. "Ashley!" She turns quickly and runs directly into Seth who is following like a summertime shadow. "Excuse me," she giggles.

Seth frowns as Arin moves like a dragonfly around the table, buzzing through the crowds with ease. He is now faced with a Serious Dilemma. Will he risk looking obvious and come around the table, or just remain where he stands and hope I'll introduce them again after the meal?

And the winner is . . . desperation. He comes and sits on the other side of Arin after she sits down next to me. Noticing his overeager grin, she smiles uncomfortably.

"Hello." She reaches out a slender hand. Again my heart twists at the action and how it's completely entranced Seth. You know, it's one thing to be dumped by a guy. Happens to the best of us, right? But when you have to watch that same guy in the courtship dance for another's heart, well, that's just wrong.

"Hi." Seth reaches toward Arin and knocks a glass of water over, spilling icy liquid into her lap.

Arin pops up like a sea lion gasping for air. "Cooold." Her hands shake, and she looks down at her jeans and then gives me a look. "Ashley, can you come with me to the bathroom?"

"Be right back," I say, hoping to hide the obvious—that we're going to the bathroom to discuss Seth and his giant, ice-water-spilling hands. I wish I could spare him the humiliation. Maybe I should have said something more at dinner that night. Maybe I should have been even more blunt— like hitting him with a two-by-four.

We head off to the women's room, and Arin breaks into childish giggles in the mirror. "Ashley, who is that poor guy again?"

She's not making fun of him, she legitimately wants to know. I'm no longer thinking of my growling stomach. Arin has enjoyed this whole fiasco immensely, and that little voice inside me shouts that she's intrigued. Those beautiful gemstone eyes have transcended Seth's baldness, past his idiot clumsiness. Pain rushes up into my throat, constricting the words.

"That's Seth Greenwood," I finally manage.

"Why's he following me?"

"He probably thinks you're cute, Arin," I say. To be twenty-four again and actually have this explained to me. Sigh. And double sigh.

Arin dabs a paper towel on her jeans, and I notice our contrasting shapes in the mirror's reflection. I swear her jeans wouldn't house half of me, and now my appreciation for Arin's *joie de vivre* is seriously threatened. I feel gargantuan. Invisible and huge all at once.

"Ashley, why don't you come with me to Costa Rica?" she asks, still staring down and working at her jeans.

My laughter echoes in the tiled, primary-colored bathroom. I fall onto the *Corona*-papered wall. "I have a job, for one thing."

"So what? It will be there when you get back. You do get something called a vacation, don't you? Don't tell me you're like these other geeks and never take one."

I am like the other geeks. But we have a strong, motivating factor. We like to eat and pay our outrageous Palo Alto rents in the hopes that someday we can escape it all with early retirement. So we stock it up like squirrels, afraid to spend a cent lest we have to work until we're sixty-five.

"I'm just like the others," I admit. I think about the pile of possible patents waiting for me at home. *Maybe I'm worse.*

"Come on, Ashley. Come with me. It's only a month. You would have such fun. Look at how pale you are. Do you ever get out of the office?"

"It's January."

"And it's sixty-six degrees today and sunny. Perfect convertible weather. When's the last time you took the top off on that TT of yours?"

"It takes time to take it off and store it."

"When are you going to live your life, girlfriend?" She

gives up on the water stain. It actually looks elegant running down her leg. She lives a charmed life.

"I am living life. I'm just older than you, and I have responsibilities." *Like using color-safe bleach at my leisure. You probably don't even know there is such an animal.* "I didn't just get out of college, and I'm not in-between jobs at the moment. I'm in career mode. Besides, Costa Rica doesn't sound the least bit intriguing to me. I'm not a real monkey or jungle kind of person. My idea of a vacation is a weekend at the spa. Don't you have a roommate or someone who'd *like* to go?"

"Nah. They're heading in different directions. What did you do after college?" Arin persists. Okay, the perkiness is truly starting to get to me. She's like a kitten full of energy and warmth, but the tenth time she's undone your shoelace, it ceases to be cute.

"I went to law school after college." I shrug, unsure where this conversation is headed, but preferring it to the Seth Discussion immensely.

"So what did you do *before* law school?" Arin's gray-blue eyes are round with anticipation.

"I went to summer school and took a few classes to get them out of the way."

She groans. "Didn't you know you were supposed to take at least the summer and do something wild and frivolous? Before fulfilling responsibilities was your main goal in life? Promise me that you'll do something fun while I'm gone. Even if it's just to take the TT to the beach on Saturday afternoon with the top down. Promise me. I'm worried about you, Ashley. You're not like the others, but you act just like them."

It's funny how something so insipid like the beach sounds completely out of the question to me. When did I get so ordered? Am I OCD? Nah, OCD is orderliness to an extreme. I'm just boring with a little anal-retentive thrown in. "You don't even really know me," I try. But she does. Somehow, this kid has me pegged.

She ignores my defense. "I want you to promise me to do something extreme. Something that challenges your life, gets you out of the rut, the way you did last night at the coffee house."

Taking in a deep breath, I answer, "I promise." Using a different brand of fabric softener is extreme. Or not TiVo-ing one of my reality shows—watching the commercials, now that's really living on the edge.

"Now, come introduce me to Seth. He's kind of sweet. Did you notice his eyes?"

"I have noticed."

Arin starts to open the door and I stop her.

"Seth is pretty sensitive. I don't want him to get his hopes up if nothing's going to happen between you two."

"I have a boyfriend!" Arin exclaims.

"A boyfriend you'd rather break up with. Besides, it only makes you more challenging. And guys like a challenge. Even engineers. Especially engineers."

She visibly swallows and nods. "Okay, I get you." She tosses her blond hair back and forth as we return to the table.

How do you tell someone who speaks flirtation as such a natural form of communication that it's playing with fire? She has no idea the authority she holds in her tiny swaying hips. I remember this great quote I heard once: "Men play at love to get sex, and women play at sex to get love." Me, I don't play at anything. I just work like the drone I am. But things are about to change. They have to, or soon I will keel over from sheer boredom. Arin may be young and naive, but she's right about me. I need to get out of this rut, or I'll live it forever.

When we get back to the table, all the men stand up and I am irritated beyond belief. These guys *do* have chivalrous bones in their bods! They just don't think I'm worthy of it. As the men stand, I see that Tim Hanson's hair plugs are filling in a bit and that's the final straw. Tim has grown an entire colony of hair while I have done, what? Nothing but moan about my sorry life. *That's it!*

I am Ashley Wilkes Stockingdale! One does not survive school with a moniker like that without a higher purpose in life. It's time I found out what it is. I don't bother to sit back down. This is my old life. This is a life that is going nowhere with a group of people who are too lethargic to yank the bell cord and get off the bus. But I have a destination! Granted, I don't know where it is yet, but I am so going to get there.

I square my shoulders. *I have breasts*, I think to myself. Now there's something you don't get with Arin's size-two frame—well, not without paying for them, anyway. I am woman, hear me roar! Maybe I will buy a sexy new bra today.

"You know, I have things I need to do. I'd better bow out of lunch this afternoon." I'm smiling like I own this incredible secret. I am going to do something wild today.

Seth's face screws up like a plump donut. "You're leaving?" His voice cracks. He's the epitome of coolness. Not.

Oddly, Arin's face is in the same contorted expression. She has just figured out that she will be left to fend off these middle-aged engineers without my years of expertise or natural ability. I have started A Scene, and my eternally-taken-for-granted presence will be missed. Ah, the power.

"I'll see you all next week," I say like Vanna White and make my way to the door. I hear the murmurs go up, like what could possibly be more exciting than a Mexican meal with this fiesta gang? I can feel their eyes on my back. For this one fleeting moment, I am Ashley, the cute one. I have the attention of everyone in the gang. And I do not trip.

Once at my car, I roll down all the windows. It's gorgeous today. Nearly seventy degrees in January and I have just figured out why I pay the weather tax of living in California. I'm going to the beach. By myself. After I buy a bra.

Seth suddenly stands at my passenger window. "Ash, is everything okay?"

"Everything's fine," I say without emotion. "I just have this overwhelming urge to go to the beach. I live in California. It's time to take advantage of it. I want to be a tourist again and find out what happens outside the four walls of my office."

Seth looks at me, his face still puckered like the end of a burrito. "Do you want me to go with you?"

I look into those crystal eyes, and I start to wither in my convictions. For a long time, I stare into his eyes wondering if he really wants to go or if he's worried about me. Then, he speaks.

"Do you want me to invite Arin, too?" he offers. Leave

it to an engineer to pick the most opportune words for the moment.

"You know, I think I'd rather just go by myself." *The company's better.* "Besides, I have to get a new red bra at the mall."

Seth's face turns bright crimson, just like the color of lingerie I'm considering. "So I'll see you soon," I say.

"Are you mad at me, Ashley?"

"You know, Seth, I'm going to let you figure that one out." His face is even more contorted.

"I wish you'd just tell me, Ashley. We've been friends for years, and lately I don't understand a word you say."

"Have fun with Arin today." I don't say it nastily, but in effect I am saying, *Have fun with another man's girl.* Does this not register?

I've only confused him more. I race my car out of the parking lot, leaving him standing alone with his thoughts. But I don't feel any victory. It's more like the agony of defeat going on.

Now I know why I work so much. Work is so much easier than this relationship thing. Maybe I should invest in a good PlayStation II so I don't have to discuss feelings, but instead talk about secret codes and keys in chambers. Maybe then I'd understand men.

9

With the wind in my hair and Seth in my rearview mirror, I am cruising the El Camino. I'm still Arin for the moment, princess extraordinaire! On the off-chance that her husband, John, is busy, I call Brea on my cell phone. She's had enough time to recover physically, and I'm hopeful she's feeling better emotionally. I nearly squeal with excitement when she tells me she is free as a bird.

Let the heavens rejoice, I will not be on my Underwear Quest alone. Brea's anxious to lingerie-shop since the doctor said they could start trying again in two months. Do not want to go there, discussing the intimacies of her marriage, but I'm glad Brea wants to shop just the same. It makes the call of the beach pale in comparison.

Once I pick her up and I'm listening to Brea chatter about the meals she's tried to cook recently, I realize it's a necessity to have a friend who doesn't question your immediate desire for a red bra. When one is single, celibate, and a patent attorney, a new red bra is never a priority. Brea knows that, but she never questions me. She just understands instinctively that my psyche needs the new red bra. And so we shop.

Stanford Shopping Center is the crown jewel of the Bay Area's excess. It houses designer shops that most of middle-America has never heard of—and a pair of panties can set you back a week's pay. I don't shop in those stores, but I can afford Bloomingdale's, so that's where we head under a bright California January sky.

The negative aspect about Bloomie's is that you have to pass all the gorgeous "special occasion" dresses, and you must conquer the idea that, not only do you have no place to wear one of these fabulous gowns, but you probably never will. I take a deep breath, blocking out my negativity, and we climb the escalator. I can wear the red bra anywhere I want to!

"So what happened with the gang today?" Brea asks.

"They went to Chevys," I respond. "Same ol' stuff. Mexican style. *Arriba!*"

"Did you go?"

I shrug. "I didn't stay. That group is going nowhere, and I'm already there. I'm turning in my singles group pass. I need to allocate my time better."

"You're just upset about Seth. You'll get over it. And what else are you going to do? Work some more?"

"Oh, I am over him." I proceed to tell Brea about Seth's pathetic attempts at romance with Arin, right in front of my eyes. But my throat still fills with a big lump when I tell the story, so I'm not as over it as I'd like to be. I'll save news of my brother's wedding for later. One can only stomach so much of my life at once.

Brea sucks in a deep breath. "I'm sorry, Ash. But you

had your chance with Seth years ago, and you never took it."

"What?" I laugh. "When did I have my chance with Seth?"

"He followed you around just like he's doing with Arin now, and you never noticed. You were so busy with patents, and trips to Taiwan, that you never noticed him. Not until he noticed Arin."

"Marriage has dulled your memory. Seth and I have never had anything going on."

"You and Seth have been partners on the canoe trip, won the potato-sack races together, cuddled up for warmth on the hay ride . . . I could go on, but give me a break that you two didn't have something going. You talk about him being clueless . . . sheesh."

"We were friends." I hold up my palms. "Besides, my leaving The Reasons doesn't have anything to do with Seth. He's just the catalyst. I've been in the same spot for three years running. Nothing ever changes. Nothing ever happens. How am I supposed to leave a mark on my world when I don't even have a pen? I'm ready to color outside the lines. And my first project is this red bra." I pick up a luscious scarlet brassiere. Demi-cut with lace scalloped edges. "I'm going to try this on."

Brea lifts her eyebrows, but says nothing.

Entering the dressing room, I undress and try the designer bra on for size. Major problem: The mirrors show your whole body. If I could just stare into a little half-mirror and see my cleavage propped up, I'd be fine, but that's not what I see. There's a three-way mirror in this dressing room. So I not only see my buxom chest, I see my little extra tummy hanging over my grandma seamless panties and the little extra handles in the back under the bra straps. Living with all these petite Asians, my frame feels like something out of the Amazon jungle, and this mirror agrees.

Call me tainted, but I'm expecting more of a model look here. But my real-woman figure looks like an ad for Michelin ready-treads, not lingerie. I'm starting to hyperventilate. I will definitely go to the beach when I'm done, and I'm going to have another big chat with God.

I dress and slam the dressing room door. "That's just depressing," I say to Brea, but she's wearing a smile as wide as a canyon.

She is already at the register, purchasing a black see-through number with a thong back. Ugh. I turn away, my face now the color of that first bra. Thinking of your best friend in lingerie is akin to thinking about your mother in it. It's just not right.

I pick up another item to escape the visual I've just encountered. This one is violet. And has little push-up pads. *Maybe that will help the back pucker* . . .

This is the reason women shop. We're ever hopeful that we'll get into that dressing room and one particular item will give us the reflection we desire in that mirror. That ungodly three-way mirror.

Trying the purple one on, I focus only on the top half of my body and this one is not bad. I must have it. Even if it sits in my drawer for an eternity. I can tell Arin I did something wild.

Outside the dressing room, I see Nancy Hollings talking to Brea. Nancy was in our high school church teen group. The cheerleader who was so enthusiastic she had a constant, plastered-on smile. She's one of those Christians who makes you wonder if she really lives in there. You know, the kind of person who hears someone's died and she comes back with the bouncy phrase, "He's gone to be with the Lord. What a blessing!"

I try to turn back into the dressing room, but it's too late, she's seen me. "Ashley!" Nancy has a baby with her, and I can tell it's upsetting Brea. So I know I must face the music or watch Brea break down publicly. I march over with determination.

"Nancy, how great to see you. Is this your baby?" I ask.

"This is Fitzsimon William Hollings Core." She holds her baby up like the Lion King on Pride Rock, and I have to admit little Fitz is dreamy. He's got full, chipmunk cheeks and a toothless grin to die for. "He's four months old," Nancy adds.

Four months! Nancy's stomach is flatter than mine and that alone is enough to make me want to hurt her, but Brea's expression of nausea gives me even more reason.

"He's so cute. Congratulations," I say in monotone, trying not to make much of the baby for Brea's sake.

"He's my third. The other two are with their dad today. He took them to the zoo to get them out of my hair." She lets out a withered sigh. "I'm so glad to see you two. What have you both been up to?" Then she shifts little Fitz onto one hip and grabs my left hand. "Ashley, you're not married yet?"

"I've been working on The Career. I'm a patent attorney."

"You always were the smart one. But I'm so glad

you're still single! So's my brother. I'm having him call you. Give me your business card." She puts the baby back in his stroller. The kid is still grinning. He obviously takes after Mama, happy to a fault.

"Oh, Nancy, I don't think . . ." But then I see Brea's ashen face, which hasn't left the baby. "That sounds like a great idea, why don't you have Dan call me? Brea and I have a lunch date, so we have to run, but it's really good to see you again. Really good." I take out a business card and hand it to Nancy. "Have a great day," I say with practically a kick of the toe.

I place the violet bra with Brea's vision of sleaziness, and she buys them both. I'll get lunch, and we'll get out of here all the quicker. With Brea, I don't even need to explain. The deal is unspoken and obvious to both of us.

Brea is struggling not to cry. Her procedure is fresh in her mind. Normally, Brea cannot keep her hands off a new baby, and she didn't go near little Fitzsimon. This is a crisis that can only be solved with food. We head to the Fountain Creamery for burgers and milkshakes. It's the only known antidote for grown-up cheerleaders.

I don't say anything to Brea. I just order us lots of fat and calories. Suddenly, as we're waiting for our food, Brea starts to laugh. "You gave her your phone number! You loser! I can't believe you did that. Do you remember her brother?"

I scowl. "Yes, he was in glee club with me."

"'Nuff said, huh?"

"I'd rather not discuss it. I've been dumped by lesser men than Dan Hollings. It's the least of my issues. I had to rush my purchase for Nancy Hollings—that's the real struggle here." I tap my forefinger on the table. "I came to buy underwear, and my thought process was rushed. I didn't even get undies to match."

"You can take it back. It's kind of ugly," Brea says.

I open my mouth to discuss the mesh thong, but decide enough is enough. "I don't really care if it is ugly. I bought it, and maybe wearing it will give me some new aura." It's now two o'clock in the afternoon, and I know Cinderella's glass slipper is in jeopardy. "Does John expect you home?"

Brea's ready to break down again. "I think I can't be away from him much longer today. I'm a wreck."

"I'm going to the beach today, so I'll drop you off back home as soon as we finish. You need to eat."

"You're going to the beach by yourself?" Brea asks. "That's kind of sad."

"Today is the first day of my new life," I explain. "I'm going to cut my hours back to fifty a week." My attention is suddenly arrested. "Hey, look over there. You see that guy?"

"The one who looks like Hugh Jackman?" Brea asks.

"Yes, him. I think that's Arin's boyfriend. I've seen him once or twice at church." I gaze at him. If Arin has this kind of gorgeous in her back pocket, is there any reason she shouldn't leave Seth to me? I think not.

"I wonder if he knows where his girlfriend is today," Brea smirks.

"He's having lunch with a pretty girl himself. I'm going to ask." I get up, being the new, pushy broad that I now am, and walk over to this stranger's table. *He's a hottie.* I'm trying very hard not to notice because I don't want to trip over my tongue when I get to the table. But the fact that he has brains is just painful because he's beyond gorgeous. With his looks, he should be a grunt construction worker, kind of on the level of that Joe Millionaire, a clean-up carpenter. With a tool belt. Yeah.

The table seems miles away and the walk endless because his to-die-for smile is focused on me. I get to the table and stand there like an idiot. I know I had something to say. *Lord, what was it?*

"Hi," Hugh says first.

"Hi, I'm a friend of Arin's." *No, no, no. I was supposed to say, "Are you a friend of Arin's?"*

"Sure, I've seen you at church on a few occasions. I'm Kevin Novak." He stands up and takes my hand. I can barely speak. His green eyes are now hovering somewhere about six inches above my head, and his hand is warm to the touch. *I really need to get a life.* He extracts his hand from mine, which is plastered tightly around his. "And this is my study partner, Joanie Bradley."

Joanie nods at me. She's a bit overweight and clearly shy about meeting me. I hold my hand out and use my eyes to tell her I understand. Girls like us don't usually mingle with handsome doctors, but it's okay, because he's taken. She smiles and shakes my hand.

"Nice to meet you," I say.

"Arin told me she was having lunch with you and the singles group today," Hugh/Kevin says.

Actually, she's flirting with a bald, middle-aged engineer I once had a crush on, but we won't focus on that. Next subject. "I wasn't up to lunch with the gang, so I bailed. I'm here with my best friend." I point toward Brea, who is relishing her milkshake and watching the events like they're playing out for her own private entertainment. "But she's got to get home."

"Me too." Joanie stands up. "Thanks for the help on that brain stem portion. I was lost." Throwing her napkin on the table, she says goodbye and leaves.

I am standing with the Christian Hugh Jackman. Me. Ashley. Even if it's only momentarily, I want to drink it in, so that someday I can tell my nieces and nephews that I did come in contact with greatness once.

"We've got a big test coming up," he explains. "I've been studying constantly."

"So I've heard. What kind of medicine are you studying?"

"Pediatric surgery. That's why I'm at Stanford; I want to work at the Lucille Salter Children's Hospital."

Sigh. Okay, so not fair. Men who look like this do not have a right to be decent human beings. He should be the pig I want him to be, that everyone *expects* him to be.

Why on earth is his girlfriend flirting with Seth Greenwood? Is she blind? Deaf? Stupid? All three? I just want to rail on God a bit for putting such a lack of intelligence into that little figure. I like Arin, but she's rapidly grating on my nerves.

"That sounds like challenging work, Kevin. Congratulations, it's not many men that pick pediatrics anymore."

"How did you know that?"

Oh my, how do I tell him I read it in People *or something equally benign?* I decide to just shrug it off. "Well, I should get back to Brea. I need to drop her back home before I go to the beach."

"You're going to the beach? You know, I've been here at Stanford for a year, and I've never ventured over to the beach since I arrived."

"You haven't been to the beach?" Okay, that's a little weird. "Your girlfriend made me promise her I'd do something wild. I'm afraid that's as racy as it gets for me. Going to the beach by myself with my convertible's top down. I have to go home to take it off. My top, I mean. The convertible's top." I laugh, a little too loudly. *I am a geek. Do I have to announce it?*

"You want some company?"

Okay, breathe. Take a breath. Was I not just lambasting Arin for flirting with Seth? Would I dare take her boyfriend to the beach? No, the new Ashley Wilkes Stockingdale lives by faith, not by selfish desires.

"I'm not sure what Arin would think of that."

"Let's call her and ask." Kevin takes out a cell phone and dials his girlfriend. I swallow hard and try to remain calm, but my foot is tapping out my restless energy.

I am setting myself up for failure. And Brea is watching the entire fiasco while sucking down a milkshake. That's as good as having it on video because she will replay it and replay it and replay it. TiVo has nothing on Brea.

10

Must I remind myself that this is *my* life, not a romantic lead's on the silver screen? I am not Julia Roberts. I am not Meg Ryan. My brief moment with greatness was briefer than I'd hoped. After Kevin called Arin, she suddenly needed help moving furniture. He ran over there like an engineer to morning espresso.

I had no intentions of actually going anywhere with Kevin, anyway. This is the new Ashley. The upstanding, non-workaholic Ashley. Still, Brea tried to pick up my shattered pieces off the Fountain Creamery's floor. It was just the realization of being "ditched" by two guys for the same woman in the same day. New realm of pathetic.

Granted, maybe my motives weren't exactly godly in my desire for company, but I still want to stamp my feet like a toddler. Why, when the men outnumber the women here in Silicon Valley, do they all want one in particular? Can't they share the wealth?

While Kevin was schlepping Arin's furniture, Seth was probably home strategizing his next move for Arin's heart—a game of romantic chess in which I am the pawn.

Since I feel no compunction whatsoever to keep a promise to the bubbly blonde who has coaxed all of the male species into her lair, I nix the idea of the beach alone. Now I don't blame Arin. She can't help it that men fall at her feet, but I don't have to delude myself that a trip to the ocean will suddenly make me a wanton goddess, either.

I watch *Masterpiece Theatre's The Forsyte Saga* on videotape and wallow in my present misery. I cry out for sexy Soames Forsyte and his delicious red hair pining after stupid Irene who doesn't want him. Doesn't she get it? Soames is ever faithful—he just has a little control issue. Some women wouldn't know a good man if he bit them.

Monday morning comes finally! I walk into work, ecstatic to be there, and throw myself into something I understand—because the game of love is far too complicated for my simple mind. Purvi is already at her desk. That means my desk is now covered with what she's been doing all morning, and I will not accomplish anything on my own daily agenda until after six p.m. It's going to be a late night. But I'm here, and I won't have to think about my non-existent love life for five whole days.

Purvi sees me and puts her coffee cup down with a clunk. "Ashley, I'm glad you're finally here." *Finally? It's eight a.m.* "I need you to go to Taiwan next week."

Like my life is not bad enough here in Silicon Valley . . . I should definitely get sent to a third-world, earthquake-prone country with bad food, where I'm six inches taller than all of the men, just to really make my pitiful existence complete.

"Good morning, Purvi," I say, hoping to put off the

Taiwan talk until my first cup of java. "How was your weekend?"

Plan diverted. "We're suing for patent infringement," Purvi explains.

"Patent infringement?" I rub my hands together. "I get to defend a patent?" It's every patent lawyer's dream to defend a patent, well, a solidly-written one, anyway. A patent is not truly yours until it's been defended in court, and this is my chance to make history. To ensure my name will be on the record books forever and my name on the payroll for another year.

I know it's my chance to shine, but thinking about the bad food gets the best of me. Here in California, we have organic free-range chicken rather than ducks browned and glossed, hanging in shop windows with heads still attached. I will never understand the Asian mind-set of looking into the eye of something you're eating. Fleeting thoughts of vegetarianism often come to mind during my business trips.

To say nothing of those earthquakes. It's like a bad dream, traveling elsewhere on the Pacific Rim. Sure, I may live in earthquake country now, but we have these things here called building codes. Our hotels won't fall flat like a stack of sesame pancakes when the Big One hits. All those pictures of earthquakes of yesteryear and their aftermath will roll through my mind in slide form while I'm trying to sleep in a stinky Taiwan hotel, making me thankful I have eternal life—in case I screw this one up and end it with business travel . . .

"Purvi, do you think this patent is important enough for newspaper coverage?" *Translation: Will I be able to single-handedly save our free market with this trip? Will Seth read about my wondrous acts of valor and be sorry? Will Hugh/Kevin leave Arin because he will only have eyes for me?*

Purvi's normally beautiful uptalking Indian accent drives me crazy in lecture form. "The important thing is that we must uphold our patents in these foreign countries." She crosses her hands at her desk. "Without such action, American and Taiwanese companies will flood the market with this—this inferior garbage. They will steal our market share. Not to mention selling our product for a tenth of fair market value. It's a show of force that must be carried out." She says it like Patton. "Are you up for the job?"

"Yes, ma'am!" I salute her. Of course I understand all she's saying, but I want to know what's in it for me. Not that she would ever care about that. At this point, I'll just have to try to focus on the weight I will lose. "When do I leave, Purvi?"

"You're booked on the Sunday flight out. EVA Air, not United. We're serving the Evil Empire with papers this time, too. I'll be going to Seattle this week."

My chest drops. *She gets to go to Seattle? That's where the career building case is! All while I get sent to a third-world country to fulfill the humor factor.* Defending a patent in Taiwan is a bit of a joke since they rarely adhere to any promises made in the meetings. Meanwhile, Purvi becomes the next VP, and I languish in the trenches. Not only does Purvi get the better case, she gets gourmet coffee too!

Once at my desk, I see it's covered with the work Purvi has been attending to all morning. When her neighbor takes her son to work, I certainly pay the price. There's a sense of dread as I notice an envelope my landlord dropped off last week. I'm sure it's only the dates they'll be spraying for ants, but I never opened it, and now I'm wondering if I've already been asphyxiated and perhaps that's the cause of my latest dating skirmishes. *Ant poison.*

Ripping open the envelope, my eyes scan over everything and rest on the words: "One month to vacate the premises." On careful inspection, I see that due to the failing economy, my landlord has decided to get out of the rental business. He will be turning the apartments into condominiums and selling them off one-by-one as affordable housing. On an up note, I can have first crack at purchasing said condo after the remodel, for a mere $40,000 down payment. *Gag. Cough. Sputter.*

Greater panic engulfs me as I realize the notice is a week old. Which actually leaves me three weeks to find a new place to live. Two weeks if you subtract my forced labor in Taipei. Grabbing the envelope, I rush back into Purvi's office.

"Purvi, my apartment is gone. I've got three weeks to find a new place."

She looks around me toward my office and into the pile of manila that waits for me on my desk. "That's going to be tough, especially with your trip coming up."

"I had planned to buy a place in May, but not this place." Heaven only knows why I offer up this little tidbit of information. Clearly, Purvi doesn't care about my plight, and my real estate aspirations are hardly her concern. She's suing the Evil Empire. And I have a housing issue in the Bay Area. How novel.

Purvi slams a pen down on her desk for effect. "Ashley, you were already off last Monday for your friend's baby problem. You haven't been putting in nearly the hours. I never even saw you this weekend. You've got a mountain of work on your desk." Her voice softens. "Maybe until this lawsuit passes, you should just move in with your parents. That would be the easiest thing."

A stab to the heart. I clutch my chest in disbelief. Did she just say move in with my parents? She clearly does not understand that my loser brother lives there, or that he's probably bringing home his foreign bride. I slap my forehead. "The wedding."

"What now?" Purvi is obviously annoyed with me. She has the uncanny ability to drop all emotion from her work day. Me, I'm a tightly-wound wad of nerves, and for the moment I've forgotten how to hide them. I am an unraveling yo-yo with no hope of springing back up.

"My brother's getting married next month. I forgot. I've got to help my mother plan the shower."

Purvi shrugs. "Like I said, move in with your parents for a while. It sounds like you have a lot on your plate." She goes back to reading her briefings. "You should be happy you still see your parents. I haven't seen mine since I married my husband's family. They are my family now. Take advantage while you still can."

Ah, I only wish marriage and a move would fix my family issues so easily. The phone in my office is ringing, and I take the opportunity to run out of Purvi's office. Picking up the phone, I am sublimely professional, hoping to show Purvi I'm getting it together.

"Ashley Stockingdale."

"Ashley, it's Seth."

Long exhale and I slam the door to my office with my

foot. "Seth, it's really not a good time. I'm a bit over-whelmed with work and projects right now." *Far too busy to discuss your harrowing love life. Welcome to the world of Reason people. Doesn't feel too good when the season passes, now does it?*

He continues though. "I thought about what you said yesterday in the parking lot. I want to talk to you about it more, so just call me when you get more time. We've got too much history to just let this slip away."

"Let what slip away?"

He's quiet for a moment, and I clench my eyes shut. How is it he can date someone else and I'm left feeling like I'm crushing him? Where does the guilt come from?

"Just call me when you get a chance, Ashley. We need to talk." He hangs up the phone and I'm left, clutching the receiver. *Does he get it? Or am I in for another round of cluelessness, engineering style?*

I'm starting to lose it. Nothing in my life is certain anymore, and the questions feel overwhelming, like when *The Bachelor* and *American Idol* are both on—which do I watch and which do I TiVo? I must prioritize my life; I must put everything into perspective. Kay Harding seems to have it all together. Perhaps, if I just follow her lead for the day . . . that's the secret: organize. Taking out my Palm Pilot, I enter in my to-do list.

1. Find a new place to live.
2. Plan wedding shower for brother's mail-order bride.
3. Eat like a winter squirrel to store fat for upcoming freshfest in Taipei.

4. Finish patent briefs and lawsuits for contract attorneys.

5. Call Seth back.

6. Change my pathetic life into something exciting and glamorous.

7. Never wear violet bra again, as it's ramming itself into my ribcage.

8. Sign up for Internet dating.

9. Find smashing guy friend to pose as boyfriend at brother's wedding.

10. Find smashing guy friend.

I start to read through all the briefs that Purvi has left on my desk. I begin to concentrate just about the time the phone rings again.

"Ashley Stockingdale."

"Hi, Ash, it's Arin." If the two of them are calling me to announce their immediate engagement, I am going to leave for Taiwan and never come back.

"What can I do for you? I'm pretty busy." I am a powerful lawyer. I will not be undermined by a tiny, unemployed literature major.

Arin goes on in that cutesy tone that makes me want to ask if her mommy is home. "I'm leaving on my mission trip with the dentists early, and I was hoping you'd be nice to Kevin on Sunday. He's planning to come to church, and he doesn't get the chance to do it all that often. He's very shy and uncomfortable in the church environment."

"Be nice to Kevin, or keep him away from Seth?" *Shame on me.*

She giggles, like this is funny. "Ashley, you know I

don't mean that. Kevin can do whatever he likes. He's leaving for some medical technology meeting in Taiwan anyway. But he'll be there on Sunday before his flight."

"Kevin is going to Taiwan?" My hands are shaking, but I don't make mention of my trip. There is one flight to Taiwan on Sunday, which can only mean we'll both be on it. Just let me have my wistful fantasies for the week. I'm swept away by a rogue handsome young doctor who has abandoned Arin because of her uselessness wrapped in a darling package.

Arin's still rambling. "There's a new machine they want to show the young doctors for use in surgery. He's going over to watch it in production and write a report on it. You know, to see if it's something Stanford should consider in the future." Arin sounds highly annoyed, as if saving children from imminent death is in the way of her social plans. Still, there's a lot to admire about her narcissistic behavior, like the fact that she gets away with it.

"No offense, Arin, but Kevin will be just fine without me. I have a business trip myself, so I don't know if I'll make it on Sunday." The last thing I need to do is be fawning over another man who forgets my name when Arin dashes off her plane, skinnier than ever from eating Costa Rican grubs.

"I understand," Arin says. "Ashley, I'm sorry if I did anything to upset you. Friends, right?"

I swallow a laugh at her use of such a teeny-bopper phrase. "Right."

Then, I hear the light click of the phone.

I know why she's asking me to watch over Kevin. I'm thirty-one. I'm ancient to her, kind of like her mother. I'm beyond the age Arin feels is any kind of threat to her. I can almost hear her call me ma'am.

Oddly, I don't blame Arin. She's assessed the situation and put her resources where they should go. But I do wish she wouldn't tease. If she wants Seth, take Seth. He'd be a solid, if not boring, husband. Those blue eyes on a child would be worth the sacrifice. *Maybe.*

If she wants Kevin, she should marry the guy. He's a gorgeous doctor at Stanford, for crying out loud. But leaving both men dangling for a trip to the rain forest? Now that's just plain irresponsible. Oh, to be twenty-four again. Doesn't Arin know another size-two Anaconda could easily coil itself around her relationships, choking the life from them both? Before she knows it, she's thirty-one and sitting amid the Reasons and her season is long gone.

Like clockwork, the mail guy is here. No, I haven't done the wild thang this weekend. But he's learning—he doesn't ask. Surely, Seth and Kevin can master a thing or two, right? With all the degrees between them.

"Ashley, do you have any mail?" Jim asks like a robot.

"No, Jim. I don't have any mail. How was your weekend?"

He nods. "It was good. Did a little fishing, drank with my buddies." He nods his head. "Yeah, it was good. How about you?"

"I'll have to get back to you on that one. I'm looking for my life's purpose."

He shakes his head. "You lawyers think too much. My purpose is easy, fishing and beer. What else is there? You get a little money, you buy beer. You get a bonus, you buy for your friends, too."

What else is there, indeed? Maybe that's my purpose, not having a purpose. Looking at the stacks of patents before me, my purpose on earth seems a bit more practical.

11

While most people sit jammed in Silicon Valley traffic, I am a world traveler. I look up at the gray sky and breathe deeply. I have a career that people only dream of having. While my brother drives the same bus route daily, I visit exotic foreign countries.

This is my mantra as I enter the plane for sixteen straight hours of world-class fun. No fresh air, no blondes, and no newspapers without foreign symbols—it's like being abducted by aliens, experimenting to see what their food does to my system, and then plopping me back into my boring life in Palo Alto with the severest form of jet lag possible. Definitely out of the ordinary.

The highlight of my trip? I will get my choice of an American meal or a Chinese meal. Both of them still airline food: my choice of lunchmeat slapped on a hard roll or generic Top Ramen. I'm not complaining, however, because it's considered basic training for the week. Boot camp to prepare me for whatever delicacy my Taiwanese counterpart is certain that I will love. Personal *Fear Factor*, if you will, all for the sake of tech's future.

"Ashley, is that you?" Kevin's deep voice breaks my reverie.

"Kevin?"

"It's going to be a long flight. I heard you might be here. I've reserved my seat beside yours."

"What will Arin think?" I ask innocently. Blinking my eyes as though I have no control over my own destiny. This must be destiny.

"Let her think as she likes," he growls.

We stop the flow of traffic onto the plane as we kiss passionately amidst a sea of onlookers.

Immediate guilt. Women like me are not the Boyfriend Stealer type. For various reasons: common decency and lack of Arin's halo effect. I slump into my airline seat ready to face my reality.

My dreams are shattered by a rough entry into the seat beside me. Hopes truly dashed. I'm sitting next to a Taiwanese businessman who has an easy smile, a friendly manner, and a wedding ring. One thing about Taiwanese engineers, they have personalities. Where do the Americans go wrong? And why do I live in the midst of their dysfunction?

As I wait for the rest of the passengers to board, my mind settles into an easy pace. I remember all I've neglected to do this week. I forgot to call Seth back, for one. I chalk it up to fate, but what if he was calling me to tell me everything had been a mistake? That he understood what I was trying to tell him that day in the parking lot? It wouldn't have changed anything, but it would have felt really good. *That's a lie. It would have changed everything.*

My week was an unmitigated blur without a lot to

show for it accomplishment-wise: fruitless apartment search, endless patent briefs all in process, nothing neat and tidy. But I never thought to call Seth—that's progress. I did not obsess!

I had more time to pray and less time to worry. The days are definitely looking brighter. Except, of course, for Seth and the fact that I'm double obsessing because I didn't obsess in the first place. I wish I could just write him off, but heaven help me, I like the guy. He's clueless but charming just the same. As a way of small protest, I skipped church today, just so I wouldn't have to keep Arin's gorgeous boyfriend away from the competition. I also didn't have to field any Seth questions about Arin. Maybe avoidance is the key.

The pilot's voice comes on the air. *Oh, I hope he's not a talker.* "Good afternoon, ladies and gentleman. I'm sorry to say that we've had a breach of airline security, and we need you to exit the plane for another thorough search. Please take all of your belongings with you." Then they repeat the message in another language.

The whole plane is still sitting there, unable to believe the two hours we've just endured is not enough security. Eventually, one passenger stands and then exits, and soon we all follow. Out in the airport lobby they have brought special mobile units, and we are all asked to put our carry-ons flat on a table and let them rifle at will. Once we are rechecked, they put us in a separate cordoned-off area, and we wait as the plane gets its own thorough search.

Now I'm really praying and lamenting that I missed church. I'm not much of a flyer, and the idea that dogs are searching my plane for possible terrorist activity is making me a little tense.

My face tightens, and I can feel the lines etching deep into the tissue. The indentation between my brows is definitely getting deeper. My mind immediately goes to the possibility of Botox. Am I too young to use it? As I stand here feeling my wrinkle, I notice Kevin Novak finish up at the security table. My heart does a little flip and all my terrorist fears evaporate, knowing God wouldn't let anything happen to Dr. Novak. He obviously has great work ahead of him. I hate that I'm attracted to him. It's like being attracted to Matthew McConaughey. *Good luck.* And do you really want a guy prettier than you? Looking past all that, we have the unyielding knowledge of a girlfriend. *Most tacky.*

Kevin heads toward me and, if I didn't know better, I'd swear I watch it in slow motion. Is there music playing? I see his angular face break into a wide grin, and he is definitely starring in my own music video. *It's a power ballad. Something by Matchbox 20.*

Kevin emits a presence that commands attention, and my peripheral vision tells me that all eyes go to him. My own are riveted. His eyes are a deep shade of green, like something in a darkened forest. Mysterious and dramatic all at once. I look away as I realize he's seen me, and I'm staring as though I'm invisible, but I'm more than obvious. I must consciously take control of my tongue, which might fall out of my mouth and drip drool like a bull mastiff.

I suck in my tummy and wave coquettishly. I am a world traveler. Confident member of the California bar. Just check out the expensive Kenneth Cole briefcase if you don't believe me. Its soft, supple leather has Success written all over it. If I saw myself from afar, I wouldn't even know I'd been dumped like last week's trash for his very own girlfriend.

"Ashley!" He remembers my name. *Remain calm, do not jump up and down.* But it's as good as Hugh Jackman himself remembering my name.

"Kevin, hi. I heard you might be on this flight." I try to avoid the girlish thoughts, like that it's fate he's on this flight, that we had to empty the plane and meet, etc. One too many chick flicks in my mind, I tell myself. Business between Taiwan and Silicon Valley is constant, and there's one plane out of SFO today. *Total coincidence, nothing more.*

"Let's hope we're all on this flight eventually." He shakes his head, and these sexy lines around his eyes appear. Maybe he's not as young as I thought. He's even better this close up, like a Roman sculpture or other priceless work of art. God outdid Himself on Kevin. Right now I'm sure it was just to torture me.

I laugh at his little joke, and it doesn't sound forced. The angels must be smiling upon me today. I am no longer a member of the band; right now I am head cheerleader.

"Did you get to say goodbye to Arin? I assume she's off on her rain forest trip." *Ugh. Bringing up the girlfriend is not a great move.* It will force his mind to her cute, nonexistent waist. I am now Amazon woman once again. But at least I'm an honest, godly Amazon.

Kevin's face clouds, and I feel hope fester in my stomach like a natural hot spring. "I'm afraid that Arin and I said goodbye permanently before her trip. That day I saw you in the Fountain Creamery, in fact." Kevin looks around at the people in the waiting area. It gives me a chance to study his face, which is angular yet gentle. I wonder if his heart isn't too trusting, too sweet to hold up under a woman like Arin. Together they emit far too much charm. It's better to split up such energy. I think Einstein was working on that theory when he died.

"I'm sorry about you and Arin," I say, thinking back to my schoolgirl fantasies about their breakup. Did my dark thoughts cause it? This is the part where he tells me he's done with young airheads, and that this trip to Taiwan together is a sign, but I touch back down to reality quickly. "Arin is a free spirit," I offer in hopes of lifting his mood.

"A free spirit? That's a nice way of saying responsibility is not her strong suit." Kevin crosses his arms. They aren't brawny by any means, but they aren't thin and gangly either. He's got a good solid build on him, but his strong jaw line makes his whole look powerful and athletic. He's definitely out of my league. I hate that. I also hate that balding engineer Seth is out of my league. Maybe I should be looking in Florida like my brother suggested. Maybe my league is the Sun City Retired Baseball team.

"Arin's lucky in a way. I wish responsibility wasn't my *only* strong suit." My voice turns wistful. "I admire Arin for her ability to snub what we all think we should do to follow her heart. I wish I could do it just once." I look at the plane out the window. "I wish I could do it right now."

And then it dawns on me in all seriousness. I could do it right now. I could bail on this plane flight, spend the week at the beach, and find myself an apartment. I start to psyche myself up; my heart is pounding; I'm breaking a sweat thinking about dissing the rules. Kevin is obviously concerned over my quiet roiling thoughts, and he lifts my furrowed face up with his thumb. My stomach bursts with fireworks, and I can't bear to tear my gaze from those ever-green eyes that draw me in like the warmth of a dewy morn-ing in the redwoods. Everything in his expression says he's going to kiss me. This is too weird. My heart is in my throat. I can feel him getting closer to me, and I feel tingly and fan-tastic, like I'm having the best spa massage of my life.

But Kevin stops just inches from my face and whispers, "Leaving the airport isn't like you, Ashley. It's like Arin."

I swallow hard. *Ouch.* "And that's not a good thing?"

"Not if you're driven by more than what suits you for the present moment. You seem to want to satisfy a higher purpose than your own immediate desires."

But currently, I'm only thinking about my immediate desires and how I want this man to kiss me and make me all tingly inside. It's like the most luscious tiramisu and flourless chocolate cake all rolled into one great emotion. Kevin clears his throat and pulls back ever so slightly, but enough to know my hopes of PDA (public display of affection, not the personal data assistant) have evaporated like a cumulus cloud.

"What business do you have in Taiwan?" he asks.

I straighten my posture and wonder if I have just imagined the last few minutes. I would have bet my life that Dr. Kevin Novak felt something stirring within him. That we shared a *moment.* But then, I've been hanging out with engineers for ten years now. Kevin is probably only recovering from indigestion.

I clear my throat. "I'm serving papers on a company that's stealing our product patent. But it's really about negotiation and getting some cash for our patent." I stop in the middle of my very businesslike tone and stare out the window again toward the plane. "Kevin, wouldn't it be great to just leave the airport and not fly to Taiwan?"

Kevin raises his eyebrows. "And do what?"

"I don't know." I shrug. "Tour San Francisco in a loud floral shirt, hop on a ferry and see the galleries in Sausalito, mountain bike in the Marin headlands, wear a Walkman and dance on a cable car, order a Diet Coke at the Top of the Mark."

"So *why* don't you do all those things if you would enjoy them?" Kevin asks me.

I sigh, a loud, troubled sort of sigh. "Because I'm the responsible one. If I suddenly act like my brother, or Arin, the world as we know it will cease to exist."

"I know what you mean," Kevin says, his green eyes losing their sparkle. "Let's do it anyway. Take care of our responsibilities and then play. On Wednesday, I come back from Taiwan. What about you?" His voice is building with excitement, and suddenly I'm swept up in the moment, forgetting I have a horrible ride on an international flight with security issues.

"Thursday at 8:30 a.m.," I announce.

"Thursday. I'll meet you at the Top of the Mark at noon for drinks and lunch. It will help you get back on schedule sooner. We'll take the cable car to the Wharf, hop a ferry, tour the galleries, and save the mountain biking for another day."

I think about my apartment, or lack thereof, and the

wedding shower, and all the items on my to-do list. But I throw caution to the wind. Heck, I threw out the violet bra, that's something I accomplished. And a gorgeous young doctor is asking me to step out of my box. It doesn't get any plainer than this. If I'm ever going to have a season, the time is now.

Please just let me enjoy this moment, God. It doesn't have to mean anything. Just let me pull myself out of this bog. I clasp my eyes shut, knowing I'm gambling with my feelings here. Kevin is not the kind of man you can casually meet. He is Colin Firth, Hugh Jackman, and Vin Diesel all wrapped into one magnificent package with an M.D. at the end.

"Let's do it," I say.

They've just announced our flight is ready to board again. Kevin is beside me, and he's picked up my bag. As he smiles down at me, I feel that spark again. Sixteen hours is suddenly feeling like a brief blip in time. For once, my life is looking up.

12

My heart is still racing as I fasten my seatbelt and ignore the flight attendant's droning instruction on performing this task. Does anybody truly not understand the concept of a seatbelt? Surely they can't afford plane fare, can they?

Kevin is now sitting beside me; my first seatmate has traded seats with him. See? They get it in Taiwan. An American engineer would never notice I had a friend. The anxiety I feel over takeoff is drastically diminished by knowing that if I die, I go out in style beside a gorgeous doctor who might have shared a moment with me. Not a bad way to go, right? Besides, he's a Christian. We could float up together. How romantic is that, like *Somewhere in Time* for believers. I smile at Kevin, wondering if he can read my thoughts. I'm not exactly the coy type. I'm about as transparent as Saran Wrap.

I grasp Kevin's hand as the plane climbs into the air. I never did like this part. Kevin's hands are smooth and masculine with long squared fingers. He has the hands of a surgeon, beautiful and incredibly skilled at the same time.

While looking at them, I miss the parting view of San Francisco and its magnificent Golden Gate Bridge.

"You weren't at church today," Kevin says as we reach cruising altitude.

Hey, we're not dead, I suddenly realize. *The plane did not blow up on takeoff. This is good. This is very good.* "No, I didn't want to miss my flight. If I'd have known we were going to be late, I could have gone to both services." I laugh, but he doesn't break a smile.

Kevin is a bit austere, I'm noticing. In fact, I'm thinking if I were back in high school, I might have said he . . . well, never mind. I wouldn't say that now. I might acknowledge that he has Kohlitis—not colitis like the bad disease, but Kohlitis named for Sequoia High's most popular girl, Kohli Cahners.

Brea and I came up with a groundbreaking theory that people who were gorgeous their entire life, like Kohli, never had to develop a personality. This is why so many Hollywood movie stars must resort to plastic surgery and creepily never age—if they look ugly, people will know they never had a personality and their career is shot. Hence, going through the gawky stage like Brea did, and apparently I still am, produces positive results on character—and a sense of humor. Sheesh, I oughta be Adam Sandler by now.

"Arin told me you'd be at church," Kevin says.

"She asked me if I could meet you," I admit, but I'm even bolder. "Do you know why Arin asked me? You are capable of entering into worship by yourself, are you not?" *Eww. Might have been a tad bit rude there, but I want him to admit to me that Arin thinks I'm a church elder. I want to know what she said about me. Meow.*

His lips curve into a smile, and I've never seen anything so delicious. Maybe he does have a personality! My heart is dangerously close to boiling over. What is it about me that doesn't evolve? Case in point, last three love interests:

College boyfriend who wanted one thing—and apparently got it everywhere else.

Bald engineer with a penchant for fiery, long-haired blondes, and now . . .

Stunning medical doctor who *should* be on *General Hospital* and who:

1. Dated my friend.
2. Is on the rebound.
3. Might not possess a personality.

I'm currently no threat. Since Kevin is also on the rebound and one always gravitates to their ex's polar opposite after a break-up. Arin is flighty and flirty; I'm grounded and plain-spoken. But all that will change when Kevin sees me on Thursday. The new Ashley, who will bear a striking resemblance to Scarlett (without elegant hair, of course).

Kevin is still looking at me intently, his Hugh Jackman chin resting on his artful fist. He's waiting for me to say something profound. The tension is too great, and I feel like an artichoke in a pressure cooker. *Not until Thursday!* I want to shout. *I cannot possibly be fabulous until Thursday!*

"Sorry I didn't meet you this morning at church then. Was everything okay?" I ask like a concerned mother.

He shrugs. "Fine."

Should I ask for his testimony now? You know, this

meeting is just really uncomfortable. I don't want to talk about his ex. I don't want to talk about my lawsuit for fear someone's on the plane who could overhear, and I am doubting Kevin wants to hear what J. Lo is up to this week, so *People* magazine is out.

"Did I say something wrong?" he asks.

I shake my head.

"Is there something I *should* be saying then?"

Again, being the beacon of light that I am, I shake my head as an answer. Better to say nothing at all than to relive my worst moment in high school. Being class president, I was asked to make a speech at graduation, but when I opened my mouth to speak, my foot slipped off the stage. I hit my chin on the podium, silencing me from my peers and leaving a lasting impression upon the class of 1990.

"Did Arin tell you something about me?" Kevin asks, his eyes thinning.

Now I can't help but wonder, *what could she have told me? Does he have some weird fetish, like men's feet or wearing ladies' undergarments?*

"Arin told me that you study too much." I shrug. "That's all she told me. Is there something else I should know?"

"I'm focused," Kevin says. "Arin doesn't like that. I wasn't focused enough on her, but I don't want you to think—" He stops mid-sentence.

"I don't think anything, and I reserve all judgment until after our day in San Francisco. Do you agree to the same terms?"

Oh, that smile again. Just pierce me in the heart, why don't you?

"I do." He leans toward me, glancing at the pile of

documents I unload onto my sorry, flimsy tray. "What are you working on?"

I do. He's said The Words and suddenly, I see him in a tux and my feet in ivory slippers, coming down the aisle to meet him. People are oohing and ahhing over my gown cascading behind me . . .

"Ashley?"

"Uh, yes?"

"I was asking what you're working on."

"R-right. I'm preparing to make my case. I'm running numbers and just thinking about all I need to do in Taiwan. Thursday I'll think about our date and nothing else." *I'm a terrible lawyer. I give everything away and then some.*

"Fair enough. I can see I'm distracting you from your work. I'll leave you alone so you can do your best. But Thursday you're mine." Kevin winks, rises, and walks toward the front of the plane before I can say a word. After a moment, I consciously shut my gaping jaw. That's the last I see of him on the flight. Some cutesy stewardess probably gave him a seat in first class just so she could gaze upon him. I force myself to stare at my briefs, to focus on the task immediately before me and not my fabulous date on Thursday. To say nothing of what it could lead to. He was the one who intimated that there might be more, galleries in Sausalito . . . *The Briefs. Focus, Ashley, focus.*

Once in Taiwan, I'm zapped by the stench of diesel and the gray wet heat of the Asian tropics. The air just sucks the life out of me, and I begin to wonder what the average life span is here. The sun is setting and my stomach is growling, but I'm ever fearful of my options regarding food. Somehow, I didn't see Kevin again. Did he not check any luggage? Was it all a figment of my imagination? There are a lot of people on a 747-400, but I thought I'd at least get a chance to wave his direction, leave a lasting impression. I'd spent half an hour in a cramped lavatory preparing for just that. But no luck.

A car arrives and takes me to my hotel. We drive by a gorgeous Hyatt that looks like something as glitzy as Vegas, but we keep driving. My hotel is American, but it's a cinder-block special, painted a brilliant Navajo peach. The limo driver helps me into the hotel, bowing ever so slightly when he's finished. I return the slight bow and head to the front desk.

"Good evening. Ashley Stockingdale, checking in."

It's a young man behind the counter. He is dressed impeccably in a dark hotel suit, and his manners make me wish I could transport him to Palo Alto. "Miss Stockingdale, it's a pleasure to have you with us. I'll have your luggage brought to your room, and you can visit the hotel restaurant if you're so inclined."

I am so inclined. It's five p.m. and though food strikes terror at the heart, I must be strong. This is my opportunity. Purvi trusted me with this trip on my own, and I'm going to do her proud. I will not perish from hunger before I serve my papers.

Serving papers. I haven't had time to think of the fear of doing this alone. Usually, I'm just an ornament on Purvi's right. I know I'm to wear a business jacket with a skirt. I know I'm to present my business card with both hands and study theirs when they hand it to me, but I'm mortified that if I get lost during the meeting, there's no one to set me straight. Purvi speaks enough Chinese to be well-revered among the people, but even my hello is rusty. My mind is still churning as the waiter greets me with a leather menu.

"Good evening, Miss Stockingdale. Would you like to start with a cocktail?" Everyone's English is perfect, unlike my Chinese.

"No. No, thank you. A Diet Coke, if you will."

The waiter, dressed in a typical black-and-white ensemble, races off to get my soda and a little bit of Americana. I look around the restaurant, which is full of diners eating alone. Windows surround us in a half circle, and heavy draperies hang from the high ceilings. There's nothing here to let you know you're in Taipei—except the dim sum and roasted duck on the menu—and even that could be Silicon Valley. There's a marble fountain creating noise so we business travelers will forget there's no conversation.

My waiter returns with my beverage. "Have you decided? Did you notice our live seafood selection?" He motions toward a tank.

I hand the menu back quickly. "I'll have a hamburger."

If he feels disdain, he shows nothing. "Right away, Miss Stockingdale."

"You should try the fish." An American businessman in his suit, jacket draped over the additional, empty chair at his table, speaks. He's eating a hamburger.

"So should you. Fish is healthy, you know."

"Where are you from?"

"Palo Alto," I say. Anyone who does business in Taipei knows Palo Alto, birthplace of Hewlett-Packard.

"What about you?"

"San Mateo," he says, naming a nearby city on the San Francisco Peninsula.

"You sound wearied. Do you have to travel here a lot?"

He nods. "Once a month." He comes over to my table and opens his wallet. "This is my wife and kids."

"You have kids and they make you travel? I thought it was only us single folk they sent off to the Far Reaches."

He grabs his hair. "You see this gray? It's a lifetime of travel in my forty-two years. They own me, and now that I have a Bay Area mortgage, there's nothing to be done about it. I'm telling you all this because you still have the puppy look. You're a novice, am I right?"

I nod. "This is the first trip they trusted me with alone."

"Don't let them do it to you, Miss. They'll buy your soul if you let them." His words send shivers down my back, and his presence suddenly frightens me. "Enjoy your hamburger." He throws a few bills on his table and stalks off toward the elevator. I feel like I've just been visited by Slugworth.

"Waiter!" I lift my finger. I think that's rude here, but I don't have time to obsess. "Would you pack that hamburger for me? I need to turn in early."

The hamburger is cold and wilted by the time I make it up the elevator. It's no In-N-Out Burger, but it's decent. My hotel room is typical. Small room, lots of phone lines, but I look at my laptop and decide I don't care what last minute advice Purvi has. My e-mail can wait.

I stare out the window down the busy Taipei street,

and I question if I can picture myself doing this in ten years. Five even.

I start to dial Seth. But it's three a.m. at home. While I know he wouldn't care, I'm too fearful to go through with it. A middle-of-the-night call is so intimate, and that's just not where we are.

Somewhere along the line, I fall off to sleep and wake up by 5:30 a.m. My morning prayer time has me questioning my career—the career I'm halfway across the world for, mind you. Why is today any different? What good is writing a patent I can't defend? I'm sure it's homesickness. *This is all normal,* I tell myself.

By Sunday I'll be back at church. Back with the Reasons, and knowing I am one of them, not above them. I don't have one particular reason as I've so obviously seen in others. I am a continuous, ever-flowing fountain of reasons, but when I work sixty hours a week and lack a social life? No one seems to notice.

I leave the hotel at seven a.m. for my 8:30 meeting. With Taipei traffic, there's no sense in chancing being late. Motor scooters are as thick as beans in Starbucks, and although the city has yet to fully come alive, my driver is stalled while waiting for the throngs of pedestrians and bicycles to cross.

With relief, we reach my destination, and, surprise, I'm still in one piece. I bow to the driver and grab my briefcase with my cheesy novel inside. At least I'll have a way to pass the forty-five minutes before my meeting. The lobby is still locked, and I find a small tea house where I have a pearl milk tea. A well-known treat in Silicon Valley, it's sweet tea with giant balls of tapioca at the bottom, resembling black jelly beans. The patrons are very excited to see an American, and I feel like Elaine in her nail salon on *Seinfeld* while they chatter and laugh over my presence.

I check over my paperwork, which contains a very scary lawsuit alleging that this equipment provider has copied, misappropriated, and infringed on my company's intellectual property for their rival low-cost product.

I practice saying it in a menacing tone several times before I head back to the office. Someone from our regional Selectech office is supposed to meet me at the meeting, and I find myself praying for his or her appearance.

The receptionist, a young female dressed like an American corporate executive, takes my name and presses buttons on her phone. In the meantime, someone enters the lobby. He's tall and looks as if he knows what he's doing. *Please, please, let him be from Selectech.*

"Corporate Patent Attorney, Ashley Stockingdale?" He bows.

The Chinese are big on titles. If you have one, they will use it. Maybe that's what I need in Palo Alto. You know, something that announces my prime address: Ashley Stockingdale, Channing Street. Or maybe my car? Ashley Stockingdale, Audi TT convertible. "Yes, I'm Attorney Stockingdale." I bow and extend my hand.

"Senior Counselman Chen Shing-Sen." He takes my hand.

"Senior Counselman, it's a pleasure to meet you."

We are quickly ushered into a dark, high-tech looking room with windows we cannot see through and introduced around. The business card fiasco takes twenty minutes. After intros, they all just sit back and stare, a silent standoff, if you will. Who's going to throw out the first number?

"Yes, well . . ." I stammer. "Your company, with its current memory card, is infringing upon U.S. Patent number 66543217, and we implore you to cease production immediately or further action will be issued." *Ooooh, I even scare myself here.*

They all look at one another and speak in Chinese until a spokesperson says no.

"Very well, shipment of your products will be stopped by the U.S. Customs department in accordance with U.S. patent law. Thank you for your time." I rise to go. *I'm like something out of* The Practice, *I'm so hot.*

"Wait," the spokesman says. "Perhaps there's a deal. Do you have a price to use this patent?"

"$350,000 for the use of our patent, as well as a steady stream of royalties at a 10 percent profit rate."

They begin to grumble. I know they have millions in product sitting on U.S. docks, and they'll go nowhere without my approval. *Isn't that hilarious? Me, who can't even get a date! I hold this company's future in my hands.*

"Do you have the contracts with you?"

"I do." I hand them the agreements.

"We'll leave word with your hotel. Where are you staying?"

"It's all on there," I say as I rise. "Gentlemen, a privilege doing business with you."

There is no laughter, and they actually bid me goodbye. I am a Legal Superstar!

For three days, I tour our company's factories and

shake hands with all the local Selectech managers. Even though I have nothing to do with the daily operation of our product, the managers are all eager to meet me and take me to lunch. Yum, all sorts of exciting local delicacies.

The Taiwanese people are wonderful, and they entertain like Martha Stewart—with a theme. The theme is always Local Flavor, and therein is the problem. Often, Asian food is too fresh for me, meaning it hasn't been dead long enough. One of my meals, a shrimp, has even been killed right in front of me. There should be some kind of waiting period, I think. Kind of like buying a gun.

My three days are absolutely non-stop until I'm dropped at the airport bound for home. *Home, home, home.* Then the horrible thought comes to me that there is no home in two weeks. Unless you count my parent's house and that is *SO* not an option. I am, after all, an international legal star. The contracts were returned signed and sealed. My company's stock rose four points on the news. My head is inflating as we speak. This is not the time to go home to Mama.

I arrive for my flight to San Francisco and my new life as a legal expert. Staring at the English flight board, my stomach tumbles at the sight of my flight and a horrific tagline beside it: CANCELED. But I'm calm. *It's probably all a mistake,* I tell myself.

No mistake. It's canceled. I'm stuck in Taiwan, and my meeting with destiny and Dr. Kevin Novak is thwarted. I rush to the counter.

"When is the next flight? I have to get to San Francisco by noon tomorrow."

The agent checks her computer. ACK! That computer! It would be faster for this woman to run down to the tarmac and ask the pilot himself when the plane is leaving. But she taps away and I wait. I'm praying for serenity.

"Flight is canceled." *As is my serenity.*

"Yes, I know the flight is canceled. I need another one. Quickly."

She proceeds to pound on her keyboard, and like the optimist I am, I'm thinking another flight will magically appear. She finally shrugs and smiles apologetically. "Tomorrow."

"No, I have to get there today." I mean tomorrow, but tomorrow is today here. "Oh, where's the United terminal?"

She points and I run, but their flight for the day has already left. "What about L.A.? Can you get me to L.A.?" I ask the United guy.

Again with the computer!

"The soonest I can get you there is six p.m. on Friday. To Los Angeles."

I bang my head on the counter.

"Ma'am?"

"I'll just wait for SFO. Thank you." I head back to the EVA terminal. I have no way to reach Kevin. Being the brain surgeon I am, I never took his card—what was that I learned about the business card being so important in Taiwan? *It's kind of important in America, too, you ditz!*

Arin is currently in the jungle, so I can't call her. Not that that would be appropriate, calling the ex and all.

Kevin will be sitting in the Top of the Mark in twenty-four hours, the soonest I can explain my absence to him. I try to think of all the ways I could track him down before then, but I'm drawing a blank. *Legal Superstar, yes. Also Doofus Extraordinaire.*

Dreams of Scarlett float away. I was named Ashley Wilkes for a reason. I was not meant to spend my life with someone who makes my heart beat wildly; I'm destined for someone practical who will sit beside me while I knit us into old age.

Kevin will undoubtedly meet some gorgeous model who's at the Mark for a fashion shoot. In the meantime, Seth and I will get a group rate on false teeth and long-term care, while simultaneously running the aging singles group. *I am so definitely a Reason.*

13

I slept in the airport and now feel like my rumpled shirt that's missing a button—and hanging on my abandoned treadmill. What is it about exercise equipment and how it always finds its way to becoming an expensive hanger? It's just like that ironing basket full of clothes that will never get worn because I'm never going to iron. "Press with a cool iron" should read, "wear once only." Good intentions buried beneath my overbooked schedule of work, reality TV, and nights out with the Reasons.

I slept sitting on my passport because I figured I'd know if someone grabbed for it there. Now I feel like it's imprinted on my bum, and I'm not about to rub that kink out. I'm remembering those nights I'd study until three a.m. in college and wake up with an actual adrenaline rush. Now, my over-thirty body is rebelling, and rather than adrenaline I'd settle for a good dose of Ben Gay. I take out a compact and try to blot my way into sanity. It's almost time for the plane to board, and I'm anxious to start the long journey home to a weird culture I at least understand.

Yesterday's plane was canceled for mechanical problems, apparently the only reason the airlines can legally cancel a flight. I checked. The plane spent the night stuck on a Japanese runway, but it's magically appeared this morning, suddenly ready for trans-Pacific travel. I'm torn between wanting to get home so badly that I could rush the plane and wondering if the "mechanical problems" have truly been assessed properly. But the call of American food wins out over my fear of actually using my seat cushion as a floating device, and so I hand the attendant my ticket with fervor.

Checking my watch, I realize it's nearly noon in the Silicon Valley. I'll call the hotel and let them know to tell Kevin I can't meet him. The thought of him traipsing up to the city in traffic for nothing has me tense, but what can I do? It's not like a surprise episode of *The Bachelor* came on—I have a legitimate excuse.

The passengers board quickly, and after takeoff I swipe my credit card into the onboard phone and wait for information. "Yes, I need to get the bar, Top of the Mark, at the Mark Hopkins Hotel in San Francisco, California."

This plane is nearly full and my neighbor, an American businessman, is listening to my humiliation with intrigue. How I wish I could offer him something more interesting than what I've got. With all those reality shows in my system, you'd think I could write myself a better script.

The phone rings through to the front desk at the Mark Hopkins, but that's okay, they can transfer me. And they do.

"Top of the Mark," a friendly male voice answers.

I turn my head ever so slightly so the businessman is not forced to listen to my sad story at full volume. "Yes, I'm supposed to meet a man there. Dr. Kevin Novak. He's about six foot two, and we're meeting there at noon. He should be sitting at the bar somewhere. He's very clean-cut looking." *Stunning,* I add silently.

"Hang on a minute."

To my absolute horror, I hear him call out Kevin's name. This bar is incredibly swanky, and the thought of my "date" being bellowed at makes me cringe. All the women must be thinking, *Who on earth is dense enough to ditch Mr. Perfect? I think I'll just comfort him.* Luckily, Mr. American Businessman can't hear the other side of my conversation. Right now, I'm only half a fool. I look at my airplane neighbor and he smiles condescendingly. *Yeah, I'm a loser, what of it?*

"No one answering by that name, Miss. I'm sorry."

"If he happens to come in and ask for Ashley Stockingdale, would you tell him my plane was delayed in Taiwan?" There, that sounds important. *I have just served papers on a major telecommunications company here in the East. My company's stock has ascended due to my incredible brief. Tell him all that, too!*

I can hear the man scribbling my note, and he offers me something to relieve the sting. "There are not very many people here now. I think I'll recognize him if he comes in." *Have I just been stood up on the other side of the earth?*

I thank the man and hang up, suddenly realizing it's probably a dollar every ten seconds to use this phone. "You were on yesterday's flight too, huh?" my airplane neighbor asks.

Mr. American Businessman is not wearing a wedding ring. I could have sworn he was wearing one five minutes ago. "Yes. I spent the night in the airport." I hope this explains my very sloppy appearance. At least my hair is in check. I kind of have a Ryan Seacrest thing going on this morning. In auburn of course, and without the expensive highlights.

"I was in Japan on the plane when they deemed it unworthy of travel." He thrusts a hand toward me. "Rob Nasser."

"Nice to meet you. Ashley Stockingdale." We shake hands. Very unusual on a flight where passing a soft drink is the only contact I generally have with my neighbor. Rob is nice looking but salesy, which doesn't appeal to me. Too slick for my tastes. Like a NASCAR racetrack, his hair is shellacked above his ears. I'm also not fond of men who have nicer nails than I do or who wear more jewelry, which Rob does.

With sudden clarity, it's obvious to me: I like engineers. This scares me because one, they don't appear to like me, and two, I know I'm forever doomed to try to garner the attention of men who'd rather watch *The Matrix* than me naked.

This is my *reason*. It must be. If I lived outside of Silicon Valley, the men would probably be knocking my door down. I'm a victim of geography!

"You're missing an appointment. That's too bad." Rob is overly concerned. I guess that he's going to offer to make me feel better in the lavatory.

And here it comes, my first fib of the flight. "It's just my fiancé. He'll understand that I couldn't make it."

"Doesn't he have a cell phone?" *Panic.* I'm the worst liar on earth.

"He's a surgeon," I hasten to add. "I hate to bother him on his cell because he gets nervous that there's an emergency or something. You know, if he's in the car, he'll pull over—that kind of thing."

"Oh. That's very considerate of you, *Ashley.* Very."

The way he emphasizes my name is reptilian. His eyes move shiftily, like a lizard, and I almost expect his tongue to snap out of his mouth at any moment.

"Well, I try to be considerate. Kevin is so busy." I dig through my bag for a *People* magazine. I want to prove how very shallow I am and hopefully add that I'm not interested in striking up a conversation. Or anything else. Pulling out my magazine, he looks at the cover.

"You like *People?*"

"Yes." *It's a form of escape for me,* but I don't say that. I want to be as undesirable as possible here. Maybe if I play up the TV Ditz part of my persona, he'll leave me alone. "I just love knowing what all the stars are up to and what they wear to every event. It also covers my favorite TV shows." I cannot wait to tell Brea this story.

The neon *L* has to be appearing on my forehead by now. *But then it dawns on me—this is the wrong approach for a man who isn't concerned with my intellect. Get out the real conversation killer and litmus test.* I pull out my Bible. It's ragged and worn edges show that it's not just a good-luck charm for the plane. I actually read this Book, and often.

The lizard swallows and shifts. He crosses his legs, looking toward the window. I open to Ephesians, and the passage about husbands and wives, which is all marked up.

Oooh, I am bad today. But I'm hoping the reptile goes home and appreciates any woman slow enough to marry him.

And thus, our conversation has ended. This Bible has told him everything he needs to know. One could argue that this isn't a very good use of the Bible, but I've been on enough business trips to know his ring-ditching type, and he has one thing in mind.

Besides, I need to think about my "reason" and plan my escape route, not spend the whole flight politely avoiding a man six inches to my left. Getting out my prayer journal, I write out my course of action. Engineers do not find me attractive, so I must plan an alternative route if I have any hope of a new season. I must either change what I find attractive or get comfortable with a life of lawyerly singleness.

I scribble heartily in my notebook. This is the first day of being fabulous after all. Isn't that what I told Dr. Kevin Novak? Well, I don't need him to prove it. I need to prove it to myself. I will not be attracted to guys who do the following:

1. Play video games.
2. Watch science-fiction movies more than once.
3. Confuse Jesus with Frodo.
4. View Dutch-treat as an acceptable first-date option.
5. Take me for a meal with a coupon in hand. (They should value me!)

Instead I will:

1. Plan more evenings out with my girlfriends.

2. Get over being the single at couple events with Brea and have fun.

3. Do something fabulous of my own volition at the Top of the Mark.

4. Revel in my single status!

5. Start up conversations with strangers more often! (Not smarmy married ones.)

My list looks good. Today is Friday, the day after I am suddenly fabulous. It's a good day for it, because really it was Friday when I left, so I have lived First Fabulous Day twice. It's been an hour, and I decide to call the bar in San Francisco again. That way, the host can tell me how disappointed Kevin looked, and I can restart Fabulous Friday feeling valiant.

The same voice answers again. "Top of the Mark."

"Hi, it's Ashley Stockingdale. Is Dr. Novak there yet?"

A pause. *Not good.*

"I never saw someone fitting his description, Ashley." Ack. The use of my first name. Host now knows I am jilted. Not desirable and pursued. Not valiant. Dumped long-distance and my pathetic phone calls only prove my desperation. I am definitely The Dumpee.

"Great!" I answer into the phone too excitedly. "That means he got my message." Insert fake breath of relief here. Neighbor businessman is smirking. I'm fighting air rage at his joy over my misery. Rob, my married buddy, knows I couldn't reach my said date. I didn't even have a cell phone number for my supposed fiancé.

I'm a liar, a loser, and a hypocrite. That's a good Christian message to send, don't you think? My spit-and-polished neighbor seems quite pleased with my failure, and I offer up a little confessional prayer silently. It serves me right for lying. Christians can be the death knell for God's good work sometimes.

I hang up the chunky airline phone and settle in for a movie I won't be able to hear through the lousy, cheap headphones they distribute for five dollars a whack, but I'll be thankful for the diversion. But after the movie starts and my humiliation wears down, I realize with crystal clarity the bigger issue here: Dr. Kevin Novak didn't *show*. Does he think fabulous Ashley Wilkes Stockingdale is someone who can just be deserted at some fancy restaurant? Doesn't he know about women scorned? Well, "hell hath no fury" doesn't begin to cover women over thirty.

Kevin Novak stood me up at a famous San Francisco landmark. He didn't call the restaurant. He didn't leave me a message. He just ditched my fabulous self! What was he thinking? Thoughts of petite Arin and her perky enthusiasm enter my mind, and I want to strangle my pastor for making me believe beauty is all about the inside of a woman. Her heart. It's so not about the inside. It's about being the perfect Christian woman wrapped in a lingerie model's body.

I can hear myself breathing. I am ticked. It's not just about today and the beginning of my new life. It's that I really don't have anyone to take to my brother's wedding as a date. No one to introduce like I would have Dr. Novak—and he's not even an engineering Ph.D., but a real doctor. But today is different. I have resolve. I'm not going back to sit with the Reasons. I am a Season girl, and I will prove it with everything in my being. Just as soon as I get beyond this mounting fury that Kevin stood me up.

After a tumultuous flight, I arrive in San Francisco angrier than I thought I knew possible. I'm repeating my new mantra for men. *Leave room for God's wrath. Leave room for God's wrath.*

Outside of customs, in my hurry, I fumble with my suitcase and briefcase and end up dropping both in a spectacularly clumsy move worthy of a Samsonite commercial. Of course, rather than help me upright my suitcase and gather the documents that are spilling out of my briefcase, businessmen are stepping *over* me. I *so* hate the Silicon Valley.

Looking up, I blink several times as I see a man *hotter* than Dr. Kevin Novak himself. He's standing with a bouquet of peach roses wearing a navy suit, and he's looking at me. Subconsciously, I rub my hair and pull up my chin. It's Fabulous Friday after all; anything is possible.

I pick up my bags and walk resolutely by Mr. Perfect. Flirtatiously, I smile at him and nearly keel over when he hands *me* the flowers.

"Ashley, it's me, uh, Kevin."

I'm blinking like I've got a permanent tick. It *is* Kevin. He looks incredible. I had forgotten he was this handsome, scaling him back in my head to something my heart could handle. And he's standing here holding flowers. Did I miss something? "But you weren't at the Top of the Mark today—I mean yesterday," I stammer.

"I know, because I checked the Internet and your flight was canceled." He shrugs. His shoulders are bigger than I remembered them. I wonder if he has shoulder pads in that jacket. Do men wear those? Or is that like male eyeliner? I pat his shoulder in a slight hug. Nope. Hard as a rock. It's all him.

"You checked my flight?" *Be still my heart. He is perfect.*

"Mine was late coming in the other day, so I wanted to make sure you'd be on time. I didn't want to sit in that elegant place staring at that beautiful view without company. I'd be like Cary Grant standing on the Empire State Building waiting."

Oh my goodness. He said Cary Grant. Not Tom Hanks, not Warren Beatty—none of the sorry remakes. It's destiny!

"I can't believe you're here," I say.

He smiles a lopsided smile like George Clooney's, and it's everything I can do not to melt into a little puddle around his feet.

"We had a date," he says. "Are you up for it?"

We did have a date. *Mr. DeMille, I'm ready for my Season.*

14

While Dr. Kevin Novak looks like he's starring on *ER*, I look like Casanova's unmade bed. This is going to be an issue—dating a man who looks like Kevin. I always considered myself well-dressed and concerned about my appearance, but it's not a natural look. I don't wake up that way. It's a process, a long process—even without flowing tresses. Doc undoubtedly looks like a million in scrubs and now I'm wondering, do I need this kind of pressure in my life? Whoever marries this guy is in for an everyday occurrence of meeting him in the morning. Oh, it's far too much to think about.

In the airport restroom, I'm rifling through my suitcase like a homeless person, trying to find something worthy of wearing to the Top of the Mark. If Kevin only told me he was coming, I would have been all made up getting off the plane. And frankly, more careful about toppling over my suitcases while leaving customs. *Whatever.*

My skin is looking thirsty, like an Arizona parched desert. I drank plenty of water on the plane, but apparently all it did was force me to visit the toilet-in-a-dank-closet four times, because my skin desperately needs moisture. After washing my face, and trying to dry it with one of those cheap, non-absorbent public restroom paper towels, all I've succeeded in doing is smearing mascara about my cheeks like war paint.

"Oh, Lord, help me," I say to the mirror, but I'm calm. I wash my face again. Can't find my $40 cleanser, so I'm making do with the sickening-sweet public bathroom soap and hoping my scent doesn't make Kevin suddenly want to urinate in Pavlovian-style.

Luckily, my moisturizer is right where I've left it, and I slop it over my skin with too much zeal. Now I look greasy, like a cooked pizza with fake cheese. Trying the soap one more time. It's been ten minutes, and I haven't even gotten to makeup, not to mention clothes. The fear of my date leaving me in the airport because I'm too high-maintenance drives me forward.

The third time is the charm. Face is washed and patted with moisture. Ready for makeup! I pick out an outfit that I didn't get to wear in Taiwan because it was too blasted hot there. It's black, long-sleeved, and made from a light wool crepe. It hugs my figure and is quite slimming. I twist and turn in the mirror. *Looking good.*

I put some soft gel in my hair, powder my face with a little blush, and dab on bright pink lip gloss. I am actually having a great hair day. What are the chances? Sucking in a deep breath, I walk out of the restroom.

Kevin's jaw drops. Okay, I am actually enjoying this. I smile coquettishly, feeling not a day over twenty-four, with the exception of my bum, which I'm sure still has the passport indentation.

"Now *that* was worth waiting for." Kevin smiles and crosses his arms.

He has to be gay or something. He's just too good to be true and this freaks me out. "Thank you," I manage.

"My car's in the short-term lot." He grabs my bags and puts his free hand on the small of my back. He is chivalrous! He must be from Savannah. Or, like I said, he's gay.

The weather is perfect. Brisk and sunny, the best kind of day for San Francisco when there's enough of a breeze to blow out the fog and allow you to see for miles past the Golden Gate Bridge. It's going to be breathtaking overlooking the scene from the Top of the Mark and with Kevin in my view to boot. I'm a Season girl! I'm like Spring and Summer all wrapped into one wonderful package! Fall and Winter are long over, baby!

Kevin is smiling down upon me like the ray of sunshine he is. Should I feel guilty that he was dating my friend a mere week ago? It's so high school to date someone's ex. The gnawing shame is making me wonder if I've got a future on TV as a catty bachelorette. You know, the one who tries to sleep with the guy to get "ahead" in her standings. Yeah, like that works. And really? Is it worth it when the whole world knows you're a hooch?

After a harrowing hallway and an elevator, we're finally in the airport parking lot. I know it's shallow, but I'm breathless with anticipation. Does he drive something cool like my TT? Or is he a more traditional guy like a Toyota Camry? I'd say he's an American traditionalist. I'm thinking Buick.

But we get to his car, and I laugh when he says, "Here we are."

Big mistake. He is not kidding. He opens the trunk—or should I say he unties the trunk because there's a rope holding it down. All bets are off. "This is your car?" I try to keep all emotion from my voice.

But my Stanford-educated doctor is driving a Datsun B210, circa who knows when. I'm not superficial about this, just curious. What's his motivation here? Is he a starving student? Or just doesn't speak vehicle?

"Sorry about the car." He smiles, but there's no other explanation. He's just sorry. Like the car.

"No, please don't apologize. I'm happy for the ride and the company." And I am, but okay, there is this gnawing princess inside.

"Arin told me you drive a fancy convertible," he says quietly. Okay, now I'm embarrassed. He knows I'm shallow and discontent. *Thanks a million, Arin.* Her parting gift, I suppose.

"Beggars can't be choosers." It's meant to be lighthearted, but sounds judgmental. I whack my forehead. What a stupid thing to say. I was really talking about me begging a ride home, but it sounded like he's the beggar. And is he? What about his medical school bills? Do I need that kind of pressure? I just have legitimate fears that without two steady incomes, we'll all end up living with my mother, in one big dysfunctional family house.

Kevin locks, or should I say knots, my suitcases in the trunk and opens my door for me. *Avoid the car as a subject, avoid the car as a subject.*

"So," I say. "How was *your* trip to Taiwan?"

He shrugs and starts the car. Three times, until it actually does what he's asking of it. "Uneventful. I don't think the technology is right for us. It has potential, but it's nowhere near something Stanford would consider now."

While Kevin is extremely chivalrous, I notice that he's almost shy in his actions. I'm used to engineers and their undeserved bravado. Kevin is the kid in school who you never really knew was in your class until the reunion—and then you're like, who is this hottie and how did he escape my high school radar?

"Hmm. Well, they're lucky to have sent you. Now you'll know when the time is right." I pause for a moment as he pays the parking attendant, not even turning to ask me for a dollar. What a hero! "So what do you like to do in your spare time?" I ask.

"I don't really have much of that. I used to like to build the great ships. You know, models? It's good practice for a surgeon's hands, but with my salary I don't have anywhere to put them in my small apartment. It was them or me."

Okay. Models. Not the lingerie type, he's interested in the hobby-house kind. Perfectly admirable interest. Much healthier than a rabid interest in science fiction.

"I did the Starship Enterprise last time."

Strike first opinion—far too optimistic. Making models of *Star Trek* vehicles enters shaky territory and is definitely not acceptable according to the list I just penned on the plane.

"Do you have any tribbles on board?" I say, praying that he does not get my joke, but he laughs heartily.

"No, no tribbles. I do have miniature-sized Spock and Captain Kirk, though. I painted them myself."

I nod and look out the window. "What a beautiful

day," I force out before my real comment cannot help but develop. Why are all men twelve-year-olds in disguise?

"Arin told me you like chick flicks and shopping." He smiles. It's a nervous smile, like he's as agitated as I am. Could Arin have made me sound more superficial? Chick flicks and shopping? Sheesh. She should have added monster truck rallies and watching *Jerry Springer* to the list and made me just as desirable.

"I do like those things." I laugh lightly. "But I like to collect teapots. And I have a rabid political bent. Secretly, I wish I was the president's speech writer. Oh, and I sing in the church band every other month. Sometimes with Arin. That's how we met." *I just love standing next to her size-two figure while we sing so I can look like the great opera diva next to her.*

"Arin told me, but I have to admit I've heard you sing at church."

And then . . . nothing. He isn't saying anything! This is a point in the conversation that calls for a compliment. The lack of one is like an immediate affront! I can almost hear him saying he heard the dogs howling outside.

"Arin said you have a way better voice than she does." He turns and faces me. (We're at a stoplight.) "She was right."

That's it. I'm bearing his children.

"No, Arin has a beautiful voice."

He looks at me with an intensity that feels laserlike. "I don't say things I don't mean."

Alrighty then. I say almost nothing I mean. Do you think that's a long-term issue? "I do sometimes. It's part of being an attorney, holding your cards close to your heart, bluffing."

"I would despise a life of that. I'm a what-you-see-is-what-you-get kind of guy. I'm illiterate when I have to read between the lines. That was part of my problem with Arin."

I don't see communication as a long-term problem, not really; I'm more worried that we're talking about the ex. He must not be over her. I am the Transition Girl. The big shoulders he will cry on until he's ready to venture out into the dating world again.

"How did you two meet?" My voice is chirpy. *Bad Ashley.* Do not continue conversation on Kate Moss. It's relationship suicide.

"We were living in the same apartment complex on campus. She was locked out." He shook his head. "I actually thought it was endearing."

"It is," I say. *If he doesn't find it cute that I'm absent-minded we're in trouble.*

"I don't want to talk about Arin. You know, when we were first dating, when I first saw you sing at church, I asked her your name."

Butterflies like bats now. Men can say these things, and a woman's heart pounds hopefully like she has spent thirty minutes on the Stairmaster. We say it, and we're cornering them and forcing intimacy so they retreat faster than a moray eel into a hole—better known as the Lack-of-Commitment Cave.

"Really? You wanted to know my name?" I ask.

"I just thought you looked like someone I'd like to know. I think you look much better with shorter hair. It shows off your facial structure, which is really beautiful."

This date is an unnecessary formality. Just get me to Vegas. "Thank you. I wasn't too sure about it at first." I'm running my hand down the back of my hair.

We're in the city now and the traffic is just horrendous, but everyone is steering clear of us because Kevin obviously has nothing to lose in the game of insurance Bingo.

As much as I don't care what Kevin drives—not when he's so handsome and charming I'm ready to bear his children now—I'll admit I'm embarrassed we'll be pulling up into the Mark Hopkins Hotel for valet parking. I actually pray about this, but Kevin is completely prepared.

"I'm going to park in the lot across from Union Square. We can take the cable car up to the hotel and then maybe do a little shopping on our way out."

"That sounds wonderful. I haven't been on a cable car since I was ten."

"I've never been on one," he admits.

"Where did you grow up?"

"Atlanta."

"Georgia?" Ah, Southern chivalry. *Well, no wonder.*

He nods, and now I am absolutely dumbfounded by this enigma in the tattered seat beside me. He is dressed like an Armani model, smells like a masculine woodsy spice that is clearly not drugstore cologne fare, and yet driving a complete piece of junk in the city.

"My parents are actually here from Georgia for a surgical seminar. They're staying at the Fairmont."

"Are they planning to meet us?" So *not* ready to meet the parents.

"If you don't mind. I realize that's bad form, but they're

too busy with the conference to come all the way down to Stanford."

"Of course not. I'd love to meet your parents."

"They're dying to meet you."

My stomach flutters at his touch. I'll admit I'm leery. Despite the dumpy car, this guy is just too right, too successful, too everything. But he holds his hand out and helps me from the car, and my stomach flutters again. I can literally feel the electricity pulsating between us. We have our own amazing current that sizzles like bacon. I swallow hard. We both stand there looking at one another hungrily, and I know I'm walking on dangerous ground.

"We should get to the restaurant," I say, to plan an escape route from this passionate current I don't want to take, but know I must.

He clears his throat. "Absolutely." As I turn away, he pulls me back gently into his arms. And he kisses me softly on my cheek, then quickly redirects to my mouth. I can feel my pulse racing, glad that there are no heart monitors present for Doc Kevin to read. This is not like me, to be kissing on a first date, but I feel completely safe in his arms and, at the same time, in desperate trouble. I'm helpless, breathless, finding it difficult to step away . . . It is he that ceases kissing first and pulls away to stare into my eyes and caress my cheek. He breaks our gaze and drops his arms from about my waist. "I'm sorry," he says. "I don't know what got into me."

Oh, Lord, I am treading dangerous undertow waters. Deliver me. I haven't actually started the date and I'm falling. Am I so desperate? Is he?

15

I'm in the elevator of the world-famous Mark Hopkins Hotel, brushing my skirt casually as if I haven't just lost all judgment. I toss my hair before remembering it's only about five inches long—kind of loses the effect. Once the elevator doors shut, I am instantly mortified. I'm overcome by the sickening-sweet scent of restroom soap fumes. My expensive cologne is vying miserably against the vaguely familiar smell. I'm tormented. Do I say something? Like, Hey, I know I smell like a public restroom, funny story actually . . . or do I just ignore it?

If Kevin has noticed my industrial-strength odor, he's keeping it to himself. I have hope, because hospital soap is much more antiseptic-smelling, so maybe he's not familiar with the standard bubblegum-meets-strawberry-meets-sanitation department fare. *I pray.*

My silence is too obvious, and Kevin is looking at me expectantly. So I smile and tilt my chin like I'm just so darling. "I am really glad you picked me up at the airport." *Ack. I hope he knows that I meant "pick me up" in the pure sense of the phrase.*

"Me too," he says, ignoring my blushing face. "It was nice to be back in the world again. My first two years of residency are officially over. This deserves a celebration. And what could be better than my dad picking up the tab for such a party?"

"It's nice your parents are meeting you here. They know I'm coming, right?"

"Of course they know you're coming. They're anxious to meet you. Remember?"

My eyes narrow, "What do you mean 'they're anxious'? What did your parents think of Arin?" *Where did that come from?*

He rubs his chin. "We were never serious enough for them to think anything, but they thought she wasn't intelligent enough for me."

I laugh. "My mother doesn't think anyone is intelligent enough for me. What is it with parents that they think their children are all geniuses?"

"I *am* a Mensa member."

Okay, little freaky. I would think most people around here are intelligent enough to join Mensa. *Actually taking the time to test? Weird.*

He shrugs and tries to laugh off my silence. "Aren't you a member?"

"Um, no."

"Did you ever try?" he asks, like it's the most natural thing in the world to join Mensa.

"Not my thing," I explain.

"Well, do you think you could pass? Have you had your IQ measured?"

"Is it a prerequisite for dating you, the IQ test?"

"I'm a strong believer in the gene pool. As are my parents." No hint of a smile here, as in, *I'm joking.*

"Is that why you picked pediatrics? Gene work?"

"Whatever I can do to correct genetic mistakes is a benefit to society, don't you think?" The elevator doors open. "Here we are."

I'm momentarily stunned by the views. The crystal blue sky pierced by the world-famous Transamerica building, and all settling on the panoramic scenery of the San Francisco Bay. "It's absolutely gorgeous. I'll never get enough of this city."

"There are my parents." Kevin puts his hand in the small of my back and guides me toward a couple. I would say older, but they aren't. Kevin's father looks as though he's just trained for a triathlon, and his mother looks like she knows the name of a very good plastic surgeon. There's no look of surprise on her perfectly-lifted brow, and no windblown face where a lifetime of living should leave wrinkles. *Now, that's some good work.* I'm studying it, trying to remove my gaze when Kevin introduces us.

"Mother, Father. This is Ashley Stockingdale." He pushes me a bit forward.

"Hello," I say reaching out my hand. "Such a pleasure to meet you both." *Although it could have at least been after our first date.*

His mother is scrutinizing me, her eyes going up and down my black pantsuit. Probably seeing if she can make out any genetic deformities.

"Miss Stockingdale," his mother says, with a crisp nod of her chin.

"Ashley, we've heard quite a bit about you." Dr.

Novak Senior says. "But my son has been holding out on how beautiful you really are."

If that isn't the biggest cliché I've ever heard. "Thank you."

"Sit down. Sit down." Kevin's father calls the waiter over with a raised finger, and I find myself looking for that guy who answered the phone yesterday. I want to shout I wasn't really dumped.

"Ashley's a patent attorney for Selectech," Kevin says. Again with the resume. "She's just been to Taiwan to secure one of her patents."

Doctor Novak is shaking his head. "Very nice, Miss Stockingdale."

"Call me Ashley, please."

"Ashley? That's a name after your time, isn't it, dear?" Mrs. asks. "I mean, usually Ashleys are about nine or ten right now."

"My mother named me for Ashley Wilkes in *Gone with the Wind*."

"Why on earth would she do that?"

I shrug. "She liked the character, I suppose."

"But he's a man," Mrs. Novak says, stating the obvious. *And the Mensa member here would be?*

"So what brings you two to the city?" I ask.

"Surgical conference. The latest in laser-assisted robots. You know, Ashley, I have an idea for a surgical tool, and I should get your help securing a patent," Dr. Novak says. "I bet I could quit this line of work altogether."

"That's my goal, too. I kept an eye out when I went to Taiwan to look at that machine, Dad. Figured out how it's done," Kevin says. "One good product, and you're set for life with royalty streams."

"Actually, you're pretty young, Kevin, and a patent only gives you a head start of twenty years. With medical products that are specialized, it can be very slow. The secret to a good patent is a high sales pattern or high desire for the product. If you found the machine that cured cancer, for example."

If I'm not mistaken, Kevin's teeth are clenched. "Who's to say I couldn't do that?"

"No one. Certainly not me."

"Miss Stockingdale, where did you go to school?"

"Santa Clara University. They have a law program that's renowned, and I just loved the campus from the time I was a child."

"Yes, didn't someone from O. J.'s case work there?" Mrs. asks.

"Gerald Uelman is a professor, but don't hold that against us; it's a very good school."

"I'd never heard of it before today," Mrs. sniffs.

Um, then how did you know about Gerald Uelman? I'm dying to ask. But I keep my mouth shut.

The waiter comes, and I want to kiss him just because he's normal and probably has an IQ like mine. "What may I get you?" he asks me.

Someone who can discuss this week's People. "I'll have a Diet Coke with a twist of lemon." *Hey, I'm classy.*

Kevin orders the house merlot and then makes a big deal swirling it around in his glass for my benefit. *Yeah, yeah, can you tell a fresh-roasted espresso bean from an old one? Well, I can.*

"I'm dying for an espresso," I say out of the blue. "Can you bring me a shot?" I ask the waiter while he's looming over, waiting for Kevin to give the okay on the glass of wine.

"Of course, Miss." And then, cute waiter winks at me. *Calgon, take me away!*

It suddenly occurs to me that Kevin's hair holds absolutely the straightest part I've ever seen. It's like his hair was created to lie in this ruler-like line. Does he use a surgical tool to get it that straight? Does his mother come from Atlanta to ensure its pinpoint accuracy? I wonder if God chooses your career by the hair you have. Big-haired people always gravitate toward marketing.

But there's this attraction between us that can't be denied. That must count for something. When I looked at Seth, there was that momentary roller-coaster-hill-thrill. I feel that same lift, only multiplied with Kevin, like a sharp airplane takeoff for noise abatement. My stomach is doing continuous gymnastics when his gaze pierces mine, but then I watch him with the stupid glass of wine and I want to hurt him. His nose is practically in the glass, and he's inhaling like a pig snorting for a truffle. What is *that* about?

Kevin has definite benefits, I remind myself as he swishes the wine around in his mouth like it's Scope. He is gorgeous, of course. He's a doctor. A doctor who loves kids. Okay, his car choice could use some guidance, but I just can't help but think, *What is this interview with the parents?* Did Arin make the cut? I mean, I love Arin, but she's no brain surgeon. And men have a way of making beautiful women into who they want them to be. Did Kevin try that with Arin and fail?

In a way, it's the men's own fault. They automatically

equate beautiful with the best, rather than the neediest, most high-maintenance chick you'll ever date. Me? I just come with regularly scheduled, five-thousand-mile maintenance. There has to be a long-term benefit in that.

But I have the distinct feeling Kevin is not making his own decisions here. "So how did you two meet?" Mrs. Novak asks.

"I'm a friend of Arin's," I say, waiting for a reaction.

"Arin's?" His mother says as though I've just said I shared an open-mouthed kiss with Madonna onscreen.

Kevin speaks. "They knew each other from church. Arin and Ashley both sing in the church band."

"Do you have a musical background, Ashley? Musical minds are very good at math," Dr. Novak states.

I listen to David Crowder in my car. "No, not really."

Now the parents are looking at each other. I'm not making the cut, and I couldn't be more pleased. Not that I don't want Kevin. He's not out yet. I'm just not up for in-laws like these two. My parents are bad enough . . .

"She reads music for the band," Kevin offers.

And then, my cell phone rings. It's my mother, and suddenly I could kiss her for her beautiful, nagging phone calls. "Excuse me," I say, as though I'm so important. "This will just take a moment. Hello. Ashley Stockingdale."

"Ashley, are you back from that horrible place yet?"

"I'm back. I'm in San Francisco. Just got home an hour ago." I am a top attorney, I should not be rattled by my mother's nagging voice. Yet, I am human—and you know how dogs hear certain sounds and then howl? It's like that with me and my mother's tone sometimes. Kevin's parents are seeming healthier by the moment.

"The church is having a festival the day of Dave's wedding, so we're moving it up to Vegas. I planned the shower for Sunday. I sent out invitations and called everyone who didn't RSVP already. We have twenty-four people coming and so you're going to need to get started."

That woman can stress me out like no VP of engineering who ever lived. I'm supposed to plan a party for what, two days from now? I walk into the foyer where I can talk in a hoarse whisper. "Mom, I am the maid of honor. I'm supposed to plan the shower."

"You were planning it, until you took off for that third-world country without telling us. I had to call your secretary to find out my own daughter was in Taiwan. Ashley, you just will never find a man if you pick up and leave like that."

"Mom, this really isn't a good time to talk. I'm meeting a friend's parents. Just meeting them for the first time." *Come on, come on. Remember all that first impression garbage you taught me?*

"Well, since you're in the city, get some good prizes for the games. I figure we'll need about six things. Spend about $15 each. What did you want to do about food?"

I'm trying to unclench my teeth, but my words come out between them. "I was planning to do the whole event at a restaurant."

"Ashley, I just told you it's at my house on Sunday. Your brother is getting married in three weeks now. We have to have a shower for Mei Ling. It's not their fault the church double-booked." Kevin and his parents are looking for me, and I edge nearer, smiling as if I'm wrapping it up. But my mother is showing no signs of slowing.

"Mom, it's tacky to have your own daughter-in-law's shower."

"I don't have time to think about that now. The invitations are out, and I've already called everyone. Listen, come over here when you're done at your friend's. We'll work on the menu. Maybe we can shop tonight."

"Mom, I'm surviving jetlag; I am not going shopping tonight. I'll be lucky to crash into bed."

"We can't all wait for you to work yourself into an early grave. Your brother only gets married once."

I'll believe that when I see it. "Gotta run, Mom." I turn off my phone, and both Kevin's parents are looking at me like I'm talking to the space station.

"That was your mother you spoke to like that?" Mrs. Novak raises her eyebrows in disapproval and looks at Kevin.

I feel like I'm in a cage at the zoo. Throw me a peanut.

"My brother's getting married. My mother's a little stressed about the swiftness of it all."

"I can certainly understand that. Is there a reason the wedding must be swift? We believe in allowing a minimum of fifteen months between the engagement and the wedding," Mrs. Novak says.

"I guess they're in a hurry. True love and all that."

Kevin's parents aren't smiling. "What college did your brother go to?"

That's it, I've had it. "He's a bus driver," I say with conviction. "A really good bus driver." My espresso comes, and I throw it back like a tequila popper. "I'm actually getting very tired; my trip is catching up with me. Kevin, would you mind?"

Kevin stands immediately, like the good son his parents

have taught him to be. He shakes hands with his dad firmly and kisses his mother's cheek. "So I'll see you both on your next time through. Kiss Emily for me." Kevin faces me. "Ready?"

"Nice to meet you, Dr. and Mrs. Novak. Have a wonderful conference and a safe trip home." *And get me a business card for that plastic surgeon. Fabulous, just fabulous work.*

We clamber into the elevator like I'm getting on the plane to America. I look up, and Kevin's stony expression has completely died. He's staring at me with those intense green eyes and a hunger I haven't seen for a good hour now. This is the Kevin I remember. He must despise his parents as much I as I do! We can elope and avoid them for years at a time!

I swallow hard as he moves in for a kiss. *Lord, let my heart stand up to it.*

16

You kissed him on the first date?" Brea's mouth is dangling open, and since we are outside the church, I can't help but look around at who heard her.

"Shh. Why don't you just use the microphone?" I ask. "Announce that Ashley Stockingdale is easy like a light-bulb-bake oven."

Brea covers her mouth in that elegant way of hers. "Sorry, Ashley, I'm just shocked. You're not a kiss-on-the-first-date kinda gal. Especially when he was just dating your friend, what's her name, that girl who sings with you? The scrawny one." Brea leans in, all concern for Arin dissipated. "Was it a good kiss?"

I'm wiggling my eyebrows. "It was a curl-your-toes, pump-your-heart, swirl-your-stomach kind of kiss."

Brea screams and grabs my hands, and we jump like a pair of pogo sticks. Before we remember we are refined Christian women who would never do such a thing.

"Where?"

"First, in a parking lot in San Francisco by his jalopy. Then, in the elevator at the Mark Hopkins." She's still staring at me. "What?" I ask. "Honestly, it was the most romantic kiss I've ever had. It could have been in a Venice gondola for all I felt." I haven't broken the parental unit issue to her yet.

"When are you seeing him again?"

"He's not off until next Thursday."

"Is he going to call you?"

Brea just has a way lately of sucking away my joy. How do I know if he's going to call me? Isn't that one of the great questions of life? Right up there with why am I here on earth? Who knows what goes through a man's mind in regard to the Phone Call. You know they create this whole debate in their mind. Otherwise, it wouldn't take until the Wednesday after your date to call.

"I don't know if he's going to call me," I say, my voice shrill.

"John called me the next day after I kissed him."

"John is a freak, okay?" Brea's husband is presently standing on the steps, once again gazing longingly at his wife. It's enough to make one sick. He doesn't stalk her or anything. He's just mesmerized by her, like normal men view football.

She licks her teeth at her husband. "Isn't he yummy?"

I roll my eyes, disgusted. Is there even another response?

"Ashley?" Seth breaks our reverie, thank goodness. He approaches with his hands in his pockets, smiling, and I'm startled that my tummy still cartwheels and his eyes still tempt me. I've just been romanced by a man with the hands of a surgeon, and yet this engineer with his hands in his pockets produces a huge lump in my throat. *This is so not funny!* "Can I talk to you a minute, Ashley?"

"Sure," I say as if he means nothing to me. But my heart is pounding and my stomach is just surging. It's everything I can do to hold it together. "Brea, I'll see you this afternoon at my mom's house. You are so dead if you don't show."

"I'll be there. Do you think I'd miss seeing who on earth would marry Dave? Please, it's like being invited for an alien showing. See ya, Seth." Brea kisses my cheek and takes off, bubbling to the next person she sees on the church steps.

Seth is looking at his feet, and I want to shake him and scream at him to tell me what he's thinking. I can hardly wait for the words.

"What's up?" I finally ask.

His stunning eyes meet mine again. "You didn't call before you left for Taiwan." He looks hurt, and I can honestly say I didn't know he had it in him. Just this smidgen of emotion sends me over the edge. I have this overwhelming desire to kiss him—on the church steps, no less! Where's that on the list of lustful sins? Did I not just kiss someone else the day before yesterday? Didn't I just tell Brea it curled my toes?

"I'm sorry." I smile. "I got so busy with the briefs, then I was off to Taiwan and yesterday I went in to work and I'm helping my mother with my brother's shower and so I just didn't get a chance."

But Seth doesn't seem to be listening to my excuses.

"I thought about what you said to me that day at Chevys." He pauses and looks around him. "You know, in the parking lot."

"Yes, I remember." *It was right before I bought the deadly violet bra. That day is just better off forgotten. Well, except for the Dr. Kevin part.*

"We've been friends a long time, Ashley. I would never do anything to hurt you."

I nod. What can I say? He did hurt me. And he made a fool out of me. And that ticks me off more than any of it. I should be skipping, telling him all about Dr. Kevin, but Seth's gaze still unnerves me. He still rattles me with every piercing engineer glance.

"Will you let me make it up to you?" he asks. "I think I owe you a real date."

A mercy date? I don't think so. "You don't have to make it up to me. I just don't want you to do that again. Not to me or anyone else, Seth. You have to be careful with how you handle your . . . friends. Call me ignorant, but I thought you were asking me out that night." My hand flies to my mouth. *Did I admit that?*

He nods and clears his throat. "When you were gone to Taiwan, I really missed you, Ash." He doesn't look at me when he says the next part. "I don't miss Arin, and I don't think about her."

Can I just yell at You, God, for a minute? I have not had a date in six months! Not six months, God! And You've got to bring me two men in a weekend? It's cruel. I'm not an irony kinda chick, You know!

"I don't know what to say, Seth. You never really knew Arin. But *we* were friends. At least I thought we were."

"Can we have lunch today? Just you and me. Not with the gang."

Ah, the Reasons. I had completely forgotten about

them. Sad that my whole identity has been wrapped up in a group of people who really mean nothing to me after a week's absence.

"I can't do it today, Seth. I'm throwing a shower for my brother's fiancée."

He looks defeated. Like he's missed out on a flower at the rose ceremony. I should stand right here and tell him that I'm dating Dr. Kevin Novak. That I kissed him and fireworks ensued. But when I think about how that would hurt Seth, I clamp my mouth shut. I'm a schlub. Maybe because Wednesday hasn't arrived yet. I don't know if I'm dating a doctor or if I just hit a momentary lustful weak spot, it being Fabulous Friday and all.

"Maybe another time then." Seth starts to back up the steps. People are entering the sanctuary in droves now, and we should be joining them.

"Seth," I say with a twinge of desperation in my voice.

He grabs my hand and squeezes. "I'll call you." He smiles.

Great. Now I'm waiting for two phone calls. Is there a sign on my back that reads SUCKER or what?

After an hour-long sermon on the importance of Christian honesty and integrity, I slink back to my apartment more confused than ever. In one hour, I'll wear that plastered smile as relatives ask me when *I'm* getting married. (Hence, the reason I went to church on this harried day. I need to be reminded that God is with me through this.) I'm generally very happy being single until I'm reminded how awful it is by well-meaning friends and family.

I can just hear them now in Scarlett Southern drawl,

"Oh, Ashley . . . however do you manage all alone like that? With no one who cares whether you come or go. My dear, it must be horrible for you."

My phone is ringing. I know it's my mother telling me to stop at the store for some aspic or something, but I don't recognize the number. "Hello."

"Ashley?"

It's a man. Wonders never cease. "Yes?" I say with a certain familiar drawl. I really need to get a life.

"Ashley, it's Dan Hollings from high school. Nancy's brother. She said she ran into you at Bloomingdale's and that you were single . . . like me."

Dang.

"Right, Dan Hollings. She's just darling, your sister Nancy." *Sticking my finger down my throat.* What was that about Christian integrity and honesty? The bolt of lightning is coming any minute now.

"I was wondering if you might be free for lunch sometime this week to catch up on old times."

Lunch is good. Lunch is short. Lunch can be severed by a simple cell phone ring. "That would be nice." *I am going to kill Brea.*

Dan Hollings was in the band in high school. That, in itself, is not a deterrent. I always did have a penchant for the geeks, but Dan Hollings *thought* he was popular. Under his delusions of grandeur, he hung around the cheerleaders while they laughed at him and sent him to get their sodas. There's a picture of him in the yearbook where he's shoved in a garbage can, surrounded by football jocks, and he always said it was staged for photography class. *Yeah, sure it was.*

Dan's still talking. "Is Friday all right? I heard you work in Palo Alto; I do too. Maybe we could meet at Fresco's."

Fresco's. Okay, well, the cheerleaders taught him one thing. A tightwad is not an attractive trait. "That sounds wonderful. That's one of my favorite restaurants." What is with the perkiness? The guy could take me to the Top of the Mark but he's still Dan Hollings.

"Great. I'll make reservations." His voice sounds like an announcer voiceover. A fake baritone tossed with a side of wheedling. "See you at noon on Friday." Just the way he says it makes it seem like he's overconfident or that my knees should be weak. *Ick. Ick. Ick. I am going to kill Brea.*

After some idle chit-chat, I hang up the phone. *Three dates.* I have been asked on three dates in a week. I know there is some terrible fate waiting to befall me and that God has some Supreme Lesson for me to learn; I'm just hoping it's not this upcoming date. I riffle through my shelves looking for that book on personal boundaries.

I'm definitely lacking personal boundaries because:

1. I'm throwing my brother a shower today, when I just got home two days ago. (It's at my mother's house, no less!)
2. I'm going on a date with a man I don't even want to see again, much less date. (Come on, would I really marry into that cheerleader's family?)
3. I couldn't be tough with Seth or tell him about Kevin, and most importantly . . .
4. I'm wearing that vicious violet bra again! I thought I threw it out.

No Boundary Book to be found. I'm going to be late. I probably gave the book away because I couldn't tell someone *No, buy your own book*. Purchasing two books on personal boundaries is certainly a symptom of some mental illness. Maybe I should invest in a DSM–IV book and diagnose myself. I'm sure whatever I have, it has something to do with my parents. I'd probably be quite normal if I came from a different family.

But I digress. I am fabulous now, remember? I look in the mirror and rake my fingers through my hair, talking to my reflection.

"You are Ashley Wilkes Stockingdale. You are fabulous. You do not have to be married to be fabulous. Anybody can be married, but you won't settle for just anyone. No, you are waiting for the Mr. Darcy of your time. The Colin Firth of the Christian set." I pucker my lips and blow myself a kiss. I am ready for anything. Even my extended family and my brother's wedding shower. Bring it on!

Phone again. Caller ID says it's Mom. Hmm. Really debating answering this one, but she'll just nag me on the cell. "Hello."

"Oh good, Ashley, I caught you. Listen, your brother wanted to get Mei Ling something nice and didn't have time to stop by the store. Do you have anything lying around the house you could wrap up?"

"Like birth control pills?"

"Ashley! Your behavior these days is absolutely appalling. I did not raise you to be such a smart-mouth. Ashley Wilkes wouldn't talk that way."

I'm stifling a giggle. I really do have a mean streak these days. "I'm kidding, Mom. I'll find something."

"Make sure your Aunt Trudy didn't give it to you for Christmas. She'll be here. I've searched in my gift cabinet, and I just don't have anything appropriate."

"I have so many gifts from men, it's no problem, Mom." Okay, I really do have a mental illness.

"I just can't tell when you're joking anymore. This sarcasm isn't going to help you find a man."

Ain't it the truth?

I log off Mom and log onto my e-mail just to check if there are any urgent e-mails from Liberia asking for money. Nothin' but some to-do lists from Purvi. But there is one from Seth.

To: AWStockingdale@NNN.net

From: MatrixMan@NNN.net

Ash, know things are hectic, but must talk with you. Call me when you get a chance. —Seth

Must talk with me. Probably about the mercy date he asked me out on, and can he, um, take it back? Or do I know so and so? Well, if he needs to know the phone number of the new girl, he can find out for himself. I'd rather go to my brother's wedding shower.

17

Please tell me that my name is not on this shower invitation! I'm standing here in stunned awe. I cannot believe this is a representation of a shower I would throw. I'm looking at the purple and gold decorations—and when I say gold, I mean metallic, not classic brushed gold. Shiny, cheesy metallic—like glitter has thrown up all over my mother's house. It's a tribute to the '80s in here, not to mention my brother's days as a high school football star. But here we are, in a bad set of *Dance Fever* waiting for the guest of honor and, of course, Deney Terrio could show at any moment.

My mother is a nervous wreck, certain that her aspic will fall or that one of her little finger sandwiches will don a piece of crust. Gone is my idea of grilled Portobello mushrooms and prosciutto-wrapped cantaloupe. In its place, we have finger-food circa 1950 and my mother in an apron.

I am most certainly adopted.

"Ashley, get your coat off and help me wrap the plasticware." Mom hands me a stack of dark purple napkins and gold curling ribbon. *Relax.* This is Mei Ling's shower, and if she likes Dave, chances are she's going for the gold.

"I brought the gift for Mei Ling." I hold it out to my mother. "From Dave," I say sarcastically as she takes it from me.

Mom places it on the coffee table with some of the other gifts. I add my own purchased gift to the pile. *From Dave*, I found some perfume I received from my boss for Christmas. The stuff smells like Jasmine and Windex mixed together, so I figure Dave will think it's divine. My boss left the price tag on it as though the financial burden would make me think the odor was actually a good thing.

Anyway, I left the price tag for Dave. Mei Ling most likely won't notice, but my brother will know he owes me. And I never miss an opportunity for that. I bought a beautiful gift for my future sister-in-law in Union Square. I'm actually very excited to get a sister-in-law—if not in complete disbelief. I just hope we can communicate. Since my brother is prone to simple grunts, I don't know what to expect of her and I'm quite nervous about meeting the poor woman.

I wrap the plasticware and set all of the snacks on the dining room table and, finally, fill the punch bowl with the standard sherbet, red dye #5 specialty of the house. I picked up the cake at the natural food store, and it is a sight to behold. Luscious, out-of-season strawberries and ribbons of whipped cream give the image of an elaborate wedding dress, and "Welcome Mei Ling" is written in soft pink cursive.

I was fine about the event—this wedding—until I saw the cake. The cake sits there, almost taunting me in its virginal whiteness. Why do I feel so single this year? It's like I turned thirty-one and I'm suddenly humiliated that

I'm unmarried. And where in the heck is Brea? She's supposed to be here with me, supporting me in my Dark Hour.

The prosciutto and cantaloupe didn't happen because I'm not the princess for the day. I'm the hired help. My lower lip is trembling at the sight of my giddy mother running with her hands in the air. I think she's thankful that there's no mother of the bride to contend with—perhaps because this might be the only wedding she hopes to ever plan. My mom is walking toward me and I just close my eyes. I can't handle it. Where is Brea?

"Please don't say anything, Mom." I hold up my palm.

She puts her arm around me. "Your day is coming, Ashley." She pats my hand and goes on about her busyness, while I have what feels like a walnut stuck in my throat. She doesn't reassure me that it's okay to be single, only that my day is coming. Well, so is the apocalypse, and I'm not holding my breath.

Doorbell. Here comes the onslaught. *Prepare.*

My mom opens the door, and Dave is standing with his arm around an absolutely beautiful Asian girl. She's petite, with flawless skin and a gorgeous thin nose that's straight out of an "after" picture at the plastic surgeon's office. Her eyes are large and deep brown, and dark hair falls around her shoulders in a modern, uneven bob. Mei Ling looks surprisingly American for someone my brother would date. She smiles at me and tentatively hugs me.

"You're Ashley," she says into my ear without an accent.

I nod. "It's so nice to meet you, Mei Ling." She is nothing like I imagined her. She looks like she could marry anyone she wanted, and I am completely thrown. I was expecting a downtrodden foreigner in bad plaid who settled for a man like Dave because she needed a green card. Mei Ling, however, has a friendly smile and a warm manner *and* designer clothes. She has really tiny, elegant hands. I want to say more, but I cannot think of a thing, I'm so taken aback by my own misconceptions. Or should I say, *prejudices.*

My mother has helped with Mei Ling's coat and is explaining how the day will go, like Mei Ling is a half-wit. But Mei Ling's English is perfect. I immediately visit the gift table and pick up the wretched bottle of cologne, which I wouldn't allow my brother to give to his tiny bride. Dave is chaperoning Mei Ling about with this deep care and concern, actually protecting her from my mother's rules.

The odds of a man treating me like this, with kid gloves, are, um, shall we say, negative six or so? So now I'm thinking, am I just this practical chick who's not meant for real romance? Maybe I'm the type a man marries and immediately denigrates to wearing sweatpants and becoming a laundry Nazi. Perhaps I'm not the type one cherishes, but the practical gal a guy gravitates toward when they have an excess of dirty shorts.

Where's Brea? She hasn't shown, and most likely she won't—because she is now part of a matched set—and like a sock in the dryer, if she gets separated, they'll never see each other again. This isn't the first time she's been a No Show when she's promised me she'll be somewhere. Not since John came into our lives.

"Ash, you okay?" Dave asks.

I nod again. I study his face. He's being nice to me. Mei Ling might be the antidote to his brotherly disease!

"You like her?"

"I do, Dave. She's beautiful, and she seems very sweet."

"Thanks." He kisses my cheek. *He actually kissed my cheek!* "I knew you'd like her. At least I'd hoped you would."

Could my opinion actually matter to him?

"I'm sorry about what I said." I shuffle my feet. "About you meeting her at the immigration department and everything. That was a stupid thing to say."

He shrugs. "I knew you didn't mean it. I'm outta here before all the biddies get here." I watch him walk over to Mei Ling, a look of deep concern growing on his brow. He really and truly cares for her, and I'm just stunned that my brother has love residing anywhere within him. It throws off all I know to be true. He speaks gently to her. "Mei Ling, if you need anything, just ask Ashley, okay? I've got my cell phone. Call if it gets to be too much. I'll be here in ten minutes."

Mei Ling nods. "Don't worry. I'll be fine. It's only your family."

Dave winks at me. "It's only my family, she says. Stick with her, Ashley. I'm counting on you."

Dave kisses Mei Ling, and she returns the kiss with a fire not acceptable in my parents' home. My mother purses her lips. Dave never sees Mom's expression, and he's out the door before she can make her annoyance known. Kissing in my family is saved for the bedroom. At least I assumed it's saved for there. Since I've never seen it, and my brother and I exist, I figure it must reside in secret. *Ick. Bad visual.*

Doorbell again. The relatives have arrived. I open the door, and three of my great-aunts are huddled together in an overweight sparkly rhinestone powwow. "Ashley!" they say in unison.

"Aunt Trudy, Aunt Val, Aunt Babe." I hug them all, and we are still on the porch when the first grenade is launched.

"Well?" Aunt Val says, as only a lifelong smoker can. She lifts up my left hand. "Look at this pretty gal still not married. What's wrong with her?" she says to her sisters.

Aunt Babe shakes her head. "It's criminal."

"We're not going to be around forever, you know." Aunt Trudy says, sounding remarkably like Marge Simpson. I question that remark. I think they are going to be around forever, sopped in their old lady perfume, preserved better than King Tut himself.

"She's no spring chicken," Aunt Babe offers.

They look to one another, my mother's same pursed lips in synchronized form, shaking their heads. It's like a rehearsed ballet. Okay, my melancholy is gone. Extreme annoyance has taken its place.

I know my great-aunts are older. I know they deserve my respect, but Lord help me, when those mustached mouths combine in raisined puckers, I'm like a cat with my back raised. I want to defend myself against this raging pit bull of judgment, yet I know it won't do any good.

"Aunties, you're all so funny. I just haven't met Mr. Right yet, but I'm dating a Stanford doctor."

Group squeal of approval.

"You're *what?*" My mother comes out of nowhere.

"It's nothing serious yet, Mom. Don't get too excited."

"We never thought we'd see the day that your brother

was getting married before you, Ashley. You must be too good for the men around here," Aunt Babe says.

"She's not too fat," Aunt Trudy surmises. "She's got a nice rack on her."

Have mercy on me.

"She's quite a pretty girl, too. Even with that awful haircut."

"Speaking of pretty, why don't you all come in and meet Mei Ling?" I open the door wider, and like three animals on their way to the trough, my aunts head to the table to check the spread. They'll apparently get to the bride after this important bit of business is resolved.

It may sound odd, but I'm kind of rejoicing that they don't see the obvious reason for my singleness. There was actually an argument about what my problem might be. Lord knows, if they did see it, I would be aware of it now. So that just goes to prove my reasons are well-hidden, and maybe that's why I confuse the men of America. It's definitely fixable. I just have to unearth it and put it in its proper place like a good Reason Archeologist.

My mother's friends arrive, and the shower attendance is complete. Mei Ling is bowing as she meets the guests, each of them whispering their thoughts aloud. Although Mei Ling speaks perfect English, it does not occur to my great-aunts that she understands it as well.

"I doubt he could find an American girl."

"He's not the sharpest knife in the drawer."

"Let's get started with some games," I announce. I break the women up into small groups, and we do the toilet-paper-wedding-dress gig. Hey, how creative do you expect me to be with two days notice? My aunts, as avid quilters, embellish with tissue rosettes and bows and, while it's hard, I announce my aunts the winners with their streaming floor-length toilet paper veil.

Big exertion breath here. One game down. One to go. But the women are talking, and I can't do anything to break apart their fun. "I have another game," I say, but no one ceases talking.

Mei Ling shakes her head. "It's all right, Ashley. I don't think they want to play a game, and I got to meet everyone. That's all that matters."

"We have to do the gifts."

"We will. You worry too much. Your brother said you worried too much."

I can't believe my brother talks about me at all. "He said that?"

"Your brother told me you're the smartest woman he knows and that I would love you."

"My *brother* said that?"

Mei Ling laughs. "Why wouldn't he? He's your staunchest supporter, you know. He said that you go to Taiwan all the time, and perhaps we could join you on an upcoming trip so I could locate some of my family relations."

"Where did you meet my brother?" Now I'm really leery, like this is some elaborate joke for my benefit. My mother said they were getting married at a Chinese church, but this—

"A friend of mine brought him to our Bible church about six months ago. They didn't stay together, but Dave stayed. He's been coming ever since and even learning a bit of the Chinese language."

Dave bumming a trip to Taiwan, I can handle, but him attending church? That's just beyond Roswell, you know? A Raelian, I could believe. Even your garden variety Jehovah's Witness, but a Bible-believing, Chinese-church-attending Christian? No way. There's just no way.

"Your brother is a very sweet man, Ashley. I know you two have had your moments, but it's time you both forgave."

Did I not just get a sermon? From my brother's Christian fiancée? Nothing is as I've seen it. God can turn my lazy brother into a Christian, but He can't make Seth see I'm the woman for him. My eyes clamp shut. *Seth*. I meant Kevin, didn't I? Dr. Kevin.

18

I arrive home and find my answering machine is blinking. I'm embarrassed by the exhilaration this brings me. Yet, it's only Sunday night. Not Wednesday, not even pathetic I-don't-have-a-date-yet Thursday. It's Sunday and I have a message; can I possibly help my elation?

I skip to the phone and press the red light of hope.

"Hey Ash, it's me Brea. I know you're ticked. But hear me out. John was—"

I push the button again. Do I really need to hear the excuse? I mean, John comes first. What more do I need to know? There are no further messages. It's times like these I need my Bible. Taking it out, I start to read in James when the phone rings.

"You're mad at me," Brea says.

"Uh, yeah."

"Did you even listen to my excuse?"

Brea knows me too well. *I hate that.* "No, but let me guess. John suffered an excruciating bowling accident and you spent the afternoon in the emergency room."

"Very funny."

My arms cross defensively. "You know I'm really happy for your marriage and all, but you still have to have friends, am I right? John can't be your entire life because that's as pathetic as not dating. I was really counting on you today, Brea. It was extremely awkward with my great-aunts. Not to mention my mother giddily planning a wedding. This means nothing to you, does it?" I accuse.

"Would you please quit your whining?"

I am whining. I hate being caught. She annoys me sometimes.

"Ashley, other people are going to get married. Your friends are going to have children. It's not my fault I fell in love, but how long are you going to be bitter? Move on, will ya?"

"Me? You're going to blame this on me? Let your yes be yes, and your no be no, Brea." Ha, got her with Scripture. "You said you were coming. This has nothing to do with me being jealous, or a loser with no friends. This has to do with you, my best friend from childhood, standing me up worse than Seth did in Fresh Choice."

"The violins are playing, Ash."

"I *so* deserve some sympathy. Purple and metallic gold decorating scheme—need I say more?"

"I'm sorry, Ash. I really am, but it was Dave's day and you knew it was going to be bad. Listen, there's this young gal at my mother's church. She's pregnant, and she wants to put the child up for adoption."

Her words stun me into silence.

"My mother told her about us, and she wanted to meet us today. She's due in three months, and you just don't say no to a volatile, pregnant teenager."

I feel utterly alone. When did my best friend decide to adopt a baby? Her life is moving in fast forward, and I am completely standing still.

"Brea, when did you decide you wanted to adopt?"

"I didn't, until my mother called me. Then it felt right. I prayed about it and I'm just beside myself. After I met Tracy, we connected, and I feel like she's carrying my baby, Ash."

"What about your own children?" *She was pregnant two weeks ago, was she not?*

"We'll still try to have them, of course, but a baby is a precious gift. Who cares where it comes from? They all come from God, and this one needs a home with two stable parents."

"And those stable people would be?" I can't tell if Brea is trying to convince me or herself. She's the kind of person who takes on everyone else's needs as her own personal mission.

Brea will make a great mother, there's no denying that, but I'm worried her heart is still broken over losing her baby. I'm worried she'll end up with a house full of kids before she ever gets the opportunity to start her own family. I want Brea to make this decision because it's right for her, not because she wants to save the world. But I realize I can't make Brea do anything. This is up to her and John. Not me.

"Okay, I know I flaked today. What else is new?" Brea asks. "When am I ever where I say I will be? That doesn't mean I'm unstable. Just flighty."

"But that is going to be important if you're a mother, Brea. You have to be where you say you're going to be."

She's quiet for a moment. "You know how much I want a baby."

"Yes, I do, but do you have to have one right now? They generally take nine months."

"You are so completely selfish, Ashley. That's why you're not married, you know. You never think of anyone but you. You can't be happy for anyone but you! *How does this affect Ashley?* Your mother should have named you Scarlett!" She slams the phone down in my ear, and this must be what quicksand feels like. I've tried everything to stay afloat, but life is just bringing me down.

"You know, God, I said I wanted to know my reason; I didn't say slap me from every angle or shout what a loser I am from the highest mountain, now did I?" My ceiling is not answering me, and now I have this rush of guilt over Brea. What a terrible thing to say to her! This is the perfect way to start my week. The phone rings again.

"Brea, I'm sorry—" I answer without checking the caller ID.

"Ashley?" a familiar accent asks.

"Purvi?" I ask, knowing it's my boss.

"Yes, I just got off the phone with Taiwan," She's all business. This can't be good.

"It's Sunday night, Purvi." That's my way of saying she needs to get a life, but I'm obviously no one to talk. I've spent my afternoon at yet another bridal shower, which I could give professionally by now. And a thousand times better than my mother.

"It's Monday morning in Taiwan," Purvi says with resolve, like I don't have my own foreign clock ticking in my head. I know what time it is in Taiwan. Purvi is still talking, but I fluttered out. I focus back in on her words. "They're not going to manufacture our patent product any longer."

I squeal. I heard that part. This is Way Bad. "No royalties?"

"Those royalties made our stock rise, Ashley. You've got to get them back. Our contract is null and void if they write off the products for the American market."

I just hate this feeling in my stomach. It's a cross between roller coaster drop and bad ramen roiling in my belly.

"Dare I ask?" I grip the phone until my knuckles are bone white.

"You're going to need to head back to Taiwan soon." *Back to Taiwan*. Were more depressing words ever spoken? Back to fish parts, brown air, and my luxury view of the cinder-block building next to the cinder block hotel.

"How soon?"

"Can you be here at six a.m.?" Purvi sounds annoyed I'm not there right now.

"I'll be there." Lord knows I have nothing else to do. Then Brea's words come back to taunt me that I'm selfish. Everyone's selfish to an extent, am I right?

"Purvi, can I ask you a personal question?" I ask before she hangs up. She sighs. It apparently invades our android personas, but I continue undeterred. "Do you think I'm selfish?"

She laughs. "All single people are selfish. If you weren't, you'd be married."

"Uh huh," I say meekly. Not quite the answer I was looking for. Is it selfish to give up any semblance of a social life to run off to Taiwan at the drop of a hat? Is it selfish to work sixteen-hour days when I know I won't have an apartment in two weeks? I think, if anything, I've been downright generous with Purvi and Selectech. They own me. I hang up the phone. *Selfish, my foot.*

Single people are the last safe vestige of political incorrectness. It's okay to point out our flaws and contemplate freely why we're all alone like a mannequin in a couture window. I didn't write my life script. God did. And He hasn't written in the wedding yet. Maybe He never will, but what am I thinking? Some man isn't going to complete me. God is. Purvi is in a miserable marriage. Her husband lives in another country or it would be even worse, and yet I'm made to feel like she's somehow fulfilled while I sorely lack something of interest in my life. *Yeah, right.* The phone rings again.

"Hello!" I snap.

"I'm sorry," Brea says.

"You know what, Brea? Did you ever think that maybe I'll never be married? Maybe God has some big plan for me and I'm going to write the patent on something so huge, you can't even fathom it. Like the machine that cures cancer," I say, thinking back to Dr. Kevin. "Maybe my life will change the world as we know it. Maybe—"

"I just wanted you to be happy for me about the baby, Ash. This has nothing to do with you. If I thought you were such a loser, would you be my best friend for twenty-odd years? I do have some semblance of dignity to uphold."

"I just can't believe you would miss my brother's shower." *Oh my goodness, I'm inducing guilt. I have become my mother. Get thee an apron.* Brea and I are both quiet for a moment, and then we start giggling.

"Forgive me?" Brea finally says through laughter.

"You know I do. Purvi says I'm selfish too, by the way. Thank you for that. Because I really needed to ask the robot a personal question about my self-worth."

"Ash, I don't know how anyone wouldn't be selfish hanging out in that singles group. Maybe you were right about them. You need to move on."

Oooh, big truth there. Hating that. Maybe just associating with the Reasons makes me one. I don't get swooped up because I have full membership privileges in the Reasons. *Ahhhh! Definitely time to change the subject.*

"I'm getting sent back to Taiwan. The company's stock is dependent upon the outcome."

"Really? Ash, that's so cool."

"Yeah."

I hear a noise coming from my bedroom. At first, it doesn't faze me. I just assume it's a book falling off the pile to be read. All the novels sit while I brush up on memory technology and scrutinize this contested patent.

There it goes again. It sounds like a kid eating Cap'n Crunch.

"Brea," I whisper. "I think there's someone here."

"What?"

"I think someone's in my apartment," I whisper louder.

"Hang up. Call the police." I grab my cell phone, which of course is dead—and I rush out the door without shoes. I press the button on my cell hoping to get one more phone call, but it's dead, so I run down to the manager's apartment.

Mrs. Manger, rhymes with Banger, opens the door in a bathrobe with a slinky gown underneath. Since she's about eighty, it's not a sight I needed today. She's not exactly grandmotherly, but her skin is ashen from a life of cigarettes and beer. *Boy, I'm far too vain to ever smoke.*

"Do you want something, Ashley?"

"There's someone in my apartment. There's a noise coming from the bedroom."

"Did you call the police?"

"No, I just got out of there. Can I call here?" I'm shaking. This is one of the better neighborhoods in Palo Alto. Granted, my building is old, but all the apartments are. That's the only thing that makes them affordable in this city.

"Come on in. Mr. Manger ain't here or he'd come up. He's fixing a water leak at our other apartment house tonight."

I've never known the man to go anywhere without a tool on him. He could just as easily use it as a weapon. Terrific timing. I step into the apartment which has been inhabited by the Mangers since time began—or at least that's how it appears. Mrs. Manger despises me as the collection of all that's wrong with the Bay Area, and I'm interrupting her movie of the week. Shoot, I'm missing *Masterpiece Theatre* myself and have to be work by six a.m., so it's not exactly at the top of my fun list either.

I dial 911. "911 emergency. What is your emergency?"

"I think there's someone in my apartment," I whisper. Like I'm still standing in my apartment.

"You're calling from 1100 Channing Street, Apartment A?"

"Yes, but my apartment is Apartment D."

"The police are on their way. Are you alone? Do you want me to stay on the line with you?"

"No, I'm safe. Thank you." I hang up the phone. "They're sending someone out right away."

Mrs. Manger doesn't seem the least bit nervous. She sits back down in front of the television.

A commercial comes on. "Do you have a new place yet?" Mrs. Manger asks.

"No, I've been very busy—too busy to look." I shrug and give this world-weary sigh.

"You've only got two weeks, Missy." Her face is wrinkled with worry, not for me obviously. How do I explain I've been in Taiwan? That I'm going back tomorrow and that another month would mean the world to me. Big sigh. She doesn't care. She's probably as rich as Moses from owning these apartment buildings forever.

They try to hide behind some scary landlord, but I checked the title while in the city for something on a patent. They own this place and four others. Not that you'd ever know it from the orange shag carpeting they boast or the drapes brown with smoke and age. But my apartment is cute. They actually seem to care what their tenants like, just never thought about it for themselves.

Before I drum up the courage to ask for another week, a police car arrives with lights blaring but sirens silenced. I peek through Mrs. Manger's curtains and see an officer heading up to my apartment. I'm praying for his safety. Slapping myself that I left my laptop in my bedroom when it's my Life Source to the outside world.

It isn't five minutes before the officer raps on the

door. I open it, and he's laughing. He's actually trying to gain his composure before he speaks.

"That your apartment?" His broad shoulders are shaking, and he smoothes his dark mustache with his thumb and forefinger.

I nod. "It's my apartment."

He holds up a frayed phone cord.

"You have rats, ma'am." *Okay, major mortification.* Is there a way to redeem yourself in such a situation?

"Rats!" Mrs. Manger says, looking at me as though I belong in the dumpster out back.

"This building is infested. I can hear them in the wall behind your bed," the cop says, looking to Mrs. Manger with a smirk.

Hah! Take that. But, eww. For a split second I feel good it isn't my fault, then the reality that I have been Sleeping with Vermin replaces that fleeting peace.

I'm so grossed out it's not even funny. I feel like a thousand ants are crawling down my back. There's no way I can stay here for two weeks. I'm worried about how I'm going to get my things out tonight. Mrs. Manger exits the room and closes the door to her bedroom. I guess we have our answer about her ignorance there, don't we?

"Did you actually see one?" I ask the cop.

"Only the tail of one." He scrunches up his masculine face. "They're big, ma'am."

I so did not need to hear that. I'm not going to sleep tonight. Or ever. "Thank you, Officer. I'm sorry to bring you out for nothing."

He looks to Mrs. Manger's door. "It wasn't for nothing. You've got a police record now. Get your last month's rent refunded and move on." He tips his hat and walks away lit like an angel by the pool's light.

I call the only guy I know who will help me at nine on a Sunday night. The Reasons' knight in shining armor: Seth. At least I know he'll be home. It's movie night.

He answers on the second ring. "Hello."

"Seth, it's Ashley. I need your help." I feel immediately stupid, asking some guy to rescue me. All that education, all that breaking through the glass ceiling business at work, and I'm brought down by a single critter. "You know what? I shouldn't have bothered you. Never mind."

"Ashley, what is it? You've got to at least tell me or I'll worry all night."

I breathe in deeply trying to get the nerve to say this out loud. "My apartment has rats. I'm too creeped-out to sleep there, and I'm afraid to get my stuff until morning, but I need my computer and clothes for work."

He's laughing. I deserve this, but, I'll be, if it doesn't tick me off. *Knight in shining armor. Right.*

"Sam," Seth says aloud. "Ashley's got rats in her apartment." Now they're both laughing.

"I told you it was no big deal." Like I needed to be laughed at. I've already been told I'm completely selfish twice tonight, tossed onto the street without a moment's notice, and starting the most important case of my career tomorrow morning at six a.m. I wonder if the guy who wrote Murphy's Law needs a wife.

"Ashley, we only think it's funny because of how we live over here, and you're Monica on *Friends* over there by comparison. Don't you find it comical that you have rats?"

"No." That insipid lump is growing in my throat. I

hate to be laughed at. I'd rather be called selfish twice than laughed at.

Seth stops laughing almost immediately. "I'll be there in ten minutes." His voice is soothing now, but I can still hear Sam rolling in the background.

"Is Sam coming?"

"No, when I rescue beautiful women I leave him at home. I'm like Superman that way. I work alone." I can hear the smile in his voice.

Seth just called me beautiful. What's up with that?

19

I know I *said* I was afraid to enter my apartment alone. But I'm more afraid that one of the men of the Reasons might see me with day-old makeup on, so I trudge upstairs like the dutiful slave to vanity that I am. I turn every light in the apartment on, hoping to shock the rodent into whatever hole he inhabits. I shudder at the thought.

After my quick brush with beauty products, I notice I've got clothes lying on the floor—like some lovesick teenager who tried on six different outfits this morning. And, of course, the coffee-stained slacks are still hanging on the shower. I have genuinely good intentions, but the fact is I know I will never clean those slacks. They will sit there, a testimony to my laziness regarding have-tos until I guiltily throw them out.

This is just one of the reasons I belong in Silicon Valley. Most people would look at those pants, or anything they've laid money on, as a valuable stock commodity, because part of sound financial management is being frugal. But I'm not like that, and neither is the rest of Silicon Valley. Time is way more valuable to us than inconveniences of any sort. Sheesh, I'd just as soon turn in my car when it needs an oil change.

It isn't long before there's a knock on the door, and I'm wishing I did a better job tidying up in the short minutes I had—living up to Seth's vision of me as Monica on *Friends*—but at least I've gotten makeup on and have the appearance of being the poster child for Calm Behavior in a Crisis.

Seth is standing on the landing outside, and I peek through the peephole just to prepare myself. *Do not say anything stupid,* I remind myself. *It was nice of him to ask you out, but nothing more than that. You are a patent attorney. You are dating a Stanford doctor. One bald engineer will not bring you down.*

"Hi," I say, opening the door. "Thanks for coming."

Seth's intense sapphire/tanzanite eyes render me silent once I meet his gaze, and I'm trying to remember my pep talk. He hesitates about coming in the door, and I'm charmed by his initial shyness. We immediately feel the chemistry the two of us don't want to admit to. At least I feel it, so I don't see how he could miss it.

But even if Seth felt this force field, he wouldn't acknowledge it, because I'm not what he imagines for himself in that alter science-fiction world he lives in. *Hey, the dude on* The Matrix *got a hot chick, where's mine?*

You know on *The Bachelor* they take a perfectly decent guy, who makes his own living and doesn't live with his mommy . . . then, ruin him with choice. Here's my theory: All men think they are worthy of a harem; it's like this innate flaw in the male species that perpetuates with each generation, becoming stronger and stronger. So we, as a watching nation, take this unsuspecting single guy, thrust him on television, and surround him with beautiful bouncing dingbats who fight over his affection. Cattily, I might add, but isn't that the fun part?

Now, said bachelor has his dreams come true, and we, as a voyeuristic society, tell him he must choose only one. I can hear Yoda now: "One only, you must choose." He'll select one, of course—that was the whole point of his group dance with the women for six weeks—but it's too late. In his pointy little head, he is now worthy of *all* the women, and he'll never be able to stick to just one again. He'll want them all back, misunderstanding that harems in the United States are banned for good, except on reality television. Hence, the ruination of another good man.

But I digress. Seth is here, and we have nothing to say to each other. And something tells me he wouldn't appreciate my theories on television mating.

Seth finally steps in the door, managing to stay several feet away from me for fear I might attack him. And ashamedly, I admit the thought crosses my mind. For a second, I just wish we could put Arin and Fresh Choice in our history and go back to the friendship we had. We ignored the electricity then, and life was good.

"Do you have everything?" Seth asks.

"I haven't called anyone yet for a place to stay. I think I might just go to a hotel for the night because I'm probably leaving for Taiwan tomorrow."

He's looking at me. Standard conversation requires a response. Should I tell him this?

"You're welcome to my bed," he finally says.

I just stare at him, my mouth ajar like I've just been propositioned by an engineer. *Is this what it feels like?*

"I'll sleep on the couch," he adds.

I start to giggle. I cover my mouth, willing the laughter away, but it continues until I'm fanning my red face. "I'm sorry. I'm sorry, that's very nice of you."

Seth's expression clouds. "Do you find the idea of my place so abhorrent?"

I swallow hard, and all giddy laughter dies. I'm staring right into those tanzanite eyes, and I can barely speak. "On the contrary," I whisper. I can't look at him. I can't say what my heart is feeling. That I don't even remember what Dr. Kevin Whatshisface looks like. That all I remember is our history and how Seth has always been there for me. This attraction I feel is not abating.

"On the contrary?" He's standing over me now, and I'm thinking it would be so easy to kiss him. To just reach up and touch his lips with my own. I close my eyes, imagining it, but I can't do it.

I turn away so he won't learn all my secrets again. "How about the Hyatt up the street? I'll get my things."

Seth steps away, releasing me from his magnetic beam, and has his hands behind his back. He's assessing my apartment, kind of like Prince Charles dignifying an English park. "Take your time."

My shoulders drop. Seth is an anomaly. He's off-the-charts intelligent and patient to a fault, but socially he moves at a slower pace. Kind of a retarded pace.

"Do you want anything to eat?" I ask.

He scrunches his face. "No thanks. The rat thing has me a little skittish." He shudders a bit.

"Right. The rats. I personally don't have rats. The

policeman said the building is full of them. Infested actually."

"Is he an exterminator on the side?"

"No, just rodent savvy, apparently."

"Well, no thanks on the food." He rubs his stomach.

"I threw a wedding shower for my brother's fiancée today, so I never actually had a chance to eat." This is a hint. I am available for dining somewhere, even with a coupon, but there's no response. "I'm hoping the hotel will have room service." *New hint. Hello?*

"Arin called me," he blurts.

"From the rain forest?"

"She's not there yet. She's in a Costa Rican hotel. That's what I wanted to talk with you about. You never answered my e-mail."

"I was busy with the shower. What did she say?"

"She called the good doctor first. That's why she called me."

Heart is thumping a little bit here. I'm officially "the other woman." How shocking and completely unrealistic. "And?"

"He told Arin that he's seeing you. That you two went on a date."

I stop packing the suitcase and look at him. There's no reaction on his face. Is he sad about this? Mad? Dare I believe for a moment, he might be jealous?

"Are you seeing him?" he asks.

Okay, am I technically seeing the doctor? I did kiss him. Do you think that counts? I'm not sure how to take this question. Is he curious because of Arin, or me? What if he's jealous over her, and I'm the woman he wants to kiss because I've eliminated the competition?

"We went to the city on Friday when I got home from Taiwan. Do you count that as seeing him?"

He rubs his forehead. "I'm not sure. What did he say afterward?"

"He'd call me." I lift my eyebrows. *Isn't this standard guy-speak for "see ya"?*

"*Did* he call you?"

"You know, Seth? If Arin wants to date the doctor, she should call him. I'm not in high school, and I'm not going to play telephone. If you want to pass her notes for her, fine, but leave me out of it."

He shrugs. *What kind of answer is that?*

"Seth!" I wave my hand in front of those crystal eyes of his. They're glazed over with no expression whatsoever. "Do you play poker?"

"No, why?"

"Seth, what is it you're asking me?"

The thin hard line of his mouth doesn't budge. "Nothing. Like I said, I was just curious." Seth surveys all the stuff I have in my house. Too much stuff for one person. "You know, I had a coworker who now has a startup Internet business. They move all your stuff into storage for an interim. They even pack dishes."

My mood brightens. "You're kidding me?"

"No. He got the idea after the dot-com explosion when all those jobless engineers had to exodus home to Ohio and the like. You want me to call him? That way you wouldn't have to worry about moving out."

Seth *is* Superman! "I'd love it if you called him. I'm probably leaving for Taiwan on the morning plane."

"No problem. Just leave me your keys. I'm going back to work after this, so I'll take care of it."

Now I'm picturing Seth rummaging through my stuff and finding old autographed pictures of Adam Ant or my autographed *Tiger Beats*. But it's Seth. It's not going to occur to Seth to rifle through my stuff, because Seth is not me.

"Do you know what they charge?"

"I think he'd probably move all this stuff for about a thousand. I've seen him work before."

"Does he charge for storage?"

"Yeah, I think a hundred a night or so, but he'd probably cut you a deal, being my friend. You want me to get your car tomorrow?" Seth says.

"Would you? I don't want to leave it at the airport."

"No problem. Sam can help me get it." He looks at my packed suitcase. "Why don't you just call Kay for the night until you figure out what you're going to do?"

Kay Harding. Resident single anal retentive with permanent sidekick, the clipboard. But she has three bedrooms, she's not my dangerous Superman here, and she's not my mother, so technically, it's not a bad idea. I'll get my fill of hotel rooms tomorrow.

"Do you think she'd mind?"

"I don't see why she would. It's only for a night."

"I'll call her." Ringing her up, she answers like she's at work. "Hi Kay, it's Ashley. Listen, I was wondering if I might spend the night with you tonight. It seems my apartment has a slight infestation issue, and I'm leaving for Taiwan in the morning."

She agrees, albeit not readily, but at this point I'm not looking for a rousing response. I'd call Brea, but I can't help but worry I'd catch her and John on a black mesh thong night and I'd never sleep a wink worrying about it.

"She says it's fine," I whisper to Seth. "Thanks for thinking of it."

Seth still isn't sitting, and I don't know if it's me or the rats that make him more uncomfortable. I catch him glimpsing at me, but I can't tell what he's thinking about.

"You'll save money on a hotel," Seth surmises.

"Yeah, just think."

Seth picks up my suitcase. Another surprising act of chivalry! He touches my fingers gently as he takes the key while he intently stares down on me. With everything in me I want to kiss him. Not because he rescued me, or because he's going to take care of moving all this garbage, but because when I'm with Seth I feel completely trans-ported. There's a fire within him that is carefully managed, like a white-hot, days-old campfire. Not like the fireworks I see fly when I'm with Kevin. Okay, so my own pyroma-niac tendencies are coming out here, bear with me . . .

Seth takes my suitcase and moves away from me, but I catch his eye again. He feels the slow burn too, even if he's not blowing on the embers.

"So you don't want to get something to eat first?" I ask.

He looks at me, and I see him visibly swallow. "No, I should get home." I know he doesn't want to go home. I see it in his forced expression, but he will go home. If there's any chance I'll weaken his resolve, Seth will just dig his heels in further. It's over. Anything we might have shared is not something he's willing to deal with. Why can't I just get that through my thick skull?

So Seth is officially history.

I breathe an audible sigh of relief, knowing I can leave for Taiwan and Mrs. Manger won't sell my stuff to the highest bidder while I'm gone. The company car will pick me up in the morning. I'll just need to call in the request.

Once downstairs, I see Mrs. Manger peek out her curtain, but she doesn't say anything to me. Three years I've lived in this apartment house, and it's all ending at a moment's notice. But do I have time to grieve? Heavens no, Seth is about four steps ahead of me, and like a horse to the barn, he's galloping to get back home to his movie. Engineers leave no room for sentiment.

"Do you mind if I have a moment?"

He stops dead in his tracks. "A moment for what?"

"I want to say good-bye to the place. It's been good to me."

He shrugs and takes off with my bag. I'm worried just how long I have so I wave to Mrs. Manger who slices her curtain shut with a vengeance.

Seth is standing next to his beat-up Beamer with the door open. The passenger door.

"It's okay if you're dating the doctor," he says. "You should be dating the doctor. Arin doesn't want him."

"You think that's a good enough reason to date him?"

"I know you wouldn't hurt anyone, Ashley. I wanted you to know it wasn't hurting Arin if you saw her ex."

Oh, Lord, everything in me wants to ask him if it hurt him, but my mouth won't budge. Too much depends upon his answer, and I can't handle it. Will You please move him if something's supposed to happen here?

He goes on. "She doesn't want me either, by the way. You were right. She's twenty-four and wants to see the world, not an old-timer engineer."

"I never said that." I reach up for his cheek and run my hand down it. "I would never say that."

"Like I said, you wouldn't hurt a fly, Ash. You deserve the good doctor." He helps me into the seat and shuts the door.

We drive to Kay's in silence.

20

Seth is sitting right beside me in this car. We're alone. I could say a million things. I could tell him how I feel. I could tell him the good doctor and I got caught up in a momentary rush of us both being dumped by the people we cared for. Would Seth care? Or would he ask me who it was that dumped me—with those big, blue eyes of his blinking like he doesn't have a clue? The questions keep me silent, and we roll along to Kay's quiet street like two strangers in an elevator afraid to look at each other.

Kay's house is a three-bedroom bungalow just like I grew up in, but in a better neighborhood. It boasts a manicured lawn framed by flowers in January. Seth doesn't help me out, which is fine and expected by now, but disappointing just the same. I thought we had shared a "moment." But then, I'm thirty-one and single, so what do I know?

Kay is obviously expecting me. The porch light is on, as well as walkway lights along the path toward the door. I feel a bit like a plane being guided down the runway with Seth as my ground crew. And maybe a little highlighted like the loser on *American Idol* left standing there all by myself while my counterparts make the trek happily to their chosen seats.

Seth is moving on with his life, actually giving me his blessing for this other relationship. In other words, he's practically walking me down the aisle and giving me away to Kevin. OOOH, PERFECT! I can almost picture him lifting my veil and kissing me chastely on the cheek. What is it about women that we cling to familiarity? What we know, even if it stinks royally?

Kay opens the door before I reach the front step. Seth drops my suitcase like a hot potato on the porch and waves me off like a departing plane. "See ya, Ash. I'll take care of your stuff, don't worry. Larry is great. Your car key is here, right?"

Trusting a guy named Larry has me a little tense, but this is Seth, so I pass it off as my own paranoia.

"Bye, Seth. Thanks for dropping her by," Kay says.

Dropping her by? Am I a child on parental custody weekend?

The Twilight Zone continues inside Kay's house. For one thing, it smells better than my mother's house on a Sunday night, and I'm starving. Yet raiding her fridge is probably not an option. Kay's house is perfect. Not perfect as in she puts on a good show, but perfect in the letter sense of the word. Without even looking, I know that I can open a cabinet and everything will be lined up in ordered and alphabetical form.

I also seriously doubt Kay possesses a junk drawer. Don't you wonder what goes on in the mind of someone who doesn't possess at least one good junk drawer? It kind of makes me fearful of sleeping in her house, like tonight might be the night she snaps or something.

"There's leftover meatloaf and mashed potatoes. Do you want some?" Kay asks.

"Wow, meatloaf and mashed potatoes? Who did you have over?"

She shrugs. "No one. I cook for myself because I enjoy it and I delight in a good home-cooked meal."

"Are you from my planet?" I ask with a laugh.

She doesn't get it. "Seriously, Ashley. Women shouldn't wait until they get married to cook. I just think that's a shame—as though we're waiting for life to start with a man. It's so peaceful for me to cook, to throw in ingredients and get my hands dirty. You should try it." She obviously reads my doubtful expression. "Seriously."

"Oh, I'm not doubting you on the cooking aspect. For me, it's more the thought that when a man comes along I'll suddenly care about the kitchen."

"I'm forty-three. There's no man coming. And that's okay with me."

"It is?" *She may be okay with it, but it's my worst fear.* What if this is it? What if I'm forever single and delight in smooshing hamburger together with bread crumbs and topping it with ketchup? Just shoot me now and put me out of my misery.

Yet Kay possesses this Ghandi-like inner peace about life. I look around her house for clues. What on earth makes a person like her tick? There are stacks of plastic bins in an opened coat closet door. Every month is represented with a box. January is being packed away and February is out, with its plastic top lying on the pristine hardwood floor.

"Sorry about that mess, I was just getting the house decorated for the month when you called." She opens the February box and brings out tiny ceramic cupids and hearts and other Valentine memorabilia.

"Do you set something up for each and every holiday?" I ask, incredulous.

"Sure, it's festive. And every year, I add something to each collection." She smiles.

It's not my worst fear to be single. It is my worst fear that I might start collecting garage-sale fodder for fun. Or be so completely oblivious of any use for men. At the same time, I'm totally in awe of Kay. She's completely at ease with who she is. She's not a chameleon for men— and I have to appreciate that, even if I can't necessarily duplicate it.

"I like this little angel," I say, holding up a trinket. Kay quickly reaches for it, as though I will drop it and shatter the thing into a billion pieces. Judging by its light quality and badly painted lips, it was probably $3.49 at Target, but to her, it's special.

I charged my cell in Seth's car, and it's ringing so it must have worked. Though I probably have limited minutes. I pass the angel carefully back to Kay as I don't want to be indebted to her for the trip to pick up another ceramic angel with a red mustache.

"Excuse me. It might be my boss." I answer the phone, but it's not a number I recognize on caller ID. "Hello. Ashley Stockingdale."

"Ashley, it's Kevin Novak."

The good doctor. Yum. Just what I needed after a dose of Seth. Instinctively, I start twirling my short hair around my finger and my stomach is tingling. Maybe it's my desire for meatloaf, but my mouth is dry and I can hear my heart pounding. It's a cheap thrill, like asking a guy to a Sadie Hawkins dance and having him say YES like he was going to ask you.

"I'm sorry I haven't called. I've been on a twenty-four-hour shift." His voice sounds weary. "I'm just about to crash, but I wanted to let you know what a good time I had in San Francisco and to find out when we could do it again."

I'm staring at the phone like it's the biggest vegetable I've ever seen. A monster zucchini. I went out with this man two days ago. It's not Wednesday, it's not even do-or-die Thursday. It's only Sunday night. Doesn't he know standard guy phone-call etiquette and the desire to make us frantic? I haven't even had time to get nervous.

"I'm leaving for Taiwan tomorrow." This is a test. Will he care? Will it give him room to wiggle out of offered date? Will he suddenly understand that his parents were right, that I'm an idiotic workaholic from the wrong kind of genetic background?

"Again?"

"Yes," I sort of moan. "This is a big case, and it's not over. General counsel kind of stuff, so it's worth my while." *Stupid thing to say. Kind of like asking yourself to the head of the table and being asked to sit at the end.*

"Wow," he says, sounding suitably impressed which only makes me feel that much smaller.

"Yes, it's a big coup for me." I *so* don't like myself right now.

"So will you call me when you get back?" he asks. *Still he persists. He's a masochist, that's it.*

"I don't know where to reach you," I admit. Maybe that is best. There's no temptation in calling the guy if you don't know his number, but if he knows you have the number he'll be careful about juggling too many women. Am I right? Now you'd think in Christian circles one wouldn't have to worry about such things, but men are men. *Oh, Brea's right. I am tainted and sick.*

Brea. It seems like forever since I talked to her. This day has lasted far too long. Eternity comes to mind, yet now I'm talking to a doctor who is too good to be true, living with Martha Stewart-on-steroids, and trusting my life's material possessions to Seth Greenwood.

"Are you staying in the same hotel?" Kevin asks.

"Yes, probably even the same room. There's something about that cinder-block view that calls my name."

He laughs. It's a melodious, deep laugh. *He gets me at the core. But too good to be true.* I have to keep telling myself that.

"Here's my number. Call me when you get back, okay? I will take you to a proper dinner *without* my parents."

"A proper dinner?" I bet it doesn't have a coupon involved.

"Where we sit down, and I'm not on call, and I can focus on getting to know you. I know it's uncomfortable with Arin in my background, but I wanted you to know that before Arin, I broke up with a long-time girlfriend who moved to Minnesota, so I'm a little rusty on the dating scene."

I AM NOT THE TRANSITION GIRL! What are the chances? That little twig of a English Lit major was the transition girl. *I* am a Distinct Possibility. Even if his parents loathe me. Maybe especially if his parents loathe me. There's hope for Doctor Kevin yet!

"I'm a little rusty, too," I say, without the explanation that I haven't had a real date in six months.

"Good," Kevin says. "We'll relearn dating together. Call me when you get back."

I'm picturing his Hugh Jackman chin resting on that gallant hand of his, yet wondering if he's going to take me to some fancy restaurant in That Car. I'm so shallow. And I don't want to be, but it's deep inside, that little Scarlett O'Hara streak of mine. If I just didn't have any expectations, my life would be fine.

"Bye," I offer up weakly. My cell phone rings again, and I apologize to Kay with my eyes before answering. "Hello. Ashley Stockingdale."

"Ashley, it's Mom."

"Mom, what's the matter? Did everything go okay with the shower, you think?"

"Yes, of course, dear. I was just calling because you forgot to take your bridesmaid gown."

Fear and trembling. "Mom, Mei Ling and I haven't shopped for the dress yet."

"Ashley Wilkes Stockingdale, someone has to take care of things while you're halfway across the world. The wedding is just around the corner, so I found a suitable dress for you."

"Mei Ling was wearing DKNY today, Mom. Is it a DKNY dress?" I ask hopefully.

"What on earth is that? Heavens no, it isn't some trendy, fashionable thing. It's something I found at Last Lots that will be just perfect for you."

Dare I ask? "What's Last Lots?"

"It's this great store that takes clothes that didn't sell in the fancy stores and marks them way down."

"Uh, do you think Dave will want a markdown in his wedding?"

"Dave's a very practical boy, Ashley. He's not like you, where he thinks fancy things should cost a lot. Sometimes I wonder that I didn't name you Scarlett. Dave knows a good bargain. Look at all the stuff he brings home from the lost and found off his bus at the end of the year."

"Maybe you should have named him Ashley, Mom."

"I never liked that name on a man."

"What color is the dress, Mom?"

"Purple, of course. It's Dave's favorite."

As if I didn't know. My eyes slide shut. I will look like a slippery satin eggplant on Valentine's Day. Is there any question it's satin? Of course not. I so do not plan my own destiny. Kay is looking at me, between careful unpacking of the plastic and ceramic hearts. I know what she's thinking. I'm an ungrateful daughter, rude to my own mother, the epitome of selfishness.

I'm hanging up and eating an entire meatloaf, because big and purple is beautiful. Barney the dinosaur found success. Maybe I will, too.

21

Have you ever seen Ashley look more beautiful?"

"She's stunning," Aunt Babe replies. "Who would have ever thought purple was her color?"

"She could wear anything, though, such a beautiful girl."

"So true. So true."

"Look at her date. Do you recognize him?" Aunt Trudy asks. "It's Ryan Seacrest from American Idol."

"I saw him on last week's show. What a doll. Isn't it cute how their hairstyles match?"

"A flat iron and hairspray. That's what he always says on the show."

The two older women cackle and watch as Ashley tips her head back elegantly and Ryan plants a kiss on her neck.

"Oh!" The two women sigh. "To be young again."

"To ever have been Ashley. Brilliant, darling, and to look good in that hideous dress her mother selected. She should be royalty, I tell you."

"She is royalty in our family. She's a miracle of the gene pool."

"It's such a pity it didn't work out for her and that cute engineer."

"She has far too much personality for him anyway. He would just stand like a bump on a log, while this Ryan Seacrest . . . what a guy. He's lucky to have her."

"To be sure, sister. To be sure."

"Ashley!"

I shake my head out of my reverie and look up at Kay Harding's hard scowl. All of Kay's heart-shaped collectibles are now lying in an ordered row on the shelf next to her television set. "You can put your bag in the guest room. Your dinner is warmed on the table."

I'm afraid to move. Do I let the dinner get cold? Or do I leave my suitcase looking ominously large in this IKEA-clean living room. I wait a few seconds, hoping for direction. Nothing.

"I'll eat first, and then put my suitcase away," I announce. "That way I can get the kitchen cleaned up."

It's eleven p.m. and the end to an outrageously long day. I eat like a logger after a day in the woods and then crash in Kay's perfectly-appointed guest bedroom atop the featherbed and underneath the down comforter. The pillows are fresh and fluffy and the wallpaper floral and girlish. It's something straight out of *Better Homes & Gardens*, but without the true homey feel. Kay assumes she possesses excellent hospitality skills, but in truth, staying here is like touching that worthless ceramic angel. Overrated and uncomfortable. Still, I'm grateful I have a place to stay, and I fall into sleep without much thought, not even of dancing with Ryan Seacrest or his soft kiss on my neck.

I'm at work at six a.m. after waking up frantic and calling the company's limo service at three a.m. on my cell phone. Purvi is already at the office and looks like she has been there all night. Her desk is under a pile of legal files and middle-of-the-night pizza trash. Her deep brown eyes are haggard, and she looks up at me like a film star about to slip over the edge of a cliff but too worn to fight.

"What's going on?" I try not to sound chipper. Upbeat would be entirely annoying if I'd worked all night.

"Do you have your bags packed?"

"I do."

"Unpack them. They want the products released from customs. Your first deal held."

"What?" Fantasies of my spectacular legal defense pop. I'm a grunt. A grunt who makes $150,000 a year with stock options, but a grunt nonetheless. Doesn't that sound good? $150,000 a year. But the average town home here is $600,000 and that *huge* salary barely covers my Palo Alto rent and lease payment on the Audi, with a small if-I-get-laid-off stipend. No wonder I live in a dream world; it's so much nicer than my reality.

"They're going with the original deal you worked out on your last trip. Good job on that, by the way. I guess they were just trying to see if we'd come down on the royalties. I hadn't set up an appointment for you, so they assumed we weren't negotiating and released the products over the weekend." Purvi is downright giddy, even through the veil of fatigue.

The phone in my office is ringing. Who is calling me at six a.m.? I run to find out, praying along the way that no one is dead. "Ashley Stockingdale."

"Ash, it's Dave. What did you do?"

"What do you mean?"

"Mei Ling woke me up an hour ago, crying. You

and Mom picked out some awful purple dress for the wedding."

"Dave, I didn't pick out anything for the wedding. I set a time up with Mei Ling to go this week, but Mom called me last night and said it was taken care of."

"Well, it's not taken care of."

"Dave," I say slowly. "Have you ever seen me wear purple in my lifetime? Why would I do that to my sister-in-law?"

"You planned that hideous shower yesterday. Purple and gold, Ash?"

"That was your mother's doing," I said. I'm taking no responsibility for my own lineage. Not even my brother can pin this on me. "I haven't worn it since my last high school pep rally."

"It's very painful for Mei Ling not having a mother and father here, or traditional Chinese things at the wedding. You know, they're big into all that ritual stuff."

"Mei Ling's a Christian now," I say.

"She's still a woman with a dream and a history. I gotta assume you're thinking of the white traditional thing for yourself."

"Dave, I think Mei Ling is the sweetest thing since pecan pie. I wouldn't do a thing to harm her or your wedding, so tell me what you want."

"I want you to find out what makes a Chinese wedding and do it. I know I haven't been the best brother, but I want Mei Ling to feel welcomed and know that we'd do anything to make this her perfect day."

A traditional Chinese wedding in Vegas? How exactly does that work? I'm a lawyer, not an event planner. Other than my subscription to *InStyle,* I know nothing on the matter of wedding planning.

"Dave, I'll do what I can."

"Ashley!" Purvi is yelling. Never a good sign.

"I have to run. Don't worry, we'll make Mei Ling's day special. I promise." I hang up.

Purvi is yelling louder.

"Yes?"

"I need you to go pick up my son from my mother-in-law's. She can't drive, and he has to get to school before eight. You can leave him as early as seven at before-school care."

Why does any of this concern me? "I don't have a car, Purvi. I put it all in storage until I returned from Taiwan. Remember, my apartment is going away?"

She looks at me with furrowed brows. I do confuse her with my petty issues. I should just move in here and be done with it—low rent and a boss that could have me at her disposal anytime she wanted. On second thought, no.

"How did you get here?" she asks.

"The company limo picked me up."

She closes her eyes and shakes her head. "Very well, take my car. The company car won't get back here fast enough." She hands over the keys with trepidation. She drives an Accord! It's not like I'm getting the keys to a Porsche! I would think she'd be more cautious about handing over the kid. Cars, I can handle. Kids? That's another story.

"What about all these briefs?" I say, looking at the pile she's left me.

"They don't matter. You'll get to them when you get to them. You were planning on being out all this week, right?"

What happened to my non-stressing boss? Has she been swallowed by the Silicon Valley drone who must work twenty-four/seven? I went for the J.D. after my name to be a kid's chauffeur? Explain this to me. I stand up tall.

"Purvi, I don't really think picking up your son—"

She stares me down, and I clamp my mouth shut. I'm beginning to see why her husband lives a world away. "Never mind," I say like the true wimp I am. "Give me the directions."

She hands them over on a Yahoo! map, and I crumple the paper in my pocket like I'm suddenly so defiant. *Yeah, right.* I find her dumpy little Accord in the parking lot and start it up without a problem. *Of all the days to leave my car behind.*

Her mother-in-law's place is on mansion row in Los Altos. I know Purvi can't afford this place as well as her own on her salary, so I'm wondering how the family made their fortune. And is it legal?

The house has a grand brick facade. I say *facade* because real brick is not allowed here along the San Andreas Fault line. At the sight of the house, it's just now occurred to me that I'm here to pick up a living, breathing child. I shiver.

I knock softly on the door, and in less than ten seconds the child is presented with his grandmother's hands upon his shoulder. He's dark-haired, dark-eyed, and looking at me with the same scowl his mother possesses, as though I have stolen the woman from his life.

"Are you ready to go?" I clap my hands, like he's three and about to take a photo with Santa.

"Where's my mom?" he deadpans.

"She's at work, and she said to tell you how much she missed you."

"My mom didn't say that." He crosses little spindly arms across his chest. "She's working on new patents which are critical to the success of Selectech. It's imperative that she be allowed to pursue her work. Family would, of course, become secondary at this time when her presence at her company is so vital."

"How old are you?" I ask.

"Nine," he answers.

Okay, this is why the men here are such geeks and I will be forever single. Men are taught at an early age that talking like a dictionary and behaving without common courtesy is a positive personality trait. Remind me to put that in my Man Book next to the chapter on nixing beer commercial lines.

"Do you have your stuff?" I ask without emotion.

"Yes."

"Get in the car then." I smile at the mother-in-law, who by her bows I can only assume does not speak English.

I take out my Yahoo! map and drive toward the school, careful to not start any conversations with Boy Wonder. I want to tell him about Jesus, but judging by the ancestor temple I know Purvi possesses and this kid's vocabulary, I dare not. He'd probably be ready to debate the differences between religions, and it's too early to go there. Besides, Purvi would have my head when she heard. My unspoken directions are pretty clear—pick up child; do not speak; hightail it back to work.

We arrive at a private school for the gifted and without a word the Boy hops out, slamming the door behind him. A teacher comes out the door and waves me away, but I just sit there in the parking lot.

"I've got to get out of the Valley." It's like Stepford here—and one day I won't even notice I'm different. My arms will just stay straight at my sides while I pursue such harrowing choices as an IMAX movie at the Tech Museum or shooting my way through a rousing night at Laserquest.

I slam my head on the steering wheel. And then look up to the sky. "What do You want from me, God? What?"

22

I t's 7:03 a.m. I'm stopping for a coffee. Not my typical skinny latte where I imagine I'm a size two and should drink accordingly, but a realistic double-iced mocha with whipped cream where I'm at peace with my size and my grunt job . . . where I acknowledge that the average Silicon Valley nine-year-old has a higher IQ than myself, that I would be more attractive to engineers if I had buttons like a game controller. *That* kind of coffee.

Stanford Roasting Company is still empty. A testimony to the fact that I'm up entirely too early. You'd think this was a regular party town with all the people who start work at 9:30 a.m., but the fact is that with China and Taiwan so tightly interwoven, work often goes late into the evening, and the office is a ghost town in the morning.

"Tall non-fat latte?" the regular barrista, Nick, asks as I saunter up to the counter. "No," I slap my hand on the counter. "Make it a double-iced mocha with whip," I say, like I'm ordering a scotch whiskey in a western.

Nick lifts an eyebrow, but fills a cup with ice and hastens on to the next customer. He's afraid I might pour out my guts. Tell him why I must have sugar—and lots of it. I cross my arms and wait in the corner for my drink to be called. Looking around the place, I see Kevin slumped over a book with a straight espresso cup set before him. The cup is empty. At least I think it's Kevin.

"Kevin?"

He looks up, his eyes red and his brown hair in disarray. Still, he's gorgeous. So unfair. Of course, I'm thinking about my makeup being fresh and am overly excited about this fact.

"Ashley, what are you doing here? I thought you were leaving for Taiwan."

I shrug. "The trip was canceled. I've got a million drawings to go over today anyway, so I suppose it's just as well."

"Drawings?"

"To see if our patent ideas conflict with anything already out there. There's a national database I have to scan. It takes forever. Tedious work." I sound more exciting by the moment.

Nick calls my double-iced mocha with whip, and I stand here looking at it. Do I reach for it and admit to Kevin that I have hips for a reason? Or let it sit on the counter? He's a doctor, after all, and clearly a purist judging by the empty espresso cup. I wonder if he'll learn liposuction as part of his training. That might be a good quality in a future husband.

"Ashley." Nick stares at me. "Your mocha's up."

"Yeah." I smile and nod, but I roll my eyes before taking it. "Oh, you added whip," I say innocently. Nick merely shakes his head.

Kevin stares at the frothy, fattening concoction, but says nothing. He must have sisters. "I'm glad you're staying home. I have a night off tomorrow. Are you up for that proper dinner I promised you?"

I can feel my face flaming. This is the man I kissed in San Francisco, the most romantic city on earth. So why do I feel like I'm talking to my high-school English teacher? What's his motivation here? He's one of those out-of-reach sort of guys that make you want to suck in your tummy full-time. Could I live with that kind of pressure? Not to mention his folks. Could I live with them?

"Right. A proper dinner." I sit down at his table behind my mammoth chocolate explosion. "What is that exactly? A proper dinner?"

He laughs and winks at me. It's a single move that clearly wasn't practiced. It's just natural. He owns way too much charm. "A proper dinner is at a restaurant with a maitre d' and sans my parents."

"Do they have those restaurants here in Silicon Valley?" I wink back at him, but my mascara catches the lashes and I don't open my eye right away. Great. Now he thinks I have a tic. So much for the perfect makeup scenario.

"They have excellent restaurants here. Nearly as good as San Francisco itself. I'm surprised you don't eat at them more often with your position."

My position. Right. I'm a lawyer. Sounds so impressive until you find out I'm going to be poring over documents on the computer today, and I've just dropped my boss's son off at before-school care.

"My boss does most of the schmoozing. She's a natural."

"So what do you say to dinner?"

I smile. He actually asked twice, and I do have Seth's blessing. Arin's too, though neither bring me any peace. "Dinner sounds wonderful. It's been so long since I've been anywhere but Chili's or the like, I hope I know which fork to use."

"I never *did* know which fork to use, so you'll be ahead of me." He grins. Have I mentioned his perfectly-squared jaw? Because it's movie-star perfect, and I find myself staring at it each and every time I see Kevin.

"I should get back to work. My boss will be waiting. She's in a bit of a mood today." I stand up, and I watch his eyes float over my figure, then a sly smile come over his face. *Scandalous!* But, um, kinda hot too, and I feel one hundred feet tall.

"You look incredible in that suit. That's not sexist to say that, is it?" he asks. "I never know these days what's okay."

"It's never sexist to tell a woman she looks good. Trust me on that one."

"So tomorrow night?" He sits back in his chair and crosses his arms over his chest, which is far too brawny for someone brainy.

"I feel like I should say something in French."

"You might have more luck if you spoke Chinese or Spanish to me. My French is non-existent."

I grab my purse, which has snaked itself around the chair. One good tug from me sends it crashing to the floor. All heads turn to stare like I'm an unruly toddler in their last bastion of peace. *I feel like I should say something in French? Sheesh, I feel like I should put a bag over my head while someone puts me out of my misery.*

Grinning, Kevin rights the chair, and my eyes are glued to the muscles in his forearm.

"Bye," I say quietly and scamper before he has time to change his mind about the dinner.

My coffee is strong. And with the heady chocolate flavor, I just take a long drawn sniff when I get out the door: today's smelling salts.

There's a message on my cell when I get to the car, and I listen to voice mail, which has Purvi yelling that she wants to leave for some sleep and *where is her car?* Like I wanted to drive this heap all morning to cart Boy Wonder around.

I didn't take time to pray today, and I feel it. It's not something I can do without, so why do I try? A dead-stop on Highway 101 and only Purvi's sad radio system to entertain me. I'm just wishing for my six-CD changer.

While sitting in traffic, I dial up Brea. She's not a morning person, but she's also never really grumpy either, so I take my chances. She answers on the first ring.

"Hi, Ash. Seth called me and told me you were all right last night. Thanks for calling back!"

"I'm sorry. I wasn't thinking last night. I spent the night at Kay's. What's going on with you?"

"John just went to work. We didn't sleep a wink last night worrying about the adoption."

"When is she due again?"

"Two months, we think. Originally, we thought three, but she hasn't had an ultrasound yet, so we're trying to get her covered under our insurance. John is taking care of all that today. Hopefully, it will go without a hitch, but you know these companies."

"Brea, are you sure about this?"

She clicks her tongue. I know she's mad, but is she being realistic? Two months is hardly enough time to get used to the idea of having a child, is it? I know she thinks I'm the selfish single, but a baby! A baby is big work, and eighteen or more years of it. I just don't want her jumping into anything because of her miscarriage. She's not in the right frame of mind.

"You sound just like John."

Ah, so John is not so sure either. "Brea, I think that adoption is one of the greatest things in the world. I just want you to be sure it's right for you. You have a way of reacting when someone else is in trouble. Remember that God is big enough to handle this without you if that's His will."

"Ash, you couldn't commit to a cable company for a long-term relationship, and you're going to tell me how to run my life?"

"Look, I didn't call to fight. I'm just trying to tell you to go into this with open eyes."

Brea goes on, "I just feel like I committed to this young girl and now I'm not so sure. Because John isn't so sure, but now that this girl is willing to give us her baby—"

"There are a million Christian couples who would love to adopt this baby, Brea. Does it have to be you?" I don't like how I sound, but isn't it better to present her with the truth? She's lived such a charmed life, and I'm worried this could bring her down. That she's not as ready for this as she thinks.

"Why did God present her if it wasn't meant to be me?"

"I don't know. Let's just keep praying about it. If this

is meant to be your baby, Brea, nothing can stop it. Not us, not the insurance companies, nobody."

She sniffles. "I really want this baby, Brea. I want John to want it, too."

I smile. "John would do anything to make you happy, Brea. He had to know what he was getting into when he married you. He's lucky he doesn't have twenty-seven foster children by now."

She laughs. "That sounds like something he'd say. You'll support me?"

"If this is what you want, I'll support you to the grave." And I will. But I'll pray a lot in the meantime.

"What's going on with you?" Brea asks.

"I've got a date tomorrow with Kevin Novak."

"The doctor again?"

"Yes, we're going to a nice dinner and all my clothes are in storage. But of course, I'd rather shop anyway."

"What do you mean your clothes are in storage?"

"Oh, I never called you back last night. I have rats in the apartment building. I had to get out."

"That's right. I completely blanked that out when we got off the phone. Meant to call you back, but we were pretty deep in discussion here last night, and Seth called and said you were safe."

"It's a big decision."

"Do you want to go shopping tonight?" She doesn't sound excited at the prospect, which makes me less so.

"Nah, it's okay. It sounds like you and John need some more time."

"I'm sorry, Ashley. I know I haven't been a good friend lately."

"I'll talk to you later." I'm crying when I snap my cell phone shut. Friends are probably the hardest commodity to earn in Silicon Valley. People move, people work, people have busy lives that don't include close friendships. But I could always count on Brea. Until she got married. Then I became just another island floating in the middle of the San Francisco Bay.

23

The three women sit against the floral wallpaper staring as if at their first ballet. Open-mouthed and gaping, their expressions show their admiration and awe. Ashley Stockingdale twirls about on the arm of Dr. Kevin Novak, her floor-length Donna Karan halter dress clinging easily to her shapely figure. Her dark auburn hair, once again grown out, is swept into the perfect up-do and framing her face, her gentle alabaster skin contrasts with the bright red lipstick she wears. Watching the attractive couple dance is like hearing that song from The Lion King. Can you feel the love tonight?

"It's almost like she's floating on air," Kay says with a sigh.

"You can't see her shoes in that gown, but I bet they're Blahniks," Arin adds.

"Is there any question?" Brea asks with disdain.

"Brea, you've known Ashley for twenty years now. What makes her so different?" Kay asks.

"Ashley always possessed something special. Something that made you want to have just a tiny piece of her with you. Some might call it charisma or charm, but I think it's an aura. Ashley has a definite aura about her."

"Like a halo?" Arin asks, with her eyes wide.

"Sort of, yeah. Like a halo." Brea nods.

"Ashley, that's not a tiara. It's a traditional Hindu amulet. Do you mind taking it off your head?"

I snap to attention, like a poor soldier awakened by a bugle. "I'm sorry, Purvi, I was just—" What was I just? Daydreaming with some false idol on my head. How do I explain this one? Sometimes I really must worry about the witness I am for Christianity. I think I'm more of a witness for neuroses.

"Ashley." Purvi is practically wilting over the car door. "I haven't slept all night." She waits for me to get out.

"I'm so sorry, Purvi. I know you worked hard. I hope you get a good day's rest. Your son is happily ensconced at school. I can pick him up if you need me to."

"Thank you, but I'll get him. I'm sorry about this morning, but my mother-in-law has a cataract and hasn't been driving. And my neighbor's out of town."

"No trouble, Purvi." Now I feel badly for whining. She worked the whole night rather than pull me into it. Normally, a boss would allow employees to work all night and go home to watch *Fear Factor* or the like. But not Purvi. She's one in a million. I grab my empty cup from her car and bid her good-bye.

My first move of the day is going to be to locate my car. I feel naked without my car. *May I never have to drive a sedan again in this lifetime.*

I dial up Seth's number, still miffed at how easily he handed me off to the "good doctor." Apparently, I meant less than nothing to him, and I punch the last number hard.

"Ashley, what are you doing? My caller ID says you're at work. You taking a later flight?"

"I'm not going to Taiwan. This week anyway. Purvi is battling the Evil Empire, and that's taking precedence for now."

"Sorry to hear that." And he is. Everyone in Silicon Valley is sad to hear when the Evil Empire gets stronger. It hurts everyone, especially the consumer who gets a weaker product, but obviously I have strong opinions here.

"Is my car still at my apartment?" My voice is tentative, but it's like asking *where's my child?* I miss my little convertible, even if I never take the top off or act sporty in it. I long for its supple leather seats . . . and the chance to take off for places unknown in it, even if I never do.

Seth laughs. "You know, it's funny you should ask. I thought about that at the last minute . . . that you'd want your car as soon as you stepped off the plane, so I jogged over and brought it back. It's parked in my garage."

Visions. I'm envisioning my car parked snugly in his garage next to his own car. He took care of me, thought ahead about taking care of me, and I read so much into this action. Which only makes me that much more pathetic on the scale of things. Seth always thinks of others; I could be any one of his friends.

"Seth, what would I ever do without you? If I have the company car drive me over, will you be there?"

"Don't bother. I'll drive it down when I go to work— which should be in a few minutes. I can get a coworker to drive me home. Or take the bus."

"You don't want to do that. My brother could be

driving that bus, and he's upset today. He called me at six a.m. to tell me so."

"I'll see you in a bit."

"I could drive you home myself," I offer.

"Ashley."

"Seth, really. You just don't understand how much it means to me that you took care of my apartment and my car—and getting me to Kay's house—I was just feeling so overwhelmed." I'm getting misty-eyed now. The last thing I want is to be indebted to Seth any more than I am already.

"That's fine, Ashley. Whatever you want to do. I'm looking forward to driving little Racy again."

"Seth." I cross my arms. "This is my baby we're talking about."

"A baby that does zero to sixty in five seconds flat." I can hear him laughing under his breath. *Troublemaker.* "Racy and I will be there by ten. Oh, and I have all your paperwork for your apartment. Larry is going to clear it out tonight. Do you need anything out before?"

Of course I do. I need all my clothes, but my suitcase will do, and I'm shopping for my date, so . . . "No, I don't need anything."

"You just call him when you find a new place, and *voila!* He appears with your stuff."

I'm trying to force down my fears that a guy named Larry will be emptying my apartment. "Great," I say half-heartedly.

Before I start on my own desk, I mosey into Purvi's office to see where I can help. There are briefs and documents strewn everywhere. I start by putting all the papers into the right legal folders and filing away. I could let Dianna, the secretary, do this, but I know where things go, and it will be easier for Purvi when she comes back. I don't dismiss that I'm not in Taiwan eating half-alive crustaceans. I owe this to Purvi, and I want her to know how I appreciate it. I'd much rather be drinking double-iced mochas for breakfast instead.

Man-hungry Dianna avoids me like the plague. We are the polar opposites of women. It's not that I think I'm above her; I just legitimately have nothing to say to her. Whenever I try to talk, we have no similar point of reference. Yes, we're both women, but the similarities end there. Dianna sees me watching her and cuts off her conversation with the mail guy, Jim Bailey.

"Did you need something?" Dianna asks.

"Does Purvi have the paperwork from Taiwan? I want to check something."

"I think so. Let me go look." She topples out on her heels.

I'm drumming my desk with my fingers, unable to concentrate on all the work set before me. I have an idea, and my mind won't let it go until I've seen it to its full conclusion. I grab up some files and head to my own office.

Dianna comes behind me with the paperwork. "Do you want anything else? You look pretty intense."

"Can you shut my door?" I look up at her. "And can you get me the Evil Empire case?"

Her eyes widen. "Sure." She returns, drops the briefs on my desk, and rushes out to see Manny from the sales department. I don't look up for another hour at least. Dianna is now talking to Jeff from marketing, but their conversation comes to an abrupt halt when Seth steps into the picture.

Dianna pulls away from her desk and drops the notepad she was holding. Slowly, she rises up to give Seth an eyeful. He looks away, and I want to cheer. Looking toward the window, I hear him say he's looking for Ashley.

Dianna rolls her eyes. She gambled on Seth and lost Jeff's attention in the process. Bad bet. Now she's got no one to flirt with.

"She's in there." Dianna tosses her hand and doesn't bother to escort Seth or actually do her job and announce him. The whole process inflames me. Is there an office anywhere that is not at the mercy of an administrative assistant's constant need for attention? Because if there is, sign me up to work there.

"Hi." Seth leans against the doorjamb, and my stomach twists at the sight of him. Dr. Kevin Novak is so incredible looking, and Seth is bald and dresses like an engineer. Did I miss some survival-of-the-fittest gene or something?

"Hi." I just stand there gaping like he's about to perform. It's intimate, having him in my office.

"Your baby's back."

"Uh huh." *He is.*

"I left it in the lot by your window."

"Right." I shake my head out of its fog. "Sorry, too much sugar this morning." I look out Purvi's window. There's my gray convertible, shiny and sparkling in the morning sunlight. "It looks cleaner than I left it."

"I washed it this morning. It was such a perfect day, and I find it's therapeutic."

"What can I do to make up for all you've done for me?"

"Why can't you just accept it, Ash? I'm your friend. I don't want anything more than that."

His words stab my heart. No, he doesn't want any more than that, and that's the Great Problem, isn't it? Those haunting words no one ever wants to hear. *I think we're better as friends.* But I'm supposed to be excited about this perfect doctor I'm seeing. What is wrong with me?

Seth doesn't think of me *that way.* He never will. And it's time for my heart to move on. Staring at those gemstone eyes of his, their warmth and depth of caring within, I have to wonder if I will ever truly move on. Somewhere along the line, I gave my heart to Seth. Even though he never did anything more than push it back toward me.

"Have you got my keys?" I ask. He hands them over, and I admit that just for a moment, I'm tempted to kiss him. Right here in my office. A good-bye kiss, if you will. Before I know it, my lips are touching his cheek. "Thank you, Seth," I whisper into his ear.

His eyes are round, and he's blinking excessively. Dianna is staring at me, like *I'm* the loose one, and I can see Mailman Bailey's mind churning as though maybe I am finally doing the wild thang. I feel great that I've surprised everyone; I stand taller. Maybe now they'll take notice and wonder what kind of heart beats inside this prim and proper young lawyer. Perhaps I have secrets.

I pull away and smooth my suit. "Let's get you to work."

"It's all right." Seth puts up a palm. "I'm right up the street. I can sprint."

Oddly enough I'm okay with the fact that I've scared

the man to death. I made my move. I know it's officially over now, and maybe I can move on. Maybe the reason I've been stuck in this rut so long is that I believed something would happen between Seth and me. Deep in the recesses of my heart, I never let go of that dream. And today, I did. Progress! Watching him walk away is a bit like watching a rat's tail in my apartment. He's more afraid of me than I am of him.

24

I found the cutest dress at Ann Taylor at lunch. It's '50s-looking, very retro, and black with a fitted waist and Wilma Flintstone skirt. When I slip on my sunglasses with it, I feel I'm Audrey Hepburn reborn—albeit a little wider. But alas, my date is at night, so I'll have no use for my rockin' sunglasses, and since Kevin is driving, I don't even have to plan on getting out of my car with casual grace. I still need work in this poise arena, though, as seen by my coffee house incident this morning.

I even bought myself a new lipstick: a testimony to the fact that I have left Seth in my past where he belongs and Kevin is worthy of a new color. I'm having Kevin pick me up at work, since I have no idea where I'm living tonight and that makes me sound frightfully flaky. I tried to call Kay and extend my invitation in her Sears' bedroom display, but she isn't home or in her office, so I'm taking that as a sign—kind of like when you see a skull and crossbones at the door.

Brea said I was welcome, and most likely that's where I'll end up because we'll want to gossip about the date anyway. Alas, John will become annoyed with our incessant giggling and go up to bed early. I am going to find a place tomorrow if it kills me. I know some might say I have a priority issue, what with the dress coming before the apartment search, but it's food, clothing, and shelter—in that order. Correct me if I'm wrong, but shelter comes last. I think my basic instincts are right on track.

Brea flaked on me with regard to shopping again, and I had only the cursed three-way mirror to answer the eternal question: Does my bum look big in this dress? When at the store, I just happened to remember that I still have a few items at the dry cleaners, so in addition to my single suitcase for Taiwan, I have another three outfits before life becomes critical.

It's seven o'clock in the evening, and I'm beginning to pace inside my office. To my chagrin, tonight is Dianna's late night. Since I've never really seen her work during the day, I'm curious what she does on late night, but it's probably just a reason for her to come in at ten in the morning.

"You don't have to hang around, you know. I can handle things here," Dianna says.

Looking around at all the tired husbands working late, I'm sure she can handle things here, but isn't that the reason not to let her? "Why don't you just go home, Dianna?"

"Because I'm here to answer the phone—in case Taiwan calls."

Ah, so she does have a purpose. "I'm waiting for my date." I square my shoulders, showing off my gorgeous new black dress.

"With that guy you cornered in the office today? He

looked scared out of his wits!" She snickers, and I just feel my fist instinctively clench. Catfight! I breathe in a deep cleansing breath. I am a Christian. I turn the other cheek. "No, actually it's with a surgeon I've met at Stanford." *Meow!*

"Go easy on the poor boy, will ya?"

With everything in my being, I want to tell her she's the last person I'd take advice on men from, but I just smile. It's enough that I make three times what she does and have the vocabulary to date a doctor. If only it was easier to fire secretaries here, I lament. Sadly, Dianna could get me fired faster . . .

I get this little prick of guilt, and God speaks to me about Dianna's life and how hard everything is. Yes, she makes life that way, but don't we all in a way? He'd want me to look for some good in her, beneath the cheesy outfit and heavy makeup and desperate attempts to make herself feel desirable.

"Maybe you're right. I should go easy," I say with a smile. A real smile this time, not my fake catty one.

Security buzzes my office to tell me a Doctor Kevin Novak is here for me. I'm nervous, but not as nervous as I was when Seth came sauntering in unannounced this morning. I have to remind myself there's no history with Kevin. If there's going to be, it will have to be created.

Checking my reflection in my compact, I smile to make sure there's no lipstick on my teeth and head for the front door. "Good night, Dianna. I hope you don't have to stay too late."

She winks at me. "Don't do anything I wouldn't do."

I'm doubting the possibility. But I like this new feeling

of peace between us. Dianna is not someone you want to be enemies with in this lifetime. Admins have way too much power. "See you in the morning, Dianna."

Kevin is waiting at the door with his hands clasped. He looks like the guys on *The Bachelorette* waiting for a rose. My heart gives a little flip. He's just too good-looking for words. But he's the kind of good-looking where you wonder are people thinking, *What's he doing with her?* He's in a suit. Not a shirt with a tie, but an actual navy, double-breasted, be-still-my-heart suit.

"Ashley, you look beautiful. Is that a new dress?"

I give a little twirl and nod. "Thank you. So do you. Gorgeous, I mean. Not beautiful."

He opens the glass door for me and waiting beside the curb is a black Porsche Boxter. He opens the door to the sports car and picks up a bouquet of pink roses and holds them out toward me. I look around. Isn't this the end of *Flashdance*? I break into song about what I'm feeling, but Kevin doesn't get it, so I snap my mouth shut and focus on the car.

"Thank you," I say, flirtatiously taking the flowers from him. "What's going on? Where's your real car?"

He starts laughing. "This is my real car. I always wanted a Porsche. Call me shallow, but I bought it when I started my residency, even though I could barely afford my apartment. Credit is a good thing."

"No, where's the car with the rope on the trunk?"

Now he's really laughing. "That's not my car."

"You know, I snagged a perfectly good pair of slacks in that car. Do you care to tell me about the Porsche? Explain yourself, perhaps?"

"A bunch of us interns own that car and pay the registration on it. We have a pact to use it for all first dates. Are you going to get in? My arm is getting tired."

"You let me drive around in the city in that heap for nothing?"

He presses a palm to his chest. "You're calling my other car a heap? I'm crushed."

"You know, that car doesn't say about you what you want it to. It doesn't say, *I'm poverty-stricken, will you love me anyway?* It says, *I have no self-respect and I spend my money poorly.* It makes a woman worry she's going to be supporting you."

"Is that right?" He steps closer to me and puts his arms around me while handing off the flowers. His charming sideways smile appears. "And would you support me, Ashley Stockingdale?"

I pull away. "Not on your life. Are we going to dinner or what?"

He steps back and helps me into the car. "Dinner, a proper dinner."

"We're not going to the hospital cafeteria, are we? Because if there are any more tests, count me out. The bar was the last thing I studied for." I try to find a place to put the huge bouquet, but Porsche Boxters aren't made for storage.

He slips into the driver's seat and revs up the powerful engine. It's funny. I love cars, but I have anxiety over a man who loves cars. In my mind, warped as it is, a woman who likes cars is confident, cool, bold. But a guy? A sports car tells me he's insecure, out to prove something. Besides, the Boxter is a girl Porsche: the cute, affordable Porsche.

A guy should drive a Carrera. But I shake the thought. This is my new life. Men behave differently in my fresh blossoming world. He's not an engineer. He won't drive this car until it dies a sad, fiery death on I-280.

"No more tests, I promise." Kevin puts the car into first gear, and we're off. "You shouldn't be nervous. You passed with flying colors."

"You don't really know that. With all my computer expertise on patents, I could have looked up the registration on the car and known it was a test. I might have checked your bank account or had a private eye follow you. You'll never really know if I passed. You're still a Stanford doctor."

"You're a difficult one, you know that?"

I smile at the description. "Of course I know that. It's part of my charm."

We speed along the back streets until we're in the middle of wealthy downtown Palo Alto. Although it's a weeknight, the restaurants are packed with patrons who have more money than cooking expertise. We pull up in front of a tiny exclusive type of restaurant, and Kevin pays the valet to take his Porsche.

The weather is chilly, and I wrap my new Angora shawl around my shoulders a bit tighter. Kevin sees me shiver, puts his arm around me, and hustles me into L'aime Donia, a little French bistro that appears to be all the rage.

Sage green and warm yellow walls complete with hand-painted landscapes provide a calming atmosphere. But I don't feel comfortable here. It's not that I can't hold my own in a nice restaurant, but it all seems so wasteful to me. As we're seated, the wine list is extensive and expensive. *New life. New life,* I remind myself.

"What kind of wine do you prefer?" Kevin asks.

"None, actually. I don't drink very often."

"Good for you. They have this merlot here that is absolutely fantastic, but it doesn't come by the glass."

I fluff my linen napkin on my lap. "I still won't drink any," I say apologetically. "If my mother and brother aren't here, I find very little use for alcohol."

He laughs, his warm eyes creasing. "See, you just passed my second test: peer pressure. Remember, I told you I didn't usually drink because of always being on call."

I bristle at this. Am I actually being tested? I shake the uneasy feeling.

He orders a mineral water. And myself? A very classy Diet Coke. Once again, with a lemon twist of course; I'm not a total hick. I chance a direct question. "Is everything a test for you, Kevin?"

"I am in my residency. It just feels that way, I guess."

"So what do you do now that you can't make models of ships?"

Kevin pauses, thinking deeply about my question. After a long silence, he speaks. "Nothing. I don't really do much of anything except work, sleep, eat, and visit with my parents when they come out."

Staring at Kevin is suddenly like staring into a mirror. We're two shallow people who drive sports cars and waste money on fancy food. This isn't my new life. It can't be. I wrap my angora around me a little tighter, but the expensive wrap brings me no warmth at the moment.

"Isn't that the guy Arin was talking about?" Kevin asks. "It must have fizzled quickly."

I look over into a corner table in the back, and I nearly wretch at the sight of Seth Greenwood in a cozy booth with a redhead. Long, elegant red hair which she flips in regular intervals. I can't breathe. Nor can I take my eyes off of him. He took this woman to a "proper" restaurant. There's no ignorance. Seth knows dinner consists of more than Fresh Choice with a dollar-off coupon.

"Ashley?" Kevin says, and I force my eyes back to him, but I still can't breathe. I'm blinking my tears away and swallowing past the lump in my throat. I'll never star in *Flashdance*'s ending. I'll be welding forever. My eyes keep glancing back at Seth's table because I can't believe what I'm seeing. *Oh, Lord, change my heart. Toward this gorgeous man across the table. Please.*

The waiter is at our table, rattling off specials in another language. Food I'll never be able to enjoy, at prices that remind me how much Seth is paying for another woman. Kevin is everything I should want. He's handsome, he's successful, he's ready to be serious with a woman, and I'm pining over Baldy in the corner! What is my problem?

"Miss?" the waiter asks. "Did you have any questions about the specials?"

"What? Um, no. No questions. It all sounds divine, thank you. I just need a minute." I force myself to focus.

"I should have asked you if you liked French food," Kevin says.

"You know, Kevin, I'm just glad to be out. I'm not in Taiwan. I'm having the most elegant dinner of my year with a handsome surgeon. Life is good, and I need to express a little gratitude for that. So thank you." I've almost convinced myself.

"You're most welcome." Kevin rips off a piece of bread from the loaf.

Seeing the colorful spices drenched in rich green olive oil, my stomach nearly loses it. *I have to get through this night.* If I don't, I'll never graduate, never progress past my pitiful crush on Seth. I guess it's a crush. Although, I would have never known I was interested if it hadn't been for Arin.

The waiter's back with his annoying French accent. "Have we decided then?"

"I'll have the salmon special," I say with confidence I don't feel. I think I heard salmon in that litany of ingredients he rattled off.

I cross my hands on the table and set about to learn everything about Dr. Kevin Novak, trying to ignore anything I feel about Seth being here. Bad coincidence, that's all. "You said that day in the café that you liked the beach. Do you get to go often?"

"Not really."

"So then what's your story, Dr. Novak?"

He gets comfortable with the question and then begins. "Well, I come from humble beginnings, but I guess you could see that when you met my parents."

"Really, you think? They seem like society people to me."

"They are, of course, but they're humble about which country club they belong to. They belong to the one with the finest doctors, not people with the most money."

No hint of laughter. He's not kidding. I look over to Seth, who's wearing a tie. *Seth owns a tie, go figure.*

"Will you belong to a country club eventually?"

"Why do you ask?" Kevin's eyes narrow. "Is it something you've always wanted to do?"

I shake my head. "Not really, no."

"Country Clubs offer an abundance of opportunities. It's nice to be able to mingle with people who understand you."

Again my gaze veers toward Seth. "Yes, it is." The Reasons understand me.

"My parents called me to tell me how much they enjoyed meeting you. They are hoping to meet your parents next time they're in town."

"Really?" I can't help but think if given the opportunity, his parents would ask me for a DNA sampling. "I thought I blew it with them."

"No. Not at all. They knew you were exhausted—just back from a trip. I don't run across many beautiful, available attorneys. They're excited for me."

"Ah," I manage. And there's an uneasy silence that falls between us like a Gray Davis blackout.

I'm trying to keep my facial expressions neutral. Money, I suppose, is something I've taken for granted living in the Silicon Valley. Money is everywhere, and millionaires are a dime a dozen, but I never aspired to be a socialite. I'm happy shopping at Ann Taylor once in a while and driving my sports car. I'm not considered wealthy by any stretch of the imagination, but I would imagine most thirty-year-olds are rich in Silicon Valley. *But this.* This kind of socialite money is foreign to me, and I don't like it any more than I like freshly killed crustacean.

"Do your parents come to California often?" I don't know what else to ask. It's either that or, *How many times a year will I have to endure them if we last beyond tonight's date?*

"Couple times a year. Often on their way to Hawaii or Japan. They love to travel." Kevin sits back in his chair and crosses his arms. He sees his parents as an advantage to a relationship, not the frightening deterrent they are. "So, enough about me. What do you do for fun?"

My eyes pop open. *The challenge: Make the Reasons sound normal.* Not a difficult task, except Kevin probably grew up playing polo and hasn't studied *Star Trek* since its inception.

"I hang out a lot with my church singles group. Sometimes we watch a movie at someone's house. Sometimes we head to Applebee's. That kind of thing." I shrug, like we're so typical. See, I don't mention that we see the *same* movie, or that chain restaurants are fine dining. I don't even say a thing about Talent Night and publicly humiliating ourselves in the local Starbucks. There's that little twinge of guilt again. I'm remembering that sermon on the sin of omission. But I'm not really officially omitting anything. I'm editing. There's a distinct difference.

"Arin's friend seems to see you."

I turn around and see Seth wave, but I turn before I can acknowledge him. "Seth. His name is Seth."

"Wasn't that crazy what Arin did? Taking off to a foreign country like that?"

"Maybe she'll be a full-time missionary. Who knows?"

"Missionary?" Kevin shakes his head. "Well, stranger things have happened."

"Oddly, I can picture her there in her wild capris. She really has such a magnetic personality, and she loves adventure, so who knows when we'll see her back."

"Seth doesn't seem to mind her absence, or at least he didn't for long, judging by his date over there. I can't say I miss her much."

I look back and see Seth and the redhead laughing. Well, I can't really see the redhead laughing, just her locks swaying as she tosses her head about. Her hair is beautiful, but I secretly hope she has the face of chopped liver.

"Seth and Arin never really dated," I explain. "They had just met when Arin left."

"But even if they went out once, Arin has a way of making you feel you were on the verge of marriage. Trust me on that one."

My cheeks are twitching. "Arin wouldn't knowingly mess with people's minds that way. I'm sure it's just her outgoing personality."

"My parents liked her too, until she showed up spouting all this religious talk." He rolls his eyes. "I could have died. She takes that stuff in, I tell you."

"She's rock solid in her faith, there's no denying that," I say, like I'm the pinnacle of moral righteousness. Me, who sits and covets a man across the restaurant. *I wonder if you hear the thunder after you're struck by lightning.*

But I'm rolling his words about Arin around in my head. Are his parents not believers? And why would they be upset about Arin talking of her faith? More importantly, why would Kevin not stand up for her?

I study the man across the table from me and choke down a bite of bread. I'm overanalyzing, as usual. I'm sure of it.

25

After my date, Kevin, the perfect gentleman, kisses me platonically on the cheek, which leaves me a bit puzzled. Brea greets me at the door and eagerly pulls me inside, her hands clasped under her chin. "So?"

The two little pugs she bought when she married are nipping at my feet, their pushed-in faces annoyed they must share their master. They seem to be taking it out on me.

"Tell me, tell me! Is he as dreamy as he looks?" Brea asks.

"I'll be upstairs," John announces with a shake of his head. "I can't stomach this conversation where you two plot the demise of another guy."

"Oh, you!" Brea kisses him playfully.

"Good night, John," I say, watching him skulk away. "Kevin's very nice, Brea. He's—" But I falter. I can't keep up the show. I've been working at it all night, and I feel the first sting of pain when I start to tell her how wonderful Kevin is. I dissolve into tears, and they flow freely as I realize the enormity of seeing Seth with another woman.

"We were having a wonderful time until"—sniffle here—
"I got dumped all over again." I pat myself steadily on the
chest. "I did the dumping. I kissed Seth goodbye. How
dare he show up at the restaurant!"

"Ash, what happened? What on earth are you talking
about?"

"Seth was there." (Wailing here.) "With a redhead."
(More wailing.) If I were speaking in tongues, I might be
more understandable. But I'm just wailing. The Jewish
people have the Wailing Wall; I have Brea. No pretenses,
no false fronts, just Ashley Wilkes Stockingdale unleashed
in all my pathetic glory.

Brea crosses her arms. "You have gotta be kidding me."

My tears stop with a sniffle. "What?"

"You are crying over Seth out with a redhead? He's a
Reason, Ashley. How many times have you said that when
I said he was interested in you?"

There's not an ounce of sympathy, and my pain
quickly turns to anger. "Hey, was I not with you when you
cried over whatshisname all through high school? When
he asked Kohli to the Prom . . . did I not ingest ice cream,
truffles, and Coke all night with you? You so owe me. I
probably own six pounds of your misery on these hips."

"That was different," Brea says as she plops on the
couch, quickly piled on by two dogs.

"How is it different? Did you ever even date Kyle
Lupinchec?"

Brea balks a bit, "No, but—"

"Did Kyle have your car in his garage? And put all of
your stuff into storage so you wouldn't have to worry
about it?"

"Seth would do that for anyone."

"I'm going to a hotel," I announce. "I'm going to call a counseling hotline so I can talk to *someone who cares.*"

"Ash, come on."

"No." I force fists to my hips for effect. "How come it's okay for you to be the drama queen, but when I have an emotional setback, I'm just supposed to get over it?"

"Because you're Ashley. The smart one. The stable one. The one everyone wants their son to marry. I'm the bad gene pool without the brains, remember? And now I can't even have kids, so I can't even do that part right."

"What!" I'm tempted to put my hands around my best friend's neck. She's gone nuts. There's no other answer. I will have to visit her in the "hospital" that no one calls a hospital. "You had one miscarriage, Brea. Not everything in life is perfect and tied in neat little ribbons. I know most of your life has been like that, but this is something you have to work for. I work for *everything,* Brea. There's no husband or parents to rescue me. Who rescued me when my car got impounded in San Francisco?"

Brea shuffles her feet. "My parents."

"And who stood up at my college graduation and cheered for the right school, unlike my own parents who thought I majored in business?"

"My parents and me."

"Neat little packages, Brea. You tick me off."

"Seth is a neat little package, Ashley. All tied up with a red bow, but you never unwrapped him because you always thought a better present was coming along."

"I did not! That is so not true." How dare she accuse me of being a man shopper!

"Uh huh. I think you've been in love with Seth a long time. You've just never been humble enough to admit your frailty. Well, you're human just like me! Just like Dave. Just like your mother. That just drives you nuts, doesn't it?"

"You're not making any sense."

"You pretend like you're so distraught and so mental over all this stuff Seth has done to you, but this is *your* doing. Seth has always cared for you, always been there for you, and you've avoided him because he was not your Prince Charming. Because you imagine this romantic Cinderella story for yourself."

I'm dumbstruck.

"Prince Charming can't carry off a career woman who's above the common romantic entanglement."

"Career woman? How can I be anything but? I have to support myself here."

Brea is unrelenting. "What did you say when Seth asked you on the ski trip to have dinner alone?"

"I had work to do, Brea. I'd already spent the day skiing. The Reasons were all there. It would have looked weird for us to go off by ourselves."

"What did you say to Seth when he asked you to help him lead the singles Bible study last year?"

"I was traveling every other week. How would I have prepared for that?"

"And what did you just say when he asked you to watch *The Matrix* with him on your birthday?"

"That was him and Sam and their stupid weekly ritual. That wasn't a real invitation."

"I'd say Seth has done more than his share to reach out to you, and you've clubbed him over the head one too many times, Ashley Wilkes Stockingdale. And now you *have* Prince Charming on the line, and you suddenly want the cook who's been in the kitchen all along!"

I'm shaking my head. "You're wrong, Brea. None of those instances were like you're saying. There were practical reasons he asked me for all those things. Look at the dinner at Fresh Choice? Hmmm?"

"Payback stinks, doesn't it? And practical is what you get with a man like Seth. You'd squash a romantic guy like a bug on the sidewalk."

I clutch my chest. "Ouch."

"I rest my case," Brea says. "So pine over Seth or Kevin, or whoever you're making out with this week, but get some focus. They're both wonderful from what I can see. Make up your mind and find out who you want before you end up with no one." Brea starts up the stairs. "Oh, and John and I are adopting that baby. I want the child to grow up in a Christian home, and there's one way I can make sure that happens." She slams the door upstairs.

What is it with me making people so angry lately?

I play Scarlett. *I'll think about that another day.* I sign on my computer, and there are only two e-mails. Now that I have Spamkiller, I realize I have absolutely no friends. There's one e-mail from Seth, and I open it immediately.

To: AWStockingdale@NNN.net

From: MatrixMan@NNN.net

Ash, here's your account number and password for your furniture, etc.

657584 Password: 777 (made that up, lucky?)

I explained to Larry re: Taiwan.
When you have a place, call him.
I have a working dinner tonight with one of the Barbies.
Call me on my cell if you need anything. S

I look over my shoulder, but Brea isn't anywhere to be found. Thank heavens.

"Ash."

I jump about a foot. "What?"

Brea has quietly come downstairs. "I came down to say I was sorry. What's Seth say?"

The words come tumbling out like a confession. "He had dinner with a Barbie tonight. He wasn't on a date."

Brea widens her eyes. "A what?"

"A Barbie. A lot of the sales companies employ these beautiful women to flirt with the engineers and sell product. Seth was with a Barbie." She's still staring at me, and I'm trying to tame my smile. "Barbies are usually married. And if they're not, they're dating linebackers."

"So Seth wasn't actually on a date."

"Right!" I squeal.

"But you were."

Ack. Reality. Reality so bites. "Go away."

I proceed to read an e-mail from Kay Harding regarding our Saturday night: bowling and square dancing. Is it too much to ask that my Saturday night contain more than the average seven-year-old's birthday party?

"Square dancing, huh?" Brea is still reading over my shoulder. "What's the good doctor doing on Saturday night? Maybe we could double date so John and I can meet him."

"He's probably working."

"What's wrong with *him*, Ash?"

"Nothing. And that's a problem. He makes me nervous, like he's too good to be true. He drives a Porsche, has a job, doesn't live with his mommy. But there's something really weird about his parents. I feel like they're looking for quality genetic material. They creep me out."

Brea crinkles her nose. "Ewww. He drives a Porsche? You're dating a guy who drives a Porsche. How *Wild at Heart!*"

"I can have a wild streak."

"I'm heading to bed." She looks at my briefcase. "And don't work all night. Get some sleep."

"I need to surf the Internet to figure out what makes a Chinese wedding."

"I don't even want to know."

"Dave says I need to, for Mei Ling. I can't imagine why she doesn't want a big American wedding with the Chicken Dance. Go figure."

"Good night." Brea ambles up the stairs.

I sit down at the computer and a new e-mail pops in from Purvi. I shake my head. That woman will have her coffin wired with DSL.

Taiwan trip on. Big happenings. Let you know more later. Purvi

I wonder if they need a female Elvis impersonator when I'm in Vegas. I'm definitely going to check it out. It's time to get out of my mode of madness. I might as well pick another.

After a few hours of strolling patent drawings, an instant message pops up. I look at my watch. It's two a.m.

How was date tonight?

I ignore the IM with a strange address. I'm sure it's some teen offering me a night of fun and free pics. New IM:

Wasn't that you at the restaurant, Ash? I was with a Barbie.

My fingers get shaky, but I type. *Seth?*

Call me Ken. Or GI Joe.

I giggle deliciously.

Did her knees make funny noises like the doll when she sat? I type.

Huh?

Girl joke. Never mind. Did she sell you anything?

No, but didn't drink. Saved her money.

How was her company? My fingers are twitching again. Not sure if I want this answer.

Shares Barbie's IQ.

"Yes!" I punch my fist to the sky.

Where are you?

@Brea's. Taiwan back on.

Bummer.

Had Last Supper. If I was only as good at conversation as IM.

LOL. Why are you up?

Have to look into Chinese wedding.

Something I should know?

Brother marrying Chinese woman next month.

Grew up in China. MK.

No way. He is not a missionary kid. I do not believe it. Not for a moment, but my heart is pounding out of my chest. How could I not have known this? My fingers are silent. I can't think of a thing to ask, but I'm overwhelmed with questions. Seth never speaks about himself. Not in a million years would I have guessed he was raised in China.

Ash?

Mentally processing you in China.

Left hair there.

You're better off without it.

And then there's nothing. Did I go too far? I lightly tap on the keyboard waiting for his return. I couldn't quit before the hair comment?

Back. Sam home. Locked out.

Too bad my brother marrying. Dave could room with Sam. Sam's cool. Cooks.

Cooking not so bad. Grocery shopping painful. I wrinkle my nose.

Go Friday night. No one there.

But everyone knows you're loser.

LOL. Am loser. Bald, aging engineer.

That's not in your online profile, is it? Bad for image.

What image?

I decide it best to change the subject. *R U square dancing?*

Talk about bad image.

"Ashley, what are you laughing at?" Brea's at the foot of the stairs, rubbing her eyes.

"I'm sorry. Am I keeping you awake?"

"No, I just thought I might be missing something. Who are you talking to?" She nods toward the screen.

"Seth. He IM'ed me."

"He's making you giggle?"

"He's very funny, Brea." Seth is also constant, like a brilliant star or a solid mountain. Settled in his ways and also his faith. What about Kevin? I guess I crave that stability a bit, what with my family being so flighty.

"Answer Seth. He's waiting."

Brea is here, says hi.

Tell her hi. Starting Matrix with Sam. Night, Ash.

Night, Seth. And the little bubble disappears off my screen. What an appropriate icon.

"What did he say?"

"That his date had the IQ of a Barbie. Does anything else matter?"

"I suppose not."

"Oh, and I'm going back to Taiwan. Purvi e-mailed me."

"Ashley! Would you quit that crazy job? Sheesh, you're going to be speaking another language before I know it. Or come home with someone who married you for a green card. Besides, I hate you on the plane all night. I sit up and pray and don't get any sleep at all."

"Did you know Seth was a missionary kid in China?"

"No, I didn't. There must be a lot I don't know about him, Ash, cuz I don't get it. I really don't get your sudden fascination with him."

I sigh dreamily. "I know. Neither do I."

"You need a vacation. You have no place to live, your clothes in storage—which totally scares me—I mean your shoes could be out of style by the time you get to them. Your job owns you, like you're chained to a desk, only worse because it's a plane, and the church band is making a CD and I heard you told them you haven't got time to help."

"I don't." I shrug.

"The singles ski trip is coming up—a whole year has passed. You are going on that, right? Even if it is with the Reasons."

"I hate to ski."

"I know you hate to ski. Get a facial in the spa up there, but you need a vacation. I think your priorities are way off, and I'm worried you're going to be a Reason forever if you don't get out of this Valley. When I find you at the *Star Wars Negative Four* premiere dressed in costume, it will be too late."

"I'm going to Vegas in two weeks for my brother's wedding."

"Dodging porn leaflets and passing slots is not going on vacation for you, Ash."

"They have spas there."

"Promise you'll go to one?"

The question leaves me antsy. I used to love anything girly like that, but now things are different. I don't lay back and relax. I worry about all that I forgot to do before I left. All the briefs that must be looked over one more time. Thinking of all the ministries I used to do, I just feel so inadequate. And I hate to feel inadequate, so I don't like to think or stop my momentum of hurtling forward at light speed. Lack of motion is definitely where it gets you.

"I promise I'll go to the spa. Now unless you're up to planning a traditional Chinese wedding, or studying patent drawings, go to bed."

"It was good to hear you giggle again. You've been so strange since I got married. I came down to hear you giggle, and if Seth makes that happen, well then, I'd give him another chance."

26

Things to look forward to about Taiwan trip:

1. Seth might miss me (absence makes the heart grow fonder, and all that).
2. Get to cancel nightmare lunch date on Friday with (gag) Dan Hollings without lying.
3. Don't have to wait for any might-be phone calls all week. I'm so busy!
4. Can put off apartment search for another week.
5. Can pick up traditional Chinese elements for brother's wedding.

Brea enters the kitchen as I'm typing away on my laptop. "Did you sleep at all last night?" she asks.

"I got enough."

"I worried you might have stayed up all night talking to Seth. What did he say?"

"Nothing really." I shrug. "We got off when you went to bed. He was going to watch *The Matrix*." *Oh, that was just painful to admit.* "I'm going to use the phone if you don't mind. I'm leaving today from what I gather, so I want to cancel my date with the Dark Side on Friday."

"I can't believe you ever said yes to him in the first place." Brea has a look on her face like she just chewed a brussel sprout.

"It's your fault I'm in this situation." I look up the number in my PDA. "If I call now, I'll get his voice mail."

"Dan Hollings."

"Oh, hi," I stammer. "I was expecting voice mail."

"The early bird gets the worm, you know. Besides, this rings through to my cell. I'm actually in my car. On my way to get a client."

I am a woman on a mission. "I need to cancel our lunch tomorrow, Dan. I'm going to Taiwan this afternoon." I give that special mixture of serious business tone combined with deep regret. It's Academy Award quality.

"Perfect," he answers. "Maybe I could meet you at the airport for lunch before your flight out?"

Ack! I knew I threw too much sorrow in the voice. I should have gone for all business. The Screen Actors Guild would revoke my card.

"I'm flying out of SFO," I say, waiting for him to tell me no, he was expecting San Jose.

"Right. So noon okay?"

I slap my forehead. I gave him way too much info. When will I learn to shut up? If I'd just said I was too busy to see another man in one week . . . "Yes, noon is fine," I murmur.

"Great. I'll see you at noon. At the Japanese place."

"Wonderful."

"You're such a loser," Brea says as I hang up.

I choose not to rehash the Bloomingdale's incident, or that this date is courtesy of Brea's insecurity. I rise above it. I'm that good of a friend. "Yeah, thanks for your support."

Brea is wearing her running gear, a darling gray and pink sweat suit, most likely from Nordstrom. She looks way too cute to sweat and, considering her size, it seems wasteful of good clothing to me. Her pugs are nipping at her feet, ready for their morning run.

"The dogs can keep up with you?" I ask, looking at their stubby legs.

"No, they go with me in the Burley."

"The what?"

"The Burley. It's a jogging stroller." She points out the window, and there is a bright red and yellow stroller contraption for children, complete with the raised orange safety flag and rain jacket.

"You do *not* take dogs in that."

"They're my babies." She picks one of them up and cuddles it close to her cheek. "At least for another two months."

"I'm seriously worried about you. You need that kid. Get one. I'm going to work."

"Aren't you going to eat? There are Atkins bars in the closet."

Poor Brea. She thinks sugarless soy bars are breakfast. You at least need caffeine to call it breakfast. "I'm stopping for a mocha."

"Hitting those kinda heavy, aren't you?" Brea's pert little nose crinkles.

"Yeah, well, I'm trying to get off the sauce, but you know."

She slaps me in her playful way. "Shut up. I only meant that you're always complaining about clothes not fitting and all."

I shrug. "I can buy new clothes. Speaking of which, I'm leaving my laundry here," I announce. "Can I pick it up clean after my trip?"

"After you just cut down my babies?" She starts baby-talking to the dogs.

"Lunch date with Dan Hollings," I say. It's all the push she needs.

"Yes, I'll do the laundry. E-mail me when you get there, okay? I'll be happy when you get a normal job and stick around."

"This is a normal job in Silicon Valley. Jogging your dogs in a Burley? Not so much."

Brea has the thighs to prove she runs her dogs. I have the thighs to prove another mocha isn't going to hurt my svelte figure.

Brea kisses my cheek. "Plan a vacation." Those are her parting words, and I ramble into work, excited to have my precious Audi back. At least some things in life work right.

Dianna is out this morning. Last night's harrowing phone answering session must have done her in. *Be kind,* I admonish myself. But Lord, does it have to be to *everybody? Can't we pick and choose?* I silently whine.

Purvi's here but on the phone, probably keeping some poor soul up in Taiwan. It's midnight there. I clean up my desk as best I can and leave as much for Dianna to do as humanly and humanely possible. Then, I make some phone calls while I wait for final marching orders from

Purvi, which will send me back to the confounded airplane and brown air. In the meantime, I'm jamming to get the newest tech drawings outlined for the patent office.

"I'll have final paperwork to you within the hour," Purvi shouts as she passes my office.

"Wait. Am I on the three o'clock flight?"

"Yes, you're booked. Dianna has your confirmation information on her desk."

Purvi waves me off for the attention of some VP.

I turn around, and Dianna is in my face with a piece of paper.

"I thought you weren't in yet," I say to her.

"Been here for an hour."

"I worked at home," I say in some mock competition. "Tell Purvi the docs for the Incline project are on her desk." I flip my hair, which of course, doesn't move.

"How was your date last night?" Dianna wiggles her eyebrows as though I'm going to share some intimate detail of my date with her. If I had an intimate detail, maybe I would. "Saw his Porsche. Very impressive. Where'd he take you?'

"Some little French place in Palo Alto."

"Not L'aime Donia," she says in a perfect French accent. "I love that place."

Knock me over, but I'm surprised she's been there. She doesn't strike me as the French restaurant type. I'm beginning to notice there's a lot I don't understand about Dianna.

"It was nice," I say with no inflection.

"You know, Ashley, you're smart enough where you don't need a rich guy."

I'm struck. Since when am I marrying for money? When am I marrying for anything is the topical question.

"I know what you're thinking," she continues. "I'm no one to give advice, but you know, I'm the best one to give advice. I'll never let a man control me again. I control them." She winks and takes off for her desk, where another admin is waiting to talk to her.

Is it controlling a man to let them look down your shirt? Maybe it is, but it's reminiscent of Jezebel, and I'm going more for the Esther or Ruth essence. But not the Virgin Mary. I've done that for thirty-one years. I want a husband, and I want him now! This morning I don't really care if it's Kevin or Seth. Someone just has to make a move and I'm down that aisle, baby. Okay, maybe I'm not that desperate. But I'm close.

Purvi shoves a few last minute documents in my briefcase and bids me adieu. "This is big," she reminds me. "Those royalties are keeping our stock price high. We lose them and stockholders, and our board is going to be looking directly at the patent department."

I salute her. "I can handle it."

"You get the next trip to Seattle. I promise."

I just nod. If there's one thing I know, Purvi will make this worth my while. Getting a patent for the company, I get a $1,000 bonus every time. Defending a patent with a stream of royalties? I'm going to Hawaii baby! I'll get my facial there. I'm going to learn to relax if it kills me.

Driving up to the city, there is no traffic. Leave it to me to find the one day the 101 to San Francisco has no traffic. Remember that movie of the week, *The Day After*? That's what the freeway looks like, so I have clear sailing to the airport and my date with destiny on the one day I'd much rather be late.

You know, I need an attitude adjustment. Dan Hollings might be perfectly dashing by now and my attitude could be ruining it for me. Reboot. I must reboot. He's no longer a cheerleader stalker. He's a successful businessman in the Bay Area. He has call forwarding to his cell phone, for heaven's sake. That shows a little initiative anyway. *Okay, Lord, I'm putting this in Your hands. This is Your plan for my life today. I accept it. I embrace it. I will represent You today to Dan Hollings.*

I'm an hour early to the airport. All I need. More waiting. But I check in at the curb and hand over my luggage, which has now been packed for nearly a full week with everything I own that I have access to.

It doesn't matter what time of day you're at SFO, it's packed. The new glass walls make the people seem so small, like bustling ants each going in a different direction. I thrust myself into the flow and head to the international terminal with all the other Valley drones and tourists.

I decide to download e-mail on my PDA and check it while I wait for Dan. I'm waiting for Dan Hollings. If that doesn't give an accurate picture of my love life, I don't know what does. As I look across the grand hall toward the Japanese restaurant, Dan is there waiting. He waves like I've come all the way across the country to see him. He hasn't changed a bit. And this is not a good thing.

He's got the same wiry, dark curly hair and scruffy, uneven beard. Yes, he had a beard in high school. Not a good look in the '80s when mousse was making its debut.

Pasty. That's the best word I can think of to describe

him. Although his hair is dark and thick, his sallow skin is colorless except for some remaining pockmarks. But it's not his looks that throw me; I'm not that shallow. It's this sticky oozy feeling he gives off. Like that awful ring-ditcher on my last trip to Taiwan. I can't explain it, but I feel defiled being around him.

"Ashley!" he says, coming toward me for a hug.

Enveloped, I answer against his shoulder. "Dan, so good to see you."

"I see we're both early," he says.

"Uh huh, so we are. What a coincidence."

"Well, sit down. I've already gotten us a table. Let me catch you up on myself." I sit down, and Dan removes his files, phone, and briefcase from the table.

"Looks like your office."

"Everywhere's my office these days."

"So what have you been up to?" I say enthusiastically, remembering my promise to the Mighty One.

"I'm a CFO for a small startup."

Small startup. Is there another kind of startup? "What do they do at your startup?"

"Business application."

Ah, nothing. No real product. "Do you have any critical patents?" I ask.

"That's right, you're a patent attorney. We have a few."

"Pending or granted?"

He looks upset. "In process." Okay, no product, no patents. This means he has a job for six months at best. But I'm not on a job interview, I'm on a date. Act accordingly.

"I bet it's fun being in a startup." *If you like not knowing where your next paycheck is coming from.*

"Oh, yeah. Lots of perks, my own hours, granted they're in the eighteen-hour-a-day range, but it's starting to happen."

I want to ask him how many stock options he took in lieu of salary, but I can tell by his bravado it was a lot.

"Let me order us some drinks." He lifts up his arm and nods at the waitress. She's a petite Asian gal who blends the right amount of smile with standoffishness.

"Can I get you started with some drinks?" she asks.

"Diet Coke would be great," I say, before Dan has the chance to order for me. Just by his open mouth, I can see he's the type to do that.

He laughs again. "You always were the good girl. I'll have a Bloody Mary." He waves off the waitress.

"So I saw your sister and her darling baby at Bloomie's. Are all her kids that cute?"

"Yeah, she pops out some nice looking kids, doesn't she?"

I nod.

"You got any? Kids, I mean," he asks.

"No, I'm not married."

"That doesn't mean much these days. I have two." He takes out his wallet.

"Kids?"

"And ex-wives." He laughs as he shows me a picture of twin girls about three years in age. "Marriage hasn't really agreed with me."

"Do you see your daughters often? They're darling." And they are. Springy golden curls and wide smiles with turned-up noses. They must resemble their mother.

"About once a month. I travel a lot in this stage of the

game. I guess that's why marriage hasn't worked out. I think I need to find someone who expects the same things out of life as me."

Brea's words are haunting me about being a career gal. "That's funny you should say that. I was just rethinking all my travel."

"It's the only way to get ahead in this game. I told my wives that all the time." *Wives.* He's only thirty-two, and he's had *wives.* Silicon Valley is a wicked place on marriage. Unless you happen to be of the same sex, then it's quite friendly toward the union. I'm awestruck by how old he appears, like he's lived two lifetimes in his years. Does any plastic surgery fight that haggard, too-much-stress lifestyle?

"Maybe getting ahead is not the answer."

"Now you sound like my sister. She's always ragging on me to get back to the basics."

I hand him back the picture of his daughters. "I think that's good advice, actually."

The waitress leaves our drinks, and Dan puts cash on her tray. "What are the basics?" He laughs. "Around here, it seems to be a 5-series Beamer and a four-bedroom house in the right section of Menlo Park."

I scratch my head. "That is what it seems like, huh? I can see the argument for the great car. You spend so much time in it, but your house? Who the heck ever gets to go home?"

Dan smiles. "I often think my maid spends more time there than I do."

The waitress comes back around. "Are you ready to order?"

"Sashimi hamachi and vegetable tempura." I hand the waitress my menu.

"Sounds good. Me too." Dan sucks down his drink and orders another one, but sees my worried face. "Make that a Coke." With what's left of his drink, Dan lifts his glass. "A toast to success. And finding out what the heck that is."

We clink glasses. "You know I was voted 'most likely to succeed.' I should have an idea of that, huh?"

"Ah, well, let's ask the expert then, shall we? What do you think success is, Ashley Stockingdale?"

I pause and ruminate on this question. It's a good question, but I can't answer it for anyone else. "I think that it's living life without fear. We're afraid we'll lose our jobs, so we work like robots. We're afraid we don't look successful if we don't have the right cell phone or the right car. It's like being in one big high school clique for your entire life. I want to live and be unafraid. If I make a fool out of myself at Starbucks, so what?"

"Yeah, so what?"

"And if I never get married, and people think I'm bus bait for the rest of my life, so what? Didn't God put me here for other reasons?"

"Amen, sister! Preach it." We both fall into an easy laughter, which surprises me.

"What about you, Dan? What's success to you?"

He slides the picture of his girls toward me, and all remnants of his laughter fades. "Being a father to my girls. A real father."

The somber moment leaves us both too filled with questions to talk. We eat our sashimi with barely any words.

"It was so nice to see you again, Dan. And I mean that. I'm going to be praying for you and your family."

Dan wipes his forehead with the linen napkin. "It's been a long time since anyone said anything about praying for me. But I'll take it. Can't hurt, that's for sure."

"We're part of God's tapestry, Dan. Let's find where our string goes, huh?"

He laughs and gives me a hug. "You're still most likely to succeed, Ashley." I pay for lunch and watch as Dan gets all his belongings together. As I watch him walk away, my mind grieves for his family. *Lord in heaven, restore that family.*

I wave good-bye to him and go through security to my gate. Once inside, I have the distinct desire to call Seth. I can say it's to check on my apartment. I dial him up before I think too hard on the matter.

"Hi, Ashley," he says.

Love caller ID. I exhale into his ear. "Oh, Seth, I am so glad to hear your voice. I'd give anything to not get on this plane. To tell Selectech to take their job and shove it."

"Well now, Ashley, have you been listening to country music again?"

"Very funny. No, I'm rethinking success, actually. Having an Oprah moment, if you will."

"Ah, you've been to a company productivity meeting." He laughs. "The meaning of life. Besides Christ? To watch *The Matrix.* Why don't you come over?"

I laugh. Seth can always make me laugh. "You didn't really watch *The Matrix* again last night."

"No, I didn't. I had work to do, but I know you think that's all I do with my time. Why not let you believe it?"

"You are an anomaly, Seth." I will never understand Seth fully, and I guess that's part of the charm.

"You're pretty hot yourself, Ash," Seth says, pleading ignorance on my big word.

"Right back atcha, babe. So, I'll see you when I get back?"

"Can't wait. Bye, Ashley, be safe."

And I hang up looking at my phone longingly. I need to make some changes in my life, or I'll never feel successful. I tap my notes into my PDA, pausing thoughtfully between each one. But they pour out of my fingertips and onto the screen like an e-mail from God, I swear.

THINGS TO DO FOR LONG-TERM SUCCESS:

1. Make peace with my *Matrix*-loving self. (It's okay to be a geek!)
2. Learn to let my limbs dance freely in public. (It's okay to look like a geek!)
3. Embrace the engineer within. (And maybe the one without, too! It's okay to love a geek!)

27

H IGHLIGHTS OF TAIWAN TRIP:

1. Stepping off dank plane
2. Stepping back onto dank plane after week in brown air
3. Friendly people (unlike Silicon Valley)
4. Trip longer than expected (apartment hunt pushed out further)
5. But home in time for *American Idol* (Yay!)

There are fourteen voice mails from my mother regarding my brother's wedding. Most of them asking if work will cover the cost of said calls. I've tried to call her back from several places around the planet, but her line is busy constantly. Hasn't my mother's generation heard of call waiting? I was tempted to break in on her phone call, but then I thought, why? She'll just have a litany of things for me to buy in Taiwan!

But I call her an hour after touchdown because I am an exceptional daughter. Besides, I have five minutes to spare before the landlord gets here to show me a new place. Craigslist, an on-line classified, has a million listings for rentals, and I got pictures and everything—while in Taiwan—so I think this is the place I want. But I digress.

"Hello?" My mother's voice is overwhelmed, like answering the phone is an aerobic exercise.

"Mom, it's Ashley."

"Ashley, where have you been? For goodness sake. I couldn't get you on your cell phone, and you never returned my calls. You could have been dead, and I would have never known. That little Indian woman you work for never tells me a thing."

"Actually, Mom, I returned your calls many times. Your line was always busy."

"I'm going crazy with this wedding. It seems like all I do is talk on the phone."

"You should have e-mailed me."

"You know I hate that computer. I can never remember how to turn it on."

The button, Mom. The little button that lights up. "So what's so urgent?"

"Do you have everything we need for the wedding?"

"Yes, Mom. I bought Mei Ling a *kwa*. It's so beautiful. It's a traditional gown that a Chinese bride would wear to her reception," I say, like the big Chinese expert I have become over the last week. "She'll wear the regular white dress she bought for the actual ceremony, but this is for after, if she's interested. At least she'll have it for a reminder of her heritage anyway. It's red brocade and just beautiful. I was tempted to get myself one."

"Get a groom first, Ashley."

She's dealing out right hooks to the head! I choose to ignore her snide comment. I'm too tired to tangle with her. "Uh . . . yeah, Mom. Oh, I also got favors with their names in Chinese writing on them. They're little Chinese clothes and chopsticks."

"Well, Ashley, no one will be able to read them if they're in Chinese."

Have I not just toured the entire downtown of Taipei to find traditional wedding elements for a wedding that is not my own? Have I not just tried to communicate with an old Taiwanese man who paints names individually on every chopstick in his own sweet time? Could I get just a smidgen of appreciation here?

"We'll *tell* them what the symbols say in the toast, Mom. This is what marrying two cultures together is all about. Explaining the differences and embracing them."

"They do drink at Chinese weddings, right? Your father payed a fortune for an open bar."

"Yes, Mom, they drink. It doesn't matter that we have everything they do in China, only that Mei Ling feels like we cared enough about her history at the wedding. It's hard enough that she won't have parents there." I pause. "This is for her and Dave, not us."

"This wedding is enough work as it is without worrying about the Chinese business, but I suppose you're right."

"I got fifty of everything. That should be enough, right?"

"Oh, heavens, yes," Mom says. "Really only my aunts will be there. They like to gamble and planned a trip to Caesars after the wedding. Your father's side of the family doesn't think the marriage will last, so they won't buy plane fare to Vegas."

Typical. That's a nice way of avoiding the subject that Dad's relatives are total bigots and won't pay to see Dave get married to a non-Caucasian. Granted, my feelings on Dave being married are cautious at best, but it's got nothing to do with race. It's got everything to do with Dave being Dave. And even Dave as a Christian is still Dave. A new creature in Christ? Maybe. But there's always a bit of the old creature left lurking within.

"We'll have enough of everything then. Listen, Mom, I'm looking at an apartment right now. I'll call you back later, okay?"

I'm eyeing the landlord with trepidation. There are two types of landlords in Silicon Valley. There's the wealthy entrepreneur who keeps buying more houses and renting his old ones as he moves up. I like to call them *absentee landlords* because they're never around and you never hear from them. Even when your plumbing is backed up.

Then there's the curmudgeon who rents in bulk. He usually lives in the building and has a bird's-eye view of everything that goes on in his complex. And it is *his* complex; you are simply a guest—a temporary guest. That means all parties, visitors, and pets will be the subject of much inspection and subsequent discussion.

As I'm watching Mr. Harvey White approach, his polyester pants from 1957 (still perfectly good to him) landing just about at the chest, I see he is obviously the latter type of landlord. He's walking around my car, surveying it carefully. I hop out with a friendly smile. I won over Mr. Manger, if not Mrs. Manger. This guy's got nothing on me.

"Mr. White, I'm Ashley Stockingdale. Such a pleasure to meet you." I'm candy-apple sweet. I cannot wait to get my hands on these granite countertops he's just put in! Granted, I won't ever cook anything on them, but they'll look divine.

He waves some papers at me. "You filled this out?"

"Yes, I faxed them to you. It looks like you got them okay."

"Your credit's bad. No sense showing you the apartment, because I won't rent to you with bad credit."

I'm shaking my head. The cedar closet . . . the hardwood floors. Now I'm nervous. "Mr. White, I can assure you my credit is excellent. Did you call my former landlord?"

"She's the mark against you." He shuffles through the paper, and he's obviously thoroughly enjoying my humiliation. "It says you took things that didn't belong to you, like the microwave."

I'm shaking my head. "No, I didn't do that. I lived there for three years and never had a late rent payment. Call Mrs. Manger."

"I did. Mrs. Manger said the refrigerator got stolen as well. Said she woulda never expected it of you."

And then with spellbinding fear, it comes to me. Seth's friend, Larry. I never told him I didn't own the appliances. "There's a misunderstanding," I say desperately. "I've been in Taiwan, and I had a company move things. Perhaps they moved too much. If you'll just let me straighten this out—"

"Nothing to straighten out." He spits into the bushes.

"Thieves. Mrs. Manger's going after you. You'll pay for that stuff and then some."

"Please, Mr. White. I can explain everything."

"A good con usually can." He points to his temple. "But you have to get up pretty early to fool Harvey White." He disappears into his apartment, and I'm left standing on the sidewalk. *It's no use panicking. It just means this isn't the place for me,* I tell myself calmly. Successful people do not panic. God's people do not panic. *Fear is not of the Lord, fear is not of the Lord,* I chant.

I pace up and down the sidewalk. Even with this gorgeous clean sidewalk within walking distance of downtown Palo Alto, I try to convince myself there's a better place waiting. I dial up Seth for Larry's number. Someone is going to pay for this "misunderstanding," and it's not going to be me.

Voice mail. ARRRRGH! I pound the numbers to his cell. Voice mail. I need caffeine. A big ol' triple mocha with a double shot of whipped cream. I start walking downtown to one of the coffee houses. My phone rings within a minute. It's Seth. I pummel him.

"Seth, your friend stole the fridge and microwave. My credit is in the dumpster, and this landlord thinks I'm a thief. I just got home from Taiwan. I have no place to go, and my clothes are I don't know where. *What is going on?*"

"Ash, calm down. There's something I need to tell you."

"Seth, I totally trusted this guy. I know it's a misunderstanding, but I need my stuff. I need a place to stay." People are looking at me as I walk down the street screaming into my cell phone. Here I go again. Christian witness?

Not so much. Freak psycho homeless person yelling on a street corner? Bingo.

"Can I come pick you up? We need to talk." Seth sounds like a psychologist. Now I'm frantic.

I swallow hard. "No, you tell me right now." I stop in my tracks.

"Larry's out of business."

My breath rushes from my lungs. From lack of oxygen, I just sit down on the sidewalk. In my brand new outfit from Bebe! It's clear I'm not thinking straight.

"Ashley?"

"Seth, I have nothing. When will I get my stuff back?"

He pauses for a long time. "Ashley, I feel terrible."

"Forget all that. I don't care about any of that. I'm not blaming you, but where's my stuff?"

"Larry hired this guy. Apparently, he was removing extra things from apartments. On purpose. Then he was selling it. They caught him selling your appliances in a back alley in San Jose."

I cradle my head in my hands. I can barely believe this. "So where's the rest of it?"

"It's been impounded by the City of San Jose Police Department. They're cataloging everything and trying to get it back to its rightful owners ASAP, but you have to fill out forms stating everything that's missing."

"Seth, this wasn't a suitcase! It's my entire apartment. You know how unorganized I am. How would I know what's missing?"

"You just have to try and remember. I'll help you."

Remember. I have to remember. The only problem is I can't remember my first name at the moment. I'm looking down at myself trying to figure out just who I am—who I've become. I'm dressed well; that's a positive. I have great Jimmy Choo shoes, so I've come out of this disaster with my style intact. But I'm sitting in the middle of a city sidewalk crying into a cell phone. Everything I've worked for is gone.

More importantly, everything I've worked for is useless and temporal. Except maybe these shoes . . .

"I'm going out for a coffee," I say to Seth. "I really need to think. And pray."

"Ash—" There's such pain in his voice, and I feel awful for him. I know he would never purposely steer me wrong.

"Seth, I'm not mad. This didn't happen because of you. It happened because I'm too overwhelmed to think straight. I need some time to sort it all out."

"Where are you going to be tonight?"

I stand up and brush off my bum. "I don't know. I'll be on the cell phone though."

"Me too. Call me when you're ready to go to the police station. I don't want you going to downtown San Jose alone."

"Will they let me get anything? My clothes?"

"I'm sure they will. The problem will be finding them. There was a lot of stuff. Larry's just sick about it all. He's out on bail."

"And out of jail, while my stuff languishes in custody." I pause, remembering Seth didn't want this to happen. "'Bye, Seth." I snap up the phone and walk past some of the gorgeous old Victorians and Craftsman-style homes in Professorville—where the Stanford faculty used to live—but now can't afford to dream about.

My feet stop in front of a traditional bungalow, which is probably worth two million because of where it is. It's surrounded by a quaint white picket fence and blooming flowers at the end of January. Is this what I want? To park my Audi convertible in front of a million-dollar home that would be $100,000 anywhere else in America? How did I ever come to believe this was success? I feel like that day in the airport when I got caught in a stream of people and never realized I was going in the wrong direction.

Do I want to prove to the world that I am Ashley Stockingdale, A Success in Silicon Valley—one of the hardest places on earth to make it? Or is there another way to be successful? I look up to the sky, realizing with clarity that I'm empty inside right now. Gazing at the beautiful shell of a house, I think I know why. But my brain's a little fuzzy from jetlag. Suddenly I'm feeling bottomed-out tired. I'd better sit down before I fall down. Maybe if I just lie down on the sidewalk for just a sec, I'll catch my breath. I'm just going to close my eyes for a sec. Just for a sec . . .

28

*T*his is Rick Ramirez reporting for Entertainment This Evening." *Rick tones it down to a golf announcer whisper. "We're at the home of Ashley Wilkes Stockingdale, bride of the infamous coffee-growing millionaire, John Folger. As we watch Ashley descend the marble circular staircase in her home, we see grace in action. Jen Jenkins reports . . ."*

"That's right Rick, we're in the home of celebrity couple, John and Ashley Folger. To watch these two cuddle is something out of a fairy tale. It's clear there's more here than your standard Hollywood romance. This is a couple in love. A couple who take their many possessions in stride to honor the love they share. Ashley, tell us what it's like to be married to one of the world's former hottest bachelors?"

"He's still a hottie." Ashley giggles and falls into the crook of John's neck. "But now I don't have to share him with the world."

Jen smiles and crosses her million-dollar legs. "John, they say Ashley's diamond is one of the rarest in the world. Can you expound on why you purchased such an expensive ring?"

"It's a canary yellow diamond, ten carats in a flawless

269

radiant cut. When I saw the diamond, I thought of Ashley. She's sunny, yet rare—so the yellow diamond was all I considered. Flawless—well, that speaks for itself. The radiant cut is a testament to her sparkling personality." He smiles down at his wife, and they collapse into each other's arms, giggling.

"Miss, are you all right?"

I look up and see a policeman gazing at me, like I might be on drugs. He's snapping his fingers in my face, and without thinking, I push his hand away. "Leave me alone."

"What's your name?"

I rub my head. What is my name? I feel like I got kicked in the head. I've never had such a reaction to jet-lag. It's like I'm hearing him speak, but from far away. "Your name, ma'am."

"Ashley Wilkes Stockingdale. Stupidest name you ever heard, huh? I'm named after mealy-mouthed Ashley Wilkes. My mother liked weak men, but I think she's coming around." I stand up, a little dazed. I turn around and see the Victorian home while trying to get my bearings. The truth is, I feel a little tipsy. "Isn't that a beautiful house?"

"Ma'am, I need to see some ID." He grabs for my Prada bag, which I instinctively pick up and unwittingly whack across his face. My hand flies to my mouth.

"I'm sorry, I just—"

"You're going to need to come with me."

"No, no, no, Officer. I'm sorry, I just thought . . . My car is a few blocks away. I'm having a very bad day. I'm tired, and I just need to go to bed for two days." I start to explain the airplane and jetlag, but somewhere I lose the words—I'm overwhelmed by his grip on my arm. "No, I'll show you. My car is right up here." I'm waving my free hand like a madwoman.

He puts me in the backseat of his car. I'm in the backseat of a police car! "Ma'am, you are in no shape to drive. We'll get you sobered up at the station."

"Sober? No, you don't understand. I'm not drunk! Give me one of those breathalyzer things." I look at the beautiful house again. "I'm not drunk." I kick up my heels into his view. "Look, I've got Jimmy Choo shoes; I'm not drunk." I look at my feet and shake my head. "These really are great shoes."

He drives me by my car, and I nearly cry as we pass my baby. No wonder I feel so strongly about my car. My life blows otherwise.

"Officer, look! There's my car—see how nice? This is a mistake, a travesty of justice. This is the only crime here. My stuff has been stolen in San Jose. Oh wait, that's two crimes. But they're not *my* crimes. I'm innocent. I'm just lacking caffeine; that's no crime, but it's giving me a terrible headache." I rub my head, but I can still see his eyes in the rearview mirror.

He just looks at me like I'm crazy. "You're under arrest for drunk-and-disorderly conduct, loitering, and assaulting a police officer." He starts to rattle off my Miranda rights.

"I'm a lawyer; I know my rights! You can't arrest me for drunken behavior without a test."

"You'll get your test. At the station."

I groan. "You're going to make me pee in a cup, aren't you?"

But he just keeps counting off my Miranda rights. I

have the right to remain silent. I can have a lawyer, blah blah blah. I lay down on the backseat of the car and take a little nap.

When I wake up, I'm sitting in a jail cell. A jail cell! There's no one else in the cell with me, but it's danker than the Taiwanese jet. And the smell! Well, I won't even go there. There's a little toilet in the middle of the room. Now I ask you, who would use a toilet with a guard behind a desk nearby? Is there a beast on earth who couldn't hold it for an eternity rather than demean themselves on a public—and I do mean public—toilet? It leaves me longing for my rat-infested apartment. *I have to get out of here.*

There's a female officer behind a long, torturous-looking counter. "This is all a mistake. I need to get to work."

She looks up at me, rolls her eyes, and goes back to stamping whatever important piece of filing she's working on.

"No, really. I want out of here."

She walks around the counter. She's big and scary and looks down at me like I'm a crumb on her table. "You get a phone call. You ready to make it?"

"I've got my cell phone—" but I look around and I don't have a cell phone. "Where's my Prada bag?"

"It's in the designer section with your gourmet meal. Do you want a phone call or not?"

"Yes!" I shout. I scratch my head trying to figure out who to call. "If they're not home do I get to call someone else?"

"Yes," she says.

I can't call my mother. Dave would never let me live it down. The family must never know of this day. I can't call Purvi; I'm supposed to be at work. *Brea, I can call Brea.* Since the hulk won't give me my Prada or PDA, I'm doubly glad I know Brea's numbers by heart. Dialing her cellular, just in case, I'm mortified when voice mail comes on. I hang up immediately. I don't want it to count as my call! "Can I use a phone book?"

I page through it, thinking of one friend and then the other. I refuse to call Kay Harding, who would never let the clipboard loose long enough to get arrested, and Seth would only think I'd gone off the deep end and blame himself for losing my stuff and pushing me over the edge. Kevin . . . do I dare?

I look up the number for Lucille Salter Children's Hospital and dial. When they answer, I ask for Dr. Kevin Novak and guiltily explain it's an emergency. They page him, and within three minutes or better, he's on the phone.

"Dr. Novak."

"Kevin, it's Ashley. I need your help. I'm in jail, and I need bail posted." *This is the most humiliating moment of my life.* Kevin's view of me is now the desperado who kissed him passionately in the dark San Francisco parking garage and a convict in jail. At least his parents won't try harvesting my eggs at this point.

Kevin is laughing. "Come on, Ashley, what's the emergency?"

"I'm not kidding. I'm in the Palo Alto Police Department in a holding cell. I need to be bailed out."

He's quiet for a moment. "You're really not joking?"

"I wish I was."

"I'll be right there." He hangs up the phone, and I'm escorted back to my cell.

There's another woman here now. She's tall and lanky, and she too is wearing great shoes. They look like Cole Haan's.

"Hi," I mumble.

"Hey." She nods. "Shoplifting?"

I'm mortified. "No." But then my pride quickly diminishes. "Assaulting an officer and loitering."

"Krista Harchek." She holds out her hand.

"Ashley Stockingdale."

"You got a bail bondsman? I know a great one."

"My friend's coming," I explain.

"It's good to have friends."

Subconsciously I start singing the song about what a friend we have in Jesus, and Krista points at me. "I know that song. Heard it at rehab once."

"We sing it at church. It just came to my head."

"Yeah? What church do you go to?"

"The one that meets at Paly," I say, referring to the high school.

She curses. "I know the place."

I swallow hard. "You should join us when you get out. Those are great shoes by the way."

She nods. "Cole Haan's. Picked 'em up at Bloomingdale's."

By picking them up, I don't know if she means purchasing them or stealing them, and now I'm thinking complimenting a thief on her choice of stolen goods is probably not a good course of action. Even if it was for Jesus.

After an hour of chitchat, Kevin is at the desk, asking the great hulk about me. Even in this dungy holding area, he's like a ray of sunshine. The hulk gives him a bunch of papers, and I see him hand over cash to the bailiff. I'm a criminal. A Christian criminal. So weird. The Hulk is coming with the keys, and Doc won't look me in the eye. How humiliating.

"It was nice to meet you, Krista. Stop by the church on a Sunday morning. The stores are closed then." I wink. "Besides, you look like you've had enough of this life."

She smiles and points a finger at me. "You got it, chick. Stay on the sober side of life."

Kevin is looking at me incredulously.

"I'll tell you outside." We get out into the California sun, and I've never been so happy to see light. I do a little twirl on the sidewalk. "I'm free!"

"Not quite. Your hearing is on Tuesday." He hands me a bunch of papers.

I try to explain my story, but I sound like an idiot and I don't want to admit to urinating in a cup even if my results did exonerate me. Someone else might not understand that kind of tired, but being a world-traveling resident, Kevin gets it.

"Did you have to look for an apartment in your first hour back? You could have given yourself a break, you know."

"I didn't want to miss out on it. It was a great apartment."

"Are you hungry? Let's get a late lunch. I haven't eaten since three this morning," he says.

"Did you see that toilet in the middle of the cell? Do you think anyone ever uses that?"

"Judging by the smell in there, someone did."

Ick. Don't want to discuss this. "Was it hard for you to get out of the hospital?"

"No, you called at a good time. But I have to say your call couldn't have shocked me more than if you'd put the defibrillator paddles to my chest." He says he's shocked, but he's eating this up. He loves the Knight in Shining Armor role.

I look at Kevin with new eyes. He's not confident to his inner-core like Seth, but there's something vulnerable in that place. He wants to rescue people, and I just hate that I was the kind who needed rescuing—but somedays, you just have to give up and let 'em rescue. It's comforting to know Kevin is capable of that—should I ever need it again. It makes me feel safe.

"I can't thank you enough for getting me. I'm just not myself today, and I didn't know who to call. I knew you were close by. How much do I owe you for bail?"

He waves his hand. "Forget it, Ashley."

"No, tell me."

"Let's get some lunch." Kevin drives up the street to Revvia, one of my favorite restaurants. It's a mixture of exciting Greek flavors with the healthy conscience of California and definitely the pricing of Silicon Valley.

"You sure like to eat well," I comment.

He lets his eyes drift toward my feet. "And you like to dress well."

I square my shoulders and hike my chest out. Getting

rescued from the pokey was worth it to have someone notice my outfit!

"Do you eat this well all the time?" I ask.

"Only when the company's worth the money. And in the last two years, this is my second time to a good restaurant. The first time was with you at that little French place."

My heart is thumping. I mean, I can't even handle the fact he thinks I'm worth anything. What other man would bail me out and buy me a fine meal in the same day? I'm thinking this might be Serious Love now. Seth, who?

"What would your parents think of bailing me out?"

"Let's just say it's not something we'll discuss." He reaches for my hand and squeezes it in his own. I love his hands. They're masculine and smooth all at once, and when he looks at me with those deep green eyes, I just feel it to my Jimmy Choos. This kind of magnetism could get a girl into trouble.

"Please let me get lunch," I offer. "It's the least I can do."

He turns and looks at me, his chin cast downward, his arm straight over the Porsche steering wheel. He looks like an ad for Porsche, only better.

"Call me old fashioned, but I don't let women take me out."

"Not even with a coupon?" I ask.

"Especially not with a coupon." His voice is steamy. I fan my face. *Is it hot in here?*

He finds a parking spot easily. He lives a charmed life. Kevin comes around and opens my door and lifts me up out of the Porsche. Of course, all my weight is really on my right foot. I'm not totally naive. Let him think I weigh what Arin does.

"So did you get enough sleep in the slammer?" he jokes.

"I did. I'll be all caught up by tomorrow morning. Then I'll just go in and explain to my boss I needed a personal day."

"Isn't it amazing how they send you to another world, time-zone-wise, and expect you to work like you had your full eight hours?"

"They expect you to be a robot."

"Aren't you?" Kevin shakes his head and grabs my hand as we run across the street. Pedestrians have the right of way in California, but being right and being dead can be the same thing. People think we're so healthy out here. We're not healthy; we're jogging to get out of the way of speeding BMWs.

"I'm quickly becoming a robot," I sigh.

Kevin does that thing where he lets his eyes scan my figure and dart away. "I agree that you are a well-made machine, but not a robot." He winks at me.

I slap his arm. "Cut that out."

He starts to laugh, and it's contagious. Have I mentioned he just emits sensuality? *Down girl.* I'm sounding like Dianna, Administrative Warrior Princess.

"That's hardly reputable behavior for a Christian boy."

He's still laughing. "I-I'm not a Christian."

My smile disappears. "What do you mean you're not a Christian? I saw you at church. Arin said—"

"I went there a couple times to meet Arin for brunch.

I'm afraid my beliefs fall into the agnostic range. I just don't know." He shrugs. "But I'm very tolerant of your beliefs. Is that an issue for you? I mean, if I can be tolerant, can't you?"

29

After lunch, the tramp back to my car is excruciating. These shoes may be great, but stilettos are not meant for walking—other than that little jaunt-and-turn on a fashion runway. I have blisters the size of Epcot, and it's only been two blocks. But I didn't want another ride in Kevin's Porsche, and I told him I had some shopping to do—which wasn't a total lie. I picked up Hawaii brochures at a travel agency, and I'm dreaming of when work will give me a break and I can take a vacation. I can wear flip-flops and Lilly resort wear.

Back to Kevin. You know how I kept worrying he was too good to be true? Well, he was. Granted, not gay like I was thinking, but not a Christian and not someone who moves in the same cultural circles I do. He does the Opera. We do the Melodramas in San Jose. But he has such manners! *Lord, why on earth can't a Christian guy treat me that way?*

If I ever get married and raise boys, I'm going to teach them chivalry. When Kevin opened my car door, it should have been a dead giveaway something wasn't right. When

I think of the countless clues that were before me, I feel stupider than a cut of sushi.

Then there's the whole "tolerance" argument. Can't I be tolerant of his beliefs? When I believe someone is going to hell for their failure to acknowledge Jesus Christ, how is one capable of being tolerant of that? I mean, let's say I fall in love with this man. What's next? *Oh, I have this little harem of women on the side, you don't mind, do you? Why can't you be more tolerant?* Granted, I feel a burden for those around me who don't acknowledge the Truth, but that's a far cry from raising children with that person.

Peeling off my shoes, I carry them in my hands for the last half-block. I can see my car from here. It's missing its top. This is the second time it's been stolen, but you know, I figure with all that's going on today, it's the least of my troubles, and I just laugh at the concept. I'll head to Brea's and call the police from home. I wonder if they'll respond to an ex-con.

There's a man watering his lawn. He's watching me like I have no business in his neighborhood, and I suppose I don't. But still, being warned off with body language only makes me more confident. And I shake my little Bebe outfit and swing my shoes.

Once in my car, I'm glad I live in California—since it is winter and there's no top on my convertible. Is it still a convertible now that it doesn't convert? I turn the car on and blast the heater, and life's not bad. It's enjoyable, in fact. Loosening my Burberry scarf, I see the radio is still intact, and the CD changer resides in the trunk so that's safe. I blast my favorite David Crowder CD and rev up to third gear. I feel free again, and with the January sun on my face, I drive to my favorite road: Foothill Expressway. It has the effect of a spa on me. It's surrounded by greenery and the distant rolling, golden hills spotted with oaks, like something out of a serene painting. Taking it in, it makes me relish life. This is success: enjoying your moment. Whatever moment God happens to gift you with.

I lift my arm straight in the air, trailing my Burberry scarf behind me like a kite tail. Breathing in deeply, I realize for the first time, and with a bit of pride, that I really am a Reason! I'm probably a Reason-cubed, but I am not a victim!

I've been playing the victim. I whine about how work sends me across the world without even twenty-four-hour notice, but is that Purvi's fault? No, it's mine for allowing them to beat me into submission.

I'm a patent attorney, not a worldwide salesman. I never signed up to be jaunting all over the planet on one person's whim. Then I whine about it, like, *Woe is me, they're doing it again.* See? Victim.

I'm the one who will come in at six a.m. without a question. And I'm the one who chose to go out with a friend's ex-boyfriend, without for one moment wondering why she might have dumped him. It never occurred to me that Arin has a missionary soul; maybe she'd been missionary-dating the very elusive Dr. Novak. If anyone was strong enough in their faith to do that, it's Arin.

You know, even transferring my material goods to Seth's friend because I was so overwhelmed—my fault. If I didn't have a roof over my head, why was I going to

Taiwan to work for basking in some glory that probably won't ever come?

My arm is still straight up in the air with my $200 scarf trailing as a victorious flag. I will beat Silicon Valley, and I will do it on my own terms. I am a Christian first. A confident, take-charge woman. A grunt laborer second. Success is about living the gift, not impressing the neighbors.

I let go of the scarf and from my rearview mirror watch it drift on the wind. Then, I downshift into fourth and punch it. I am free! I'm not single for a reason. I'm single because that's God's will for me.

After all, I don't have to answer to anyone. I can get a double espresso at ten p.m. and there's no one to say, "That will keep you up all night," like John does to Brea. *Mental note: My husband—if there ever is A Husband— won't care if my girlfriend comes over once in a while and gig- gles with me like we're at a teenage slumber party.*

God didn't place me here in the tech capital of the world to play the victim. He placed me here to enlarge His Kingdom, and how can I do that whining about my pathetic life? Brea's married. She still whines—only now it's for kids. It's always something. Contentment has to start somewhere, and I choose here along my favorite road, in my gorgeous convertible, under the California sunshine in the midst of winter . . . I choose to start here.

I grab my cell phone and put the earphone in my ear. Granted, I have to roll up the window to hear, but I shout Kay's name, and the number dials automatically. I love technology.

"Kay Harding," she answers.

"Kay, I have a proposition for you."

"Yes." Kay's a bit nervous, hearing from me again without an appointment.

"Kay," I say with personality, trying to get her involved with my renewed passion. "I have no place to live at the moment. What would you say to my paying rent and living with you? You don't have to answer now, but I'm tired of the struggle. Making ends meet, to say nothing of making dinner! Life doesn't have to be this hard. We can make it easier on each other."

"Sure," she says simply, and I almost hear relief in her voice. Could she be lonely in that big ol' house?

"No, really, I want you to take your time," I say. I don't want her volunteering to house me as a mercy mission.

"I don't need any time. I'd like a roommate. Regardless of what I said, I get sick of cooking for myself. This place is too big for me anyway. But . . . will you keep the living room clean?"

"I will."

"And no wild parties?"

"I'll do you one better. No parties at all."

"Done then. $675 a month?"

"Eight hundred, Kay. It's still half what I was planning to spend on an apartment."

"Great. When are you planning to move in?"

I'm silent for a moment. "Is tonight too soon?" I ask sheepishly.

"I'll go get a key made for you on my way home from work."

We say good-bye. *There*. I will live with the great clipboard; maybe I'll learn some organization in the process. That was stepping out of my comfort zone. I feel ready to take on the world. One problem solved at fifty miles an hour with the wind in my hair and an ear speaker. *Next.*

I shout Seth to my phone.

"Hi, Ashley. Where have you been? I didn't want to call . . . thought you might be angry at me."

"Nah, I'm not angry. I got arrested today, had another date with a non-Christian—my specialty lately—but I did find a place to live, and I'm going to work on getting my stuff back tomorrow. What's up with you?"

"Ash, have you been drinking?"

"That seems to be the consensus, but no, I haven't been drinking. I might be more normal if I had. I've never been clearer-headed."

"Do you want to go by the police station after work to get some stuff?"

"Actually, I'm not going to work, and I've seen enough of police stations today. I'm going to the beach: Natural Bridges in Santa Cruz. I just wanted to let you know I'm okay and not to worry about my stuff. I'll get it tomorrow." I pause and bring out the big guns. "I appreciate how you're always ready to help me, Seth. But I'm growing up today."

"Ashley?"

"I'm going to Hawaii. I picked up some brochures while I walked in Palo Alto. In stiletto heels. I don't really recommend that. Hawaii, on the other hand . . ."

He's confused. I don't know why I can still surprise him. I'm neurotic, and I change like the wind. Why is this so hard for him to grasp? Maybe that's why I like Seth. He's fascinated by my ever-changing mental state. If you consider the fact that very few other people, my family included, notice my mental state, it's almost a compliment. I'm fascinated that he never seems to change.

"Ash, you're in the middle of a lawsuit for Selectech. Hawaii?"

"Hawaii," I say emphatically. "But first, Natural Bridges State Beach."

"What are you up to?"

I let out a long, evaporating sigh. I'm not a woman of conviction. When Arin said she was leaving for the rain forest, everyone just shook their heads. They knew she meant it. From now on, when I say something, people will cower at my conviction.

"I'm up to fifty miles per hour on this gorgeous sunny winter day, and my car has a mind of its own. It just won't go to Selectech. It's going to Natural Bridges."

Seth is stunned silent. And this is a good thing. Last week, my life had so many romantic prospects. But today, I realize there really wasn't an option in the bunch. I was valedictorian. You'd think it wouldn't have taken me thirty-one years to know what I wanted, with or without a man.

"Don't you have to look for a place to live?" Seth asks, trying once again to suck me back into the vortex of fear.

"Found one. I move in with Kay Harding tonight." Aha! I'm not a complete idiot. I can find myself a place to live with no credit and no belongings.

I look in the back of my car. Whoever stole the top didn't take the Bible sitting in the backseat. But I guess when you steal, the Bible isn't exactly what you want to take. Still, I've got all the makings for my own little retreat in this vehicle and that's what I plan to do. Revel in my single status. Rejoice in God's reasons, regardless of what they are. Plot my course. From here on out, Ashley Wilkes Stockingdale is a new woman.

"Gotta hang up now. I need to call Purvi."

"Ash—"

"'Bye!" I hang up, pretending not to hear his last call. I do not analyze the conversation. I just move on. *Next.*

"Purvi," I tell my phone, and I hear it dial.

She answers yelling, very un-Purvi-like. "Ashley, where are you? Marketing and engineering need the drawings you checked, and I need you to go over these contracts again. You're on the foreign filing deadline for one patent, a continuation deadline for the other. Where are you?"

"I'm in my car. On the way to the beach. I've worked for sixteen days straight, and I need a break before I turn postal."

Purvi's voice changes. She's sympathetic, but she still wants what she wants. "Ashley, are you looking to lose your job? I can cover you for so long, but these patents need to—"

"I spent two weekends in Taiwan, and I have eight weeks of vacation stored up—not counting my comp time. I'm not going to lose my job unless Selectech needs another lawsuit, and they don't. I just need a day off, and I'm taking one. Work will all get done. Have I ever let you down?"

She swallows her next words. I hear it, even with the convertible open and the wind rushing into one ear.

I calmly continue. "I'll be in tomorrow, and everyone will have what they need by deadline. Today belongs to God."

"Sure, Ashley. If you need anything at all, you call. I'm worried about you."

Her concern is back. I'm leaving this trail of panic-stricken people behind me, because I'm taking one day off. What does that say about me?

"Brea," I say to the phone. She answers.

"Now you're home," I chastise.

"Of course I'm home. I was looking at cribs this morning. Did you call me on my cell?"

"Yes, but in the cavernous crib store it probably didn't work. Would you get a decent phone?" I lambaste her.

"I was only in there for an hour."

"It was an hour I happened to be in jail."

"What on earth?"

"I hit a police officer. Long story, but he grabbed my Prada. That's history. Now I'm going to the beach. I'm moving in with Kay Harding tonight—just wanted to let you know I would be at your house to get my stuff and then I'm outta your hair. That should make John happy."

"Cut it out. John loves having you here."

Yeah, like one loves caring for a neighbor's angry caged cat.

"You want some company for the beach?" she asks.

"Nah, thanks though. I'll call you tonight." I hang up the phone and make one final call. The call I'm dreading the most.

30

The winding, snaking highway through the Redwoods to the beach is treacherous and beautiful all at once. Speeds often reach upward of seventy-five miles an hour, and with the hairpin turns, it's inevitable that crashes happen. The asphalt on Highway 17 is covered with black skid marks, and a plethora of paint colors tint the guardrails—kind of like a sick art experiment.

I'm not focusing on any of that for long though. I can feel the sun on my face, even though my heater needs to be on full-blast to ward off the January chill. My mood is uplifted by the majesty all around me. To think of the stories that these trees could tell from their lifetime—a lifetime stretching to when Jesus walked the earth. This roadway, cut through the forest, is like a slice of heaven on earth, except for the accidents, of course.

I'm so entranced that I put off my phone call to Kevin to tell him there's no future. There's no sense in ruining a perfectly gorgeous day. I've left my problems back in Palo Alto with the top of my convertible.

These petty issues have consumed my life for years.

Things like my coffee shop running out of "real" whipped cream and having to settle for the canister pre-whipped stuff. Or my dry cleaning not being back before a trans-Continental flight, or something really terrifying: not getting a patent secured in time for a product to go on the market.

I'm suddenly struck with the Ecclesiastes idea that they mean nothing. I can't sit and state that anything I've accomplished will be remembered.

As I exit the highway, I can smell the ocean. Its fresh salty scent reaches me, and I obey its call toward crashing waves and dramatic, rocky cliffs. I drive through town, past all the weirdos that make Santa Cruz, Santa Cruz.

I pull into a parking lot and take in the expansive view and just listen to the thunder of the rolling waves for a while. The constancy of it, the expectation always fulfilled. The color of the water overwhelms. It's where spas get their color themes.

I grab my notebook because this is a day for remembering. Tossing my Prada in the trunk, I walk onto the beach and watch an enormous gray pelican swoop and pluck a fish from the sea. The bird, which seems like something out of prehistoric times, soars gracefully over the crest of the wave, as if showing his catch to those lucky fish left behind. Letting the school know they could be next.

I sit on the dry part of the sand and gaze toward the vast horizon. For a long time I think about everything from what I'll wear tomorrow and what type of bathing suit is most flattering to God's divine plan for my life. Taking out my notepad, I decide to approach life the way

I would any new patent. I listen, and I take notes in case I forget something.

The new Ashley Stockingdale will:

1. Dance at my brother's wedding and embrace his new life.
2. Take a vacation and learn to relax—if it kills me.
3. Spend ten minutes of every day rejoicing in my surroundings.
4. Take chances. Maybe even wear Lilly Pulitzer to work one day.
5. Not ever, and I mean never, watch *The Matrix* again.
6. Not make fun of Reasons. I am one.

When I look up, the brilliant blue sky against the backdrop of the Pacific captivates me. There's a biplane kite in the air with vibrant neon colors, and I wish I could soar with such ease. I also realize I'm hungry. I've been here for three hours and never noticed a minute tick. I stand and pad barefoot toward the water and kick my big toe in the edge of an icy wave.

"Ashley!"

I laugh at the sound of my name, but it comes again. "Ashley!"

I look up and see Seth walking toward me. He's carrying a bouquet of flowers, and they're tulips, my very favorite. Pink tulips. I blink and shake my head. Maybe I *have* been drinking and forgot about it.

I wait for him to reach me, to see if I've been in the sun a bit too long. Kind of an oasis thing going on, but it is Seth. He's probably here to ask me if I think Arin or Kay will like these tulips, or because he feels guilty about my material possessions.

"Hi, Seth. Did you think I'd lost it?" I can't think of another reason he'd be here.

He doesn't hold out the flowers; he just stands there. Once again, waiting for life to happen as engineers seem to do.

"Well?" I tap my bare foot in the sand.

He doesn't say anything, but he drops the tulips at my feet and keeps his gaze upon me. His gemstone eyes against the backdrop of the ocean are haunting reminders that I haven't overcome all my demons. Seth Greenwood still stirs my heart like the creatures in a tide pool when the ocean rushes in.

Seth's hands reach for me, and I flinch and step back. He steps forward again, and I shake my head. Too much is riding on this moment for me. I stand here with all the expectations in the world, yet not one ounce of faith that any of it will happen.

"Say something," I command him.

But he says nothing. He only bites his lower lip. I remind myself not to count on a human to fulfill me—strive to remember all that I've decided this day—to be happy in every day, in every moment. I start to sing a hymn out of sheer nervousness. I begin quietly, but my volume grows in harmony with the waves.

"Come thy fount of every blessing. Tune thy heart to sing thy praise. Grace and mercy never ceasing, call for songs of glorious praise. Teach me some melodious sonnet, sung by flaming tongues above—"

"I've tried this once before," he announces. So . . . he *can* speak.

I stop singing. "Tried what before?"

"You're always in such a hurry to get somewhere. I never feel the time is right."

"I am always in a hurry. That's part of the reason I came to the beach today. I don't want to rush through everything. I'm going to be fifty and still trying on miniskirts at this rate because I haven't realized I've grown old. Quite pathetic."

His hands surround my cheeks, and he tips my chin upward. Yes, I should be enjoying this moment, but I'm wondering where he saw it. Did Bond do this? Indiana Jones? Bless his heart, I know it's not Seth's move. It's a suave move, and it unnerves me to no end. *Wait for it. Wait for it.*

His lips press hard against mine, and I can feel the heat rise to my cheeks. My makeup has long since paled, but I don't care. I kiss him firmly, and our passion grows more intense until we're fully macking on the beach. I pull away and shake my head. Breathless. *Whoah, I didn't think he had it in him.*

I have to test if it's a fluke, and I kiss him again. He returns it feverishly. Now I'm really leery.

"Is this some kind of joke?" I ask.

"This is *it*, Ashley. There's no one else coming along." (He shrugs here.) "You're the best I'm going to get."

My stomach twists, and I can't stop the tears. They rush down my cheeks like the fountains in Palo Alto's many courtyards. *This is it? This is my moment of reckoning and romance? I'm the best he's going to get?*

Seth picks up the flowers and holds them out to me, but I bat them away.

I'm moved, in spite of myself. I can tell he's saying something entirely different than his words convey. But I'm also a bit miffed. This is supposed to be Our Moment! "There's no one else? That's your romantic plea for my heart? There's no one else?"

"Come on, Ash. You know I'm not good with words."

"I'm not asking for words, Seth. What do you *feel?* Do you feel anything inside that locked box you call a heart?" I tap at his firm chest. He's been working out.

He chucks the flowers on the sand and a rogue wave carries them away.

"I feel everything." He bites his lip again. "I just don't express it right, I guess. I can't win."

"Don't look at me that way. I don't expect life to be all gumdrops and roses, but I don't want someone who feels they're *settling* for me. Do you think that's too much to ask?"

"I never said that I was settling. You're putting words in my mouth."

Which might not be such a bad idea at this point. "All right then." I step forward toward him. "Tell me what I'm missing. Did you not just tell me there's no one else—and there might never be? Am I supposed to be carried away by such sentiment?"

He shakes his head. "Forget it, Ashley. You think the worst of me. I see now there's nothing I can do to change that." He starts to walk away, but turns back toward me. "I made a mistake with Arin. I was a fool to think some flighty young thing like her was what I wanted, but I did think that for a while. Sue me for being stupid. You knew the truth. You knew it all along."

"Are you saying this is *my* fault because you didn't know what you wanted?" I ask incredulously.

Seth looks angry. It's the first time I've ever seen such emotion from him.

"If you knew about Arin, why didn't you tell me rather than let me make a total jerk out of myself? You knew what was brewing between *us* all along, yet you let me follow Tinkerbell around like a cloud of pixie dust."

"I tried to tell you! How dare you pin this on me!"

"Maybe you did." He shakes his head and focuses on a far-off point on the horizon. The sun is beginning to set, and the bright orange and pink sky darken the ocean to a smoky gray. "I came to tell you that I'm leaving California. I got a job in Phoenix, and I leave in two weeks. I thought . . . well, never mind what I thought. It was stupid."

I gasp for breath, for some sort of response to this. This!

"I really came here to tell you—" He stops and stares at my face. Once again, the words are in his eyes, but will not be relinquished from his mouth. He starts and stops again. I can see it when he turns away from me inside for good.

"I—I just wanted you to know that you can live in my condo rent-free. Sam got a place of his own, and I know you've got no place to go."

I shake my head, trying to process what he's just told me. Were the flowers really a good-bye gift? Impossible. He didn't drive all the way down here to say good-bye—

something that could've waited until I returned tonight. But I will not say the words for him! I will not!

"I didn't want you to hear it from anyone else," Seth says.

"Right." I give him one more chance. "And the kiss?"

"What's a kiss between friends?" He half-smiles at me.

What, indeed. Everything and nothing, all at once.

"Thanks for your offer. But I already worked things out with Kay. I can check on your place if you need me to. Water the plants and all that."

"No." He shakes his head. "I'll either rent it out or sell it if you don't need it. I just thought if you needed—"

"It was nice of you to think of me." I don't want to let him walk away like this, and if I don't, then everything I've just told myself is a lie. How can I possibly live with conviction if I give it all up for a simple kiss? If I don't demand enough respect for myself that others fail to respect me, too?

"You're not who you think you are, you know," Seth says. It feels like an accusation.

"I don't understand that."

"You're not some over-aged woman living in the shadow of Arin and her ilk."

Ilk? What does ilk mean? Since I couldn't fit in Arin's shadow, I know I'm not living there.

He continues. "Arin's cute. She's sweet. You're beautiful. And you're real. I can ask Arin out easily and make a total fool of myself and get over it because it doesn't matter. I don't care what *she* thinks of me."

I keep waiting to wake up from one of my fantasies. Now he feels free to tell me what he feels—now that he's turning and walking away from me, now that he's moving to another state. But does it really mean anything? I can't make him stay with me here on the beach, in California at all, and I wouldn't want to. Life is a series of choices. I've made mine. He's made his.

For better or worse, they don't coincide.

oving in with Kay Harding has been like signing up for boot camp. The clipboard hangs in a place of honor: on its own specialized hook attached to the refrigerator. Organization is not simply a character trait for Kay. It's a way of life. Kay does everything as if the clipboard is her master and she must answer to its every command. She is a slave to the clipboard.

Kay does her laundry on Monday, her gardening on Tuesday . . . the list goes on. At first, I thought I'd kill her watching the dance that is folding day. It's like those girls at the Gap folding things neatly on the board, over and over again. Something within you suddenly wants to run through the display and toss them into the air, shouting, "Quick! Make your escape!" Human nature, I suppose.

Wednesday is Reason Bible study night, and Kay made me promise that I would attend. It's been at least a year since I bothered—figuring Sundays were enough—so I imagine it's about time. Not with Bible study (I did that on my own) but *group* Bible study. There's a ritual for that, too. Kay checks her clipboard and calls those who have snack the night before to remind them. She asks someone ahead of time to lead opening prayer and then she prays over the whole house just before they arrive. I like that last part, but the first time I'll admit it freaked me out a bit. It's kind of like a priest casting out demons. Or eating casserole. Sometimes you'd just rather not know what's in there.

At seven p.m. the doorbell rings. It's Jackie Cole. She's got snack tonight, and Kay takes the plastic tub of cat-shaped cookies and turns them over. "Are these for people?"

Jackie points to the writing in defense. "See, it says right there. For people."

I smile. A snack that requires explanation that it is for human consumption is not going to create a rush to the kitchen. This will bother Kay immensely. I can see her twitching. And then she'll want to talk about it tonight. What's worse is that I'm starting to share her concerns.

"I'll put them in the kitchen," Kay says with a good effort at graciousness.

In Kay's defense, Jackie is a vegetarian. Not just a vegetarian, but a Vegan—meaning she eats only cardboard. I can hear Kay rifling through the kitchen for the perfect Martha snack, which she will prepare and arrange in a matter of minutes.

"So, Jackie," I say to cover up the kitchen noises. "How are things with you?"

"My job stinks. I have this idiot boss who has an issue with women, and I'm just tired of his passive-aggressive behavior."

"I'm sorry. That must be terribly difficult." I sit down, hoping to end the antagonistic conversation, but Jackie is just getting started.

"On Friday, he planned a beer bust, and do you know he had a barbeque? It's just like him to offend me by serving seared flesh for a work party. Him and all his cannibalistic, women-hating companions."

Now I've got nothing against vegetarians. I know some perfectly normal ones, but some, like Jackie, are more vegetarian than Christian. It's their first religion. She's been known to rattle off how early a mother cow is separated from her calf, or how that calf is then placed in a box to become my next Veal Meal. It's not that I don't respect her opinions, but I desperately want a shower after talking to her. She makes me sweat. Besides that, Jackie looks so unhealthy. Her skin is sallow with a green tone to it, her demeanor angry, and I can't help but think if I forced a good truffle or iced mocha down her throat, maybe she'd cheer up and remember the Good News.

"Well, you know how men like to celebrate their barbeques." I laugh, betting that no one has ever asked Jackie if she did the wild thang over the weekend. Maybe it's a compliment that I've missed.

"Tell me how it's celebratory to kill something!" Jackie's hands go to where her waist should be, but it's disappeared beneath an abundant bust.

"You've got me there. Why don't we sit down?" Never mind that I'm already sitting down. I'm trying to get her off her high horse and ready to embrace the Word. The doorbell rings, and I practically jump and dive for the door. It's Seth. And he looks right past me.

"Hi, Jackie," he says.

"Seth, can I take your jacket?" I ask. I step right in front of him and force him to look at me.

He eyes me momentarily and makes me wish I could take everything back I ever said to him. I want to start all over again with him, but it's too late for that. The disdain in his eyes is apparent.

"No, thanks. I'll wear it." Ah, so he wants to *show* me the cold shoulder. I get to watch him dressed for an Arctic winter all evening.

I swallow past the lump in my throat. I want him to kiss me like he did on the beach. *Oh, Lord, leave it to me to demand more when Seth offered me everything he could.* Why do I expect soap-opera romance from an engineer? Brea is right. It's no wonder I'm single.

Kay comes back, and there's a glow of sweat on her brow, too. Clearly, she's found an appropriate snack, but at some physical cost. More people arrive, and we take out our Bible study on submission. Again with the submission! Wasn't Sunday's lesson enough? Or the twelve other times we've studied this?

The group recaps their previous conversations, and then I read a key passage aloud, getting into the lesson in spite of myself. Isn't that how Bible study works? It's a pain in the keister to get there, get your brain focused, but when you do, your heart follows. That's gotta be God. "'Servants, be submissive to your masters with all fear, not only to the good and gentle, but also to the harsh. For this is commendable, if because of conscience toward God one endures grief, suffering wrongfully'—"

"You know," Jerry, a man in his late forties, suddenly speaks up. "This is a good passage. Slavery works in the world. I don't know why people protest it. Look at those little gals working as prostitutes in Asia. They eat. They have a roof over their head. We should be happy in all circumstances. The Bible says that. I don't know why we as Americans think we have any right to go into these countries and tell people how to live."

The women are all staring at him, mouths agape, waiting for him to correct himself. (Jerry has never been married, but I suppose that doesn't need mentioning.) Seth is shaking his head—wondering how Jerry will ever get out of this one—and Jackie actually looks ready to hurt him. She is definitely rethinking the whole cruelty to animals thing.

"What's the difference between them being prostitutes or being married?" Jerry tries to explain himself. "It's the same lifestyle for them in those countries."

He's completely serious. This is a Bible study! And we're entering an argument about why prostitution is not legal, nor it be. "Um, diseases for one thing," I say. "The Bible also destroyed Sodom and Gomorrah for lack of morality, and sex outside the marriage bed is detestable to God, according to Hebrews 13."

Jerry looks down at his Bible. "There's prostitutes all through the Bible."

Now I know my church is an outreach church. We have many people who come who don't know Jesus as their Savior, and that's a good sign that they feel comfortable. After all, I invited the klepto in jail, didn't I? The issues arise when someone like Jerry is using church as a social pick-up club. He's obviously failed at all the singles bars (can't imagine why!) and now graces us with his wisdom.

Normally, I would have all this love in my heart for someone so lost, but tonight I'm just ticked. You don't have to be Christian to disagree with prostitution. I mean a basic knowledge of right and wrong should do it. But to justify it by using the Bible? *Oh, heaven help me, I'm going to throttle him.*

Kay looks straight at Jerry. "If someone told you eunuchs were throughout the Bible, and that you should be happy in that lifestyle, would you believe it?"

Jerry scratches his head. "That's mixing apples and oranges."

While all of us panic, struggling to set Jerry on a path where he won't be pummeled by the women in our group, Seth is quietly flipping through his Bible and suddenly speaks up. It's almost a whisper, so it grasps our attention.

"'Marriage should be honored by all, and the marriage bed kept pure, for God will judge the adulterer and all the sexually immoral!' Hebrews 13:4. Does that sound like an approval for prostitution?"

This aura of peace descends upon the room. Why is it Christians always try to argue instead of letting the Holy Spirit do His work? We're all silent for a while.

Jerry is nodding his head. "I see." And I think he just might.

Kay looks at her watch. "Let's get to prayer. Amy, it's your turn to lead."

Amy is about to start when a knock at the door sounds and in walks Dr. Kevin Novak. I see Seth's jaw flinch, but he moves over and allows Kevin a seat. Kevin smiles at me and winks from across the room. There they are: Kevin and Seth. Sitting beside each other, I see their enormous differences. Kevin is comfortable in his own skin, but uncomfortable in this setting. He poses to try and cover it up, stretching out on the couch like he owns it, while Seth's cheek muscle is still twitching.

I wish I could just tell Seth if I had my choice. . . . Well, there is no choice. There's Kevin in all his gorgeous, non-Christian splendor, and there's Seth, the man who knows my heart but all he can offer is his condo when he goes away.

After a few short and equally shallow prayer requests and group prayer, we move on to the snack portion of the evening. The box of cardboard cat cookies are now in a cut crystal bowl, but something about them makes you want to pour milk in a bowl next to them and call Fluffy from next door. No one touches the cookies.

Kay has arranged a plate of sliced fruit with strawberries, fresh pineapple, and kiwi. In February! Next to that is a platter of warmed brie with crackers. I have to admit, I'm in awe. If this were at my place, I'd have arranged a few Vitamin C capsules next to some limp pickles and hoped no one noticed that I wasn't prepared. Kay is never unprepared, and I have to admit, I can't believe a single guy doesn't covet this skill in a potential wife. Heck, I covet it.

Seth is staying far from me, as if I have one of the diseases I spoke of earlier during Bible study. His prayer request was about his move.

"Hey, Ashley." Kevin nudges my shoulder with his own.

"Hi, Kevin. It's good to see you at Bible study."

"It makes a lot of sense. This Book." He holds up his Bible, with his name engraved in the black leather cover. Did Arin buy it for him during her missionary dating stint?

"It's the only thing that makes sense on some days," I say, but I'm watching Seth out of the corner of my eye.

He's not eating, he's not talking. He's just standing there, like a high school wallflower waiting for the right moment to cut in.

"I haven't heard from you since the day I bailed you out."

"Yeah, I've been busy," I hedge.

"Me too. This is my weekend off. Are you free?" Kevin asks.

"My brother is getting married on Valentine's Day, remember? I'm going to Vegas."

"Oh, right. That should be fun. Do you gamble?"

I do, unfortunately, and it cost me dearly. "No, no, I don't gamble. Or drink, or do much of anything I can do in Vegas. I don't even golf."

"That's too bad."

Definitely time for a change of subject. "Tell me how you're doing with that Book. What are you reading?"

"Matthew."

My heart is pounding. Kevin is standing here, willing to discuss theology and his readings of the Scripture—quite possibly his salvation—and where is my shallow head?

Watching Seth Greenwood walk out the door without even saying good-bye.

32

I t's Thursday morning, and when I come into Selectech's glass entry, security is standing at the door in droves—obviously waiting for the escort. A sure sign. *Someone's getting the axe today.* I don't think it's me because they looked me in the eye when I came in the entrance, but my phone rings the second I get into my office—startling me to no end.

"Ashley Stockingdale," I say with as much peace as I can muster.

"Ashley, this is Hans Frauer," the CEO of the company says. My heart is pounding. *Where is Purvi?*

"Yes, Mr. Frauer."

"I'd like to see you in my office right away," he says in his staunch German accent.

"Coming, sir." *Sheesh, not even time to pack up my belongings in a box.*

Dianna, queen of office gossip, looks at me and forces a smile. "It will be all right." But there's something wrong. She's lost half her Tammy Faye mascara. She's been crying!

"Where's Purvi?" I ask in alarm.

Dianna shrugs. Now, Dianna knows everything, so her pleading ignorance frustrates me to no end. My hands are trembling, but I'm mumbling prayers and mentally calculating how much I have in savings. How much I can live on until another job comes along. No easy feat in this economy, and it will definitely hurt the early retirement plan. But hey, it will help with the whole workaholic thing.

I smooth my jacket before entering Hans's office. The jacket is a cargo-style DKNY in olive and part of the settlement from my renters' insurance. As is always the case in stressful situations, I take comfort in my clothes.

When I enter Hans's office, there are men in suits in the chairs. Men don't generally wear jackets here in Silicon Valley. I guess when they're firing people, it is a prerequisite. Hmmm. Maybe they take comfort in their clothes as well.

I nod. "Good morning, Mr. Frauer."

"Good morning, Ashley."

I take a moment to send a composed nod and smile to the VPs of engineering and human resources and the general manager. *Yep, definitely getting fired.*

"Good morning, gentlemen . . . Annette." *Okay, okay, let's just get this over with.* I steel myself for the inevitable.

"Ashley, as you know, we've had an abundance of patent work this year. As well as our share of patent legal work . . . "

"Yes, sir."

"This was also the first year we decided to sue Evil Empire."

Get to the point.

"Ms. Sharma has done an excellent job leading our company into this new arena, but we feel her limitations have been reached. That it's time to do something new with our direction and focus."

Purvi has done an excellent job? She's given her lifeblood to this company! "I don't understand. Where is Purvi, Hans?" I say, using his first name on purpose.

"The board has come to the conclusion that Purvi is not ready to go head-to-head with the Evil Empire."

I pace his office. "I heartily disagree." *Did I say that?*

"The board looks at results, Ashley. Your results here have given this company key patents in our technology field, as well as a steady stream of royalties because you paid attention to the competition."

"I appreciate that you've noticed my work, but, Mr. Frauer, Purvi has directed all of it."

"We should tell you that we've let Purvi go," Mr. LaBou says.

I fall into a chair that's been waiting for me all along. *They actually did it? They fired Purvi?* She gave her soul to this company. "I don't know what to say." *Other than you're all tools of the devil!*

"We'd like you to take Purvi's place as interim general counsel," Hans says. "We've watched you now for nearly a year. We've seen our stock jump three points at the very least, due to your laying the groundwork in patents."

General Counsel. This is what I've worked for. At the same time, how can I deny what they did to Purvi? They sucked her dry and left her empty shell at the curb. How could I ever define success this way and live with myself?

I mutter a silent prayer and receive the confirmation I'm looking for.

"No, thank you," I say.

"I don't think you understand. This is your opportunity. Your only opportunity. There is not another patent job in the house."

I stand up. "I won't need another one, but I appreciate the offer. My answer is no."

"Let me reiterate, there's not another job here for you, Miss Stockingdale. It's general counsel or nothing."

"I understand that, Mr. Frauer, but I'm afraid I'm not interested in the job. I don't have that kind of time to work. I'll hand in my resignation by the end of the day."

Hans shakes his head. "You're privy to far too much information for that. Consider this your termination if you're not interested in the position."

Better yet! Unemployment and a severance package. I see the hard line on his face, but at the same time I know he's in more trouble than I am. He's got two key patent lawsuits pending, six patents in the hopper, and not one patent attorney. Pride is a Beast.

Hans lifts a finger, and soon security is surrounding me, escorting me from the building with a quick trip to my office for the obligatory box, which they check every time I add something to it. The irony that you can fit your entire career into a single cardboard box is not lost on me.

"Rough day," one of the security guard says.

"It's easier than you'd think."

"Everyone loves you here, Miss Stockingdale. You'll do fine."

"Success has more than one definition," I say. I didn't get all that legal expertise and negotiating experience for nothing. I'll have a fine severance at the end of this.

Once outside, Dianna comes running out of the office doors. "You turned it down?" *Man, she's fast.* Gossip is drawn to her like a wave to the shore.

"Did Purvi come in this morning, Dianna?"

She nods. "About seven. They fired her then." Dianna has streams of tears leaving little rivers in her makeup. "Told me to not say a word or I'd get the axe, too."

"How did she take it?"

"You know, Purvi. She was fine." Dianna is still tearing up. "She was the best boss I ever had. Hans treated her like dirt, and she shielded us all from it." Dianna practically spits. "Pig!"

I take her hand. "She will be fine. Go back in and don't get into trouble on my account."

"Why won't you take the job, Ashley? You'd be a great general counsel, and Purvi would want you to have the job."

My head is nodding up and down. "Because when they offered it to me, I knew it was wrong. God has other plans for me. I don't know what they are, but He hasn't let me down yet." I turn to walk away when Dianna speaks again.

"This'll make you feel better. They had me book you on the flight to Taiwan tomorrow morning."

I just start to laugh. "Someone else will be eating my undercooked seafood, then. And I hope he has a German accent." We hug good-bye. "If you need anything, or if you have any questions, just call me."

"Maybe marrying the rich doctor isn't such a bad idea."

"Maybe. But I don't need a man to be happy," I say. "Neither do you." I wave and head to my car with my little cardboard box—a box that represents four years of my life.

Three days pass, and I'm surprisingly over my job. I've had a few leads already, and one of them is even in Arizona, and though my heart longs to follow up on it, I nix the idea as a pathetic attempt to escape rather than create my new life. The wedding is almost here and, with it, the depressing concept of Valentine's Day. Who invented this sadistic holiday? Normally, I just forget about it, but with Kay's creepy chachki reminders all over the house, I encounter vivid red tauntings everywhere. I expect them to beat like Poe's "Telltale Heart," so I'm glad for the escape to Vegas.

I'm without a date, naturally. Even when offering a free trip to Vegas, I can't think of anyone to bring! When you can't even *buy* a date, that's not subtle loserdom— that's prime real estate, the Boardwalk of Loserville.

I asked Kay, but she feels that Vegas is not where God would lead her. I heartily agree, but I have no choice in the matter. My brother is getting married and that miracle would drag me to the bowels of the earth if necessary.

I thought about asking Dr. Kevin as a "friend," but Vegas somehow implies that sex is included in the ticket, so no. And I'm not convinced at all that his newfound

Seeker Status is anything but a ploy to bring me back around.

Seth wouldn't assume that sex is part of a trip to Vegas, but he's not speaking to me. Besides, why dredge up emotions when it's obviously over? He's leaving this week and, chances are, he's avoiding me until he leaves. I long for his friendship again, but I know that needs to be ended as well. Both for his well-being and my own.

I see my face looks like a prune, I'm so cried out from obsessing about what I should have done. What I should have said. Not about Selectech. About Seth. I'm sick of gulping into my pillow at night, stifling my tears so I don't wake Kay, not to mention manufacturing mucus in Sam's Club quantity. Having a crush on Seth was fun; getting over him is not.

I stare in my bathroom mirror with an utter lack of emotion. I never thought I was the type who would define herself by a relationship, and I don't, but Seth was a constant ray of hope in my life. The Omnipresent Potential. A reason to buy new clothes. I realize it wasn't *him*, of course. It was the hope I was addicted to. I know that God is with me, and I wouldn't want to marry without His consent, but I want a reason to buy new shoes!

My hair is finally long enough for a clip, and I pin it back. Powdering Jane Iredale foundation onto my skin, I brush some blush on my cheeks and finish with my Stila lip polish. *That's as good as it gets.* I blow a kiss to the mirror.

I'm on the two p.m. flight after church to Vegas, but I'm singing a solo in service today. I spent a long time in prayer this morning, praying for my brother and Mei Ling and their life together. I hope they'll be very happy and that I can be happy for them. I think I'm past petty jealousy, but you never know. It seems so unfair that God should give Dave a life partner and me a big lesson on living single.

Brea is coming to the wedding, so I won't be alone, but she's bringing John. So that's no fun. They'll dance, gazing into each other's eyes to old Journey tunes, while I fend off unemployed cousins with goin' nowhere stories—and fight off my aunts who try and fluff my hair to full '80s capacity. *Oh yeah, can't wait for this.*

All my good intentions to befriend my new sister-in-law have gone the way of the Intel 486. Lost amid the "have tos" of job-hunting and singing in the church band. Life with Kay has become an eclectic experience. It's *different* having a roommate. She's not like a "normal" roommate, meaning someone you can ask, "Does my butt look fat in this?" or "Can you see my bra strap from the back?" But she's a fabulous cook and is teaching me volumes about productivity and organization.

Did you know you can actually get out the door earlier if you don't try on six outfits in the morning? Granted, you'll feel uncomfortable all day because you weren't in the mood for that certain blouse, but you're there on time. Of course, now I don't have a *there* to be, but that's another whine. I am no longer a whiner. Come what may. I'm Annie, singing "Tomorrow"! I'm Maria on *Sound of Music!* Perhaps that's a bit too optimistic.

Were it not for Kay's fetish with Valentine's Day, I might even love being here in her darling little bungalow. I've made the bedroom and extra bath my own. I decorated with rich Sheridan fabrics the day before finances became an issue.

There's a knock at my bathroom door. "Are you ready, Ashley?" Kay asks.

I take one last run-through at my hair. "As ready as I'm going to be." I open the bathroom door, and Kay has that pitying look on her face. "I'm fine," I say.

"Just go and enjoy the wedding."

"I plan to. I do!"

The phone rings, and I dash for it. Every time it rings, I have this flush of guilt because it's never for Kay. *In her own home!* I've got to get my own line before she kicks me out for disturbing the peace.

"Hello," I say.

"Ashley, it's Brea."

"You better be coming today."

"Relax. I'm coming." Brea clears her throat. "I'm calling to remind you this is your brother's day and that's okay. Your brother did not 'win' because he's doing something before you, all right?"

"What are you, my conscience?"

"Someone needs to be. This is the biggest day of his life, Ash. There's no graduation; there's no promotion at work. This is big for Dave. Okay?"

But I don't feel any of the angst she's predicting. I'm actually very happy for Dave and really excited to take a break from Silicon Valley. I kinda love my brother. Granted, I've endured life with him as my human tormentor. He's told me for twenty years no sucker would marry me, given me a wedgie at the junior dance, invited his friends to read my diary, forged a love note from me to the quarterback . . . the list goes on. But Dave has changed, and it's time I did, too.

I breathe deeply. "I'm perfectly calm. I'm going to sing at church today, and I've been praying all morning, so you needn't worry. Dave's happiness is my own."

"When you're relaxed like this, that's when I worry."

"I'll see you at church." I hang up on her before she can harangue me any further.

Kay and I pile into her Honda Accord, and I warm up my voice all the way to church—which drives poor Kay into gripping the steering wheel with tense hands.

"I'm not that bad."

"Your voice is beautiful, and you know it, Ash. I'm just nervous about church today. I'm meeting someone after service."

"You are?" *Oops, too much surprise in the voice.* "I mean, that's great, Kay. Is it someone I know?" *Please, oh please, don't let it be Seth. Please don't rub that in my face, Lord.*

"No, just someone I met at another church group when I went with Sharon."

"What's he do for a living?"

She dares to face me. "What do you think?"

"He's a professional bungee jumper," I deadpan.

"Yep. An engineer."

"I hope you have a great time anyway. Did you bring a coupon with you?" I joke.

"Got one in my purse for three restaurants."

"You're all set then."

Kay and I part company at church, and I go in the back to practice with the band. The ambiance candles are all lit, and the church members are all taking their seats in the high school theatre. Seth is, of course, right in the front row. He's leaving on Friday. It's a done deal, signed on the dotted line, his place having a "For Sale" sign out front. I drove by.

The church band opens with a rockin' praise song that shakes the house. Everyone is dancing and lifting their arms in worship. While fired up, I wait for the pastor to introduce today's message, and I take the stage to belt out my song of worship. For the first time in years, I focus on Him. Not who's watching me, not even Seth in the front row. Just Him. I feel filled to capacity when I'm done.

After polite applause, I dare to take a seat next to Seth in the front row. The front row is the only half-empty one near me, and I decide to be a Big Girl and sit where God is leading me.

"Beautiful," he whispers after a moment, then takes my hand. My hand! It's a gesture of friendship, of truce, not love. Right? I force myself to steal a glance at him, but his expression gives me no answers. I squeeze his hand tighter. *Don't go,* I implore with the strength of my grip.

"You can sing, woman." Dr. Kevin Novak has just slipped into the seat on the other side of me, and Seth quickly removes his hand. I'm torn. I feel like Kevin's salvation and Seth's ego rest squarely on my shoulders, and it's all about balance.

The competition between the two men is obvious, each one determined—Seth to not be mocked, and Kevin to not lose this invisible war. After a lengthy sermon that I couldn't concentrate on for fear I was sweating too much, the last song plays and I'm left standing beside both men.

"So I'm on my way to Vegas today," I say, as casual conversation.

"Me too," Seth says.

"What?"

"I got a flight to Phoenix through Vegas for $50 round trip. One last house-hunting expedition."

"How much is that wasted hour in sin city worth to you?" Kevin asks.

Seth shrugs. "About a hundred bucks, I suppose."

The scene is really uncomfortable. I want to talk alone with Seth, but Kevin is not leaving and now that we're playing dating *Survivor,* he's not about to. I wish I had a rose. I'd have my own private *Bachelorette* rose ceremony. Kevin is here at church, however, and there could be a lot at stake in regard to his faith. The only way to get out safely is to say good-bye to them both at once.

I swallow hard, take a deep breath, and excuse myself. "I need to get to the airport. I'll see you both when I get back." But I know I won't see Seth, and the idea leaves me short of breath.

"Call me when you get in. Do you need a ride from the airport?" Kevin asks.

Bless his heart, he's a sweet agnostic, if nothing else. "No, thank you."

I try to casually beckon Seth privately with my forefinger, but he doesn't notice. My eyes connect with his. I know he feels it. There's no denying the pull this time. He comes closer, ignoring Kevin's presence. "Good-bye, Ashley." He kisses me on the cheek, and I grasp his hand.

"You're really leaving?" I whisper through my tears. Kevin senses the crowd feel and rubs my back to say good-bye. I ignore him. I only have eyes for Seth in this moment.

"I'll be a VP," Seth explains.

"In Arizona. You've always said that Silicon Valley is the place to be, Seth. This is where you stay for a long-term career in high-tech. Didn't you tell me that once?"

"I probably said a lot of stupid things. When you start looking for work, Ashley, you might not be so picky in this economy. Moving up around here has become impossible."

He steps even closer to me, and I don't even care where Kevin is at this point. I can feel the heat from Seth's chest, the energy between us. But I don't back away. I give him my own silent challenge. He's within inches of my face now, and I'm wondering if he'll kiss me right here in church. I hold my breath, waiting. It's not like we meet in a sanctuary—we're in a high school gym—but still. Kissing in church? Way uncool. But my worrying is for naught. He pulls away from my gaze and steps back. My breath rushes from me.

"I'll e-mail you when I get back. Have fun at your brother's wedding." Seth nods and turns away.

"I'll be at the Viva Vegas chapel if you want to stop during your layover," I say, pathetically throwing myself his way.

He waves me off and continues to walk away, never even glancing back. Kevin is quickly beside me again.

"Everything okay?" Kevin asks.

"Fine. Just the way things are supposed to be."

"Good. Let's get some lunch before you leave for the airport. I'll drive you," Kevin offers. And I have nothing left in me to resist. But I'll explain the equally-yoked passages over lunch. Some good needs to come from this day. And this friendship. I wave to Kay, letting her know she's off the hook as my ride, and I look to Kevin like I'm headed for the gallows.

33

The wedding chapel is gloomy dark, except for rainbow beams of light that come through the geometric stained-glass windows. There are no saints on this stained glass, only diamond and spade designs and, if I'm not mistaken, a single green dollar sign. I laugh at the thought of Dave picking the place. He loves to shock people, and I'm sure that was his intention here.

Truthfully, I'm a little creeped out, but I can see my brother's flair for drama in all the details. There are blood red curtains draping down the walls and French white sheaths of fabric on the chairs with clown-sized bows on their backs. Tiny twinkle lights blink obnoxiously like it's Christmas every day in Vegas, and I just know my brother will laugh about this until the day he dies.

Mei Ling must be a saint to put up with my brother. My traditional Chinese favors are going to go unnoticed amidst this assault circus on the senses. There are silk (nice way of saying fake) flowers everywhere, like a Jo-Ann fabric store exploded. The cathedral ceiling is enormous—cavernous might be a better word—with a black theatrical ceiling. I'm completely overwhelmed and can't focus on any one place because another light blips and captures my line of sight.

I was deluged before I even walked in by the bevy of virginal white brides in the casino. Weddings, casino-style, seem to include an abundance of cleavage.

Although the chapel seats fifty, there are nine people here besides the bride and groom. My three aunts—in full, sparkly, low-cut regalia to rival the casino brides—my parents, Brea and John, and the best man: Chip Light-me-another-one Standish. It's so Ricki Lake, and I'm really feeling for my brother, except I know this is *his* ultimate wedding. And Mei Ling doesn't seem to care. In the back room, she was actually giggling about her Vegas wedding being better than she imagined. That Dave certainly knew how to throw a party, and she loved that about him—how he was always the center of any party. She also informed me that they're going to use the wedding money to go on a cruise to the Bahamas. *She's quite a woman to be able to tolerate this, even enjoy it. And obviously even more right for Dave than I thought.*

I'm waiting at the end of the aisle, across from my brother, who looks like he could faint at any moment. I can see him breathing from ten feet away—not a good sign. Silently, I'm praying he'll get through this. I wonder what it's like to make a commitment to marriage when you haven't even graduated to living on your own yet. I guess I haven't had the proper respect for the step he's taking.

I'm actually holding my own. I must admit the whole day is a bit surreal to me, like it's not really happening.

Maybe I'll have this huge Light Bulb Moment when I realize I'm dateless at my brother's wedding, but for now I'm just thankful I'm not getting married here.

I'm wearing a navy strapless Jessica McClintock gown. It's off-the-rack, but the bride picked it, and I'm not looking like a stuffed eggplant, so I have no complaints. Mei Ling has good taste—well, maybe not in men or wedding chapels, but in fashion she's quite adept.

The wedding march begins. There's no piano, but it sounds like it's live, and I find myself looking for the speakers. Mei Ling appears in the doorway. She's absolutely beautiful in a gown she created herself—which she copied from a Vera Wang model with no pattern or anything. Who says that sewing is a lost art?

Mei Ling walks down the aisle. There's no step, touch, step. She just walks down the aisle like the practical beauty she is. She stands next to my brother and smiles at him coolly. He, on the other hand, is now completely relaxed. He's got that "I caught a butterfly" look that John always wears when looking at Brea.

The preacher has appeared out of nowhere, and I'm now wondering what he's a preacher of, exactly? Meditative Realization? Yoga? One can be ordained in three minutes on the Internet and faster in Vegas. I got a spam once that said that.

"Dearly beloved," the minister says in a deep, old-time-Baptist tone. "We are gathered here today to intertwine David Jeffrey Stockingdale and Mee Lingah Wah in holy matrimony." *Maay Ling, I want to correct him. And intertwine? That sounds a bit nasty to me, but I look to my brother and he's enraptured by his bride. Okay, intertwine it is.*

"Marriage is a holy state. Intertwining the two as one." *He's loving that word.*

I look at Brea, and she's covering her face. Now, anyone else might think she's emotional, but I know better. I know she's laughing immaturely at the use of *intertwine* by the preacher. This starts it. I look away from Brea, but it's too late; we've seen each other.

That irrepressible giggle starts to bubble. The kind you can't stop when it starts. The kind that becomes louder as you try to stifle it. I keep it under control for a few seconds, but then I just lose it. How can I be so immature? Intertwining is just a word, after all. Everyone is looking at me now, and Brea and I don't dare meet each other's eyes again. I bite down on my lips to halt the laughter.

Closing the Bible with a crack, the minister talks more about intertwining as one. *Enough already!* But my eyes must be deceiving me. Suddenly, out of the ceiling a great hole opens up, and a man and a woman dressed in powder blue leotards descend, wrapping around each other like two snakes in heat. I look around to see if I'm really witnessing what I think I am. And since everyone's eyes are on the ceiling, I have to assume it's true. There are two people in skimpy clothing clawing each other from a swinging trapeze. Like that singing female bear at Country Bear Jamboree in Disneyland, only not so much.

Oh, I can't take it. I just can't take it. My laughter is growing in intensity so it's becoming obvious. *This is just so wrong!*

The minister asks if I'd like to excuse myself and then moves on, with more intertwining talk, more slithering limbs in the sky. The preacher's on the clock, and judging by the sheer amount of white satin in that foyer, he's got to get a move-on. Other brides await. My brother and Mei Ling are told to light their unity candle.

"As you light this candle to signify your unity, Junien and Patrice will perform an arial adagio symbolizing the unity of two souls." Junien and Patrice, all limbs from the looks of them, jumble into one big human pretzel, with pained expressions on their overly made-up faces to emphasize the drama of the moment. I'm in awe.

What do you suppose Patrice says when asked about her job? *"Um, I wrap myself around a guy in tights while hanging from a ceiling."* Does no one else see what I'm seeing? I'm struggling to keep my mouth quiet while my whole body shakes with laughter. I have to fan my face. My legs are weak, and I can barely stand. My aunts are staring at me as though they cannot understand what is so comical. There are two people in the air, hanging in a hypnotic pornographic pose, and *I'm* the one with the problem. Like I said, I know I'm adopted.

Before you know it, Patrice and Junien have ascended into the ceiling, ready to be dropped onto another unsuspecting congregation. But it's of no use now, I'm still giggling like an overly enthusiastic sitcom fan.

The preacher does his best to stare me down, as does my brother. Mei Ling has started to giggle as well. And soon, my brother is joining her until we're all practically slapping our knees.

Dave and Mei Ling are pronounced man and wife, and they both try to get a solemn look, but they're still laughing. They do kiss each other warmly when asked to, though, and it's official: They're intertwined. They wait at the altar and are greeted by all the guests. All nine of them.

My brother's best man, Chip, is beside me. "Nice wedding, huh? What was so funny?"

"I was just nervous, I guess."

"I guess."

"Please join Mee Linga and David for a reception in this room." Reading the names off a clipboard—hey, another career for Kay—a middle-aged, redheaded woman ushers us into the next room. Before we're out, I see the chapel doors open and a new groom ready to take his place. So much for formality.

Dave and Mei Ling walk over to me and, go figure, I'm choked up. "I'm sorry I laughed, I guess I was nervous."

Dave starts to chuckle. "I thought you were laughing at the intertwining thing."

I just shake my head. "How did you decide on that particular theme?"

Dave shrugs. "I just thought, I'm never going to have the chance again to pay two people to drop from the ceiling. That's cool. Will anyone ever forget our wedding?"

"Not likely," I admit.

Mei Ling laughs. "You should have warned me, Dave. I nearly had a heart attack. I thought we were being invaded or robbed. In my country, it's not a good thing when people drop from the ceiling." She takes my hand. "And your poor sister. I bet she's never been to a wedding where there's actual entertainment."

"Can't say I have, but it was a beautiful wedding."

"Our second one," Mei Ling whispers.

"What?" I look toward Dave.

"We had our pastor marry us before we came here. It was nice. Traditionally Chinese and actually in the language."

I thrust a fist toward him. "And you didn't invite me?"

"We had an older Christian couple who's been mentoring us stand up with us." Dave puts his arm around Mei Ling. "It was important to us to do this before God with the people who have taught us so much. I wanted it to be intimate so I could focus on what He has done for us."

I shake my head. "Well, Dave, I didn't think it was possible, but you surprised me again."

"It's just one of the many surprises I have lined up. Wait until you see the honeymoon suite, Mei Ling." Dave kisses his bride and then faces me. "So what are you doing with your night in Vegas?" He scans the room. "Our cousins aren't here, so you've got no dance partners to fend off. Maybe you and Chip can gamble together."

I look over at Chip who is sniffing nervously, like a pig looking for truffles. Most likely, he's wondering where he can find marijuana to get through the night. "Not in this lifetime. Besides, Brea and John are here," I say.

"Like they want you around." Dave laughs.

My mother stands beside me. "Ashley, what was so funny?"

"I'm just happy for Dave, that's all, Mom."

"We all are." My mom smiles. Dave takes Mei Ling out to the dance floor, and the two of them have their first slow dance. Before the first toast. "She's a beauty, isn't she, Ashley?"

"She is," I agree. My mom has a dreamy look on her face, and I can't remember the last time I saw her this happy. "You're happy for them, huh, Mom?"

She has tears in her gray eyes. "I'm always happy when my children are happy. That's all I ever want." She turns and faces me. "That's why I worry so much about you in that job. I never know if it truly makes you happy or if it is just a way to buy more of those expensive clothes you wear."

"I lost my job this week, Mom." I'm waiting for the inevitable, her extreme disappointment at yet another of my failures. Never mind that she just said that she worried over me at—

"Good."

"What?"

"I'm glad you lost that job. That's no life, traipsing all over the world and racing to get gadgets on the store shelves. You're too good for that kind of life, Ashley. If you enjoyed it, that would be one thing, but I think you were just too good at something you didn't enjoy. That's always the way it was with you. If you tried anything, you succeeded. You need to make sure the next thing you try is something you like."

"You're not worried about me? Financially or otherwise?"

She looks me square in the eye. "Did I ever tell you why I named you after Ashley Wilkes?"

"There's a reason?"

"Of course there's a reason," my mother says. "Ashley Wilkes always did the right thing. When faced with temptation and trials, he always rose up and did the right thing. Not always the most successful thing, but always the best thing." She fluffs her corsage a bit. "Some may see him as the weak character, but he was strong because he gave everything of himself for others. Even as a baby, you were so strong-willed. You came out of the womb barking orders, and I've always wanted to see that drive put to good use."

I knew she wasn't stupid. But I never knew just how intelligent she really was. Here is proof. There is a legitimate reason behind my ridiculous name. "I think you should have been named Ashley, Mom." I kiss her on the cheek, and I see a single tear roll down her face.

"Bless your heart, dear. I was put on earth to raise two wonderful children who find their purpose. And look at you both!" She rubs my cheek with the back of her fingers. She used to do that when I was a child, and it brings me immediate peace.

"Well, my purpose can't be shopping at Bloomingdale's, since I'm unemployed," I joke.

"You'll find another job. You're too smart to do otherwise, but do me a favor and find your passion first." She winks and takes off to grab my father for the dance floor.

The DJ is playing a little swinging Glenn Miller from the '40s, my absolute favorite. Is there anyone who can hear "In the Mood" and not get happy? I think I was born in the wrong era.

Suddenly, watching my parents and my brother, the music overtakes me. Remembering how much fun I had at karaoke, I head to the center of the dance floor a la carte and start to swing. "Na na-na, Na na-na, Na-na-nah, whap wha! Sing it with me now!" I'm all over the dance floor relishing in the happy notes, and I don't care who's watching. I can see Brea laughing, and the DJ just assumes I'm drunk, as so many seem to do these days. I lift my hands high in the air, '40s style, and grab people's hands as I dance by.

This is better than any fantasy scene of my creation. This is living life the way God intended: without fear or trepidation. *Mental note: I am Ashley Wilkes Stockingdale, single, unemployed patent attorney, and Reason Extraordinaire!*

"Ashley."

I spin around and see Seth. My heart nearly stops. I blink my eyes several times, but the image doesn't disappear. "Is that you, Seth?"

"It's me."

"What are you doing here?"

"You invited me. So did Brea. She said we had unfinished business."

I look over to Brea and tear up immediately. "She said that?"

Seth looks around. "Is Kevin here?"

I shake my head. "In the Mood" ends, and "I Love You for Sentimental Reasons" begins. Seth takes me into his arms, and I cuddle into the curve of his neck, sniffing his cologne. Who would have guessed that Seth owned cologne?

Now I admit this song could make me get cozy with Chip Standish, but my head is happily resting on Seth's shoulder.

"Was your layover longer than you expected?" I ask.

"Ashley, I'm tired of that. I'm not here because of my layover, or my cheap flight. Okay?"

I pull away. "Why then?"

"You have the nerve to call me clueless!" Seth says. And then he stops dancing and just stares at me with those brilliant eyes of his. My body is all aquiver, and I know now what John feels when he looks at Brea.

He reaches down, cupping my face into his hands, and kisses me full on the mouth. My toes curl up, and every part of me feels tingly and alive. "Do that again," I say, and he presses his lips to mine and we kiss and we kiss and we kiss . . . Then, he looks up and sees my family staring at me like I'm Vegas's main attraction. *I am not Celine Dion. Don't let the hair fool you.*

Mental note: When four years of stored-up passion bursts forth, make sure your family isn't there to witness it.

He presses my head back to his shoulder and continues our dance. "You deserve the right words. The right emotions."

You know, I just feel everything with Seth. The words suddenly are not as important to me as they once were. Being next to him is so natural, yet exhilarating, all at once. My heart is pounding in my ears to think what he might say. I look up at him expectantly.

"I adore you, Ashley Wilkes Stockingdale. When I think about going to Arizona without you, my chest hurts. It would be more than a desert for me."

Be still my heart. I'm shaking like a Chihuahua. He's giving me the words! The Words!

"I'm staying in Silicon Valley to see where this leads."

"Let's hope it's not the unemployment office, because right now, we both have a little job issue. A dry spell, if you will."

"All the more time to explore what we really feel—and eat out on a coupon." Seth laughs, then leans down and kisses me again. All is right with the world.

All is right? *I'm unemployed, a bridesmaid again, and in Las Vegas, Nevada.* This is nothing like I wanted, and everything I needed. Who would have thought? It's been right here in front of my nose all along.

What a girl wants is God's will for her life.

Nothing else even compares.

Also by Kristin Billerbeck

Available at
bookstores
everywhere

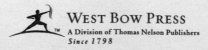

WEST BOW PRESS
A Division of Thomas Nelson Publishers
Since 1798